SAGE was founded in 1965 by Sara Miller McCune to support the dissemination of usable knowledge by publishing innovative and high-quality research and teaching content. Today, we publish over 900 journals, including those of more than 400 learned societies, more than 800 new books per year, and a growing range of library products including archives, data, case studies, reports, and video. SAGE remains majority-owned by our founder, and after Sara's lifetime will become owned by a charitable trust that secures our continued independence.

Los Angeles | London | New Delhi | Singapore | Washington DC | Melbourne

LAND ECONOMICS AND POLICY IN DEVELOPING COUNTRIES

LAND ECONOMICS AND POLICY IN DEVELOPING COUNTRIES

Prasanna K. Mohanty

Los Angeles | London | New Delhi
Singapore | Washington DC | Melbourne

Copyright © Prasanna K. Mohanty, 2022

All rights reserved. No part of this book may be reproduced or utilized in any form or by any means, electronic or mechanical, including photocopying, recording or by any information storage or retrieval system, without permission in writing from the publisher.

First published in 2022 by

SAGE Publications India Pvt Ltd
B1/I-1 Mohan Cooperative Industrial Area
Mathura Road, New Delhi 110 044, India
www.sagepub.in

SAGE Publications Inc
2455 Teller Road
Thousand Oaks, California 91320, USA

SAGE Publications Ltd
1 Oliver's Yard, 55 City Road
London EC1Y 1SP, United Kingdom

SAGE Publications Asia-Pacific Pte Ltd
18 Cross Street #10-10/11/12
China Square Central
Singapore 048423

Published by Vivek Mehra for SAGE Publications India Pvt Ltd. Typeset in 10.5/13 pt Berkeley by Zaza Eunice, Hosur, Tamil Nadu, India.

Library of Congress Cataloging-in-Publication Data

Names: Mohanty, Prasanna, author.
Title: Land economics and policy in developing countries/Prasanna K. Mohanty.
Description: Thousand Oaks, California: SAGE Publications Inc, 2021. | Includes bibliographical references and index.
Identifiers: LCCN 2021043761 (print) | LCCN 2021043762 (ebook) | ISBN 9789354790430 (hardback) | ISBN 9789354790515 (epub)
Subjects: LCSH: Land use—Developing countries. | Land reform—Developing countries. | Land tenure—Developing countries. | Agriculture and state–Developing countries.
Classification: LCC HD1131 .M64 2021 (print) | LCC HD1131 (ebook) | DDC 333.73/13091724–dc23
LC record available at https://lccn.loc.gov/2021043761
LC ebook record available at https://lccn.loc.gov/2021043762

ISBN: 978-93-5479-043-0 (HB)

SAGE Team: Rajesh Dey, Ankit Verma and Madhurima Thapa

To
Smita, my wife
who values education

Thank you for choosing a SAGE product!
If you have any comment, observation or feedback,
I would like to personally hear from you.

Please write to me at **contactceo@sagepub.in**

Vivek Mehra, Managing Director and CEO, SAGE India.

Bulk Sales

SAGE India offers special discounts
for purchase of books in bulk.
We also make available special imprints
and excerpts from our books on demand.

For orders and enquiries, write to us at

Marketing Department
SAGE Publications India Pvt Ltd
B1/I-1, Mohan Cooperative Industrial Area
Mathura Road, Post Bag 7
New Delhi 110044, India

E-mail us at **marketing@sagepub.in**

Subscribe to our mailing list
Write to **marketing@sagepub.in**

This book is also available as an e-book.

Contents

List of Boxes	ix
List of Figures	xi
List of Tables	xiii
List of Abbreviations	xv
Preface	xxi

Chapter 1	Land Economics: Concepts, Perspectives and Overview	1
Chapter 2	Characteristics of Land: Functioning of Land Markets in Developing Countries	36
Chapter 3	Determinants of Location: Theory, Practice and Lessons for Development Strategy	73
Chapter 4	Determinants of Land Use: Theory, Practice and Lessons for Land Policy	115
Chapter 5	An Appraisal of Land Use Planning: Exploring a New Paradigm for Developing Countries	145
Chapter 6	Sustainable Land Management: Connecting Transport, Land Use and Development	186
Chapter 7	Financing Land Development: Designing a Toolbox of Land-based Instruments	227
Chapter 8	Land Economics and Policy: Addressing the Challenges of Sustainable Development	264

Bibliography	309
About the Author	324
Index	325

List of Boxes

6.1 India: Classification of Land Use 191

8.1 SDG 11: Make Cities and Human Settlements Inclusive, Safe, Resilient and Sustainable 265

8.2 National Urban Policy Framework, 2018: 10 Guiding Principles 278

List of Figures

2.1	Negative Externality on Supply Side: Divergence between Market and Social Outcomes	48
2.2	Positive Externality on Demand Side: Divergence between Market and Social Outcomes	49
2.3	Merit Goods: Needs versus Effective Demand	50
2.4	Competitive versus Monopoly Equilibrium Outcomes	51
3.1	Weber Location–Production Triangle	81
3.2	Weber Model: Isodapane Analysis	82
3.3	Weber–Moses Location–Production Triangle	84
3.4	Weber–Moses Model: Input Budget Constraints	85
3.5	Weber–Moses Model: Location–Production Equilibrium	86
3.6	Effect of Increase in Transport Cost on Price and Output	91
3.7	Lösch Demand Cone: Influence of Transport Cost on Market Area	93
3.8	Hotelling's Model of Spatial Competition	96
3.9	Hotelling's Model: Spatial Competition Equilibrium	98
3.10	Hotelling's Model: Unequal Market Area Division	99
3.11	Hotelling's Model: Production Cost Differential and Market Area	99
4.1	Von Thünen Model: Extensive Margin of Cultivation	117
4.2	Von Thünen Model: Bid Rent Functions	119
4.3	Von Thünen Model: Rural Land Use Patterns	119
4.4	Von Thünen Model: Urban Land Use Patterns	121

4.5	Von Thünen Rings: Urban Land Use Pattern	122
4.6	Alonso–Muth–Mills Model: Determination of Urban Boundary	126
4.7	Alonso–Muth–Mills Model: Rent–Distance Function	126
4.8	Alonso–Muth–Mills Model: Central versus Suburban Location	129
4.9	Alonso–Muth–Mills Model: Central versus Suburban Housing	131
4.10	Alonso–Muth–Mills Model: Housing Price Distance Function	131
4.11	Alonso–Muth–Mills Model: Housing Production: Central City versus Suburb	134

List of Tables

2.1 Land Market Issues Confronting Investors in Developing Countries   45

3.1 Theories of Location: From von Thünen to Krugman   78

5.1 Chronology of Key Urban Planning and Land Development Initiatives in India   161
5.2 URDPFI Guidelines: Urban Land Use Classification   168

6.1 Population of Urban and Rural Areas at Mid-year and Percentage Urban 2018   186
6.2 Percentage of Population of Urban Areas at Mid-year (1950–2050; in %)   187
6.3 India: Demographic Trends and Projections During 1950–2050   187
6.4 India: Changing Pattern of Land Use (1950–1951 to 2014–2015)   193
6.5 India: Distribution of Landholding and Operated Area (2010–2011 and 2015–2016)   195

7.1 A Toolbox of Land-based Instruments   234
7.2 Levels of and Trends in Property Tax Revenues for Groups of Countries (as Percentage of GDP)   239

7.3 The United Kingdom: Evolution of Taxation of
Planning/Development Gain (1909–2010) 242

8.1 Committee on Urban Land Policy (1965): Major
Recommendations 275

List of Abbreviations

AMM	Alonso–Muth–Mills
ANOBs	Areas of outstanding natural beauty
AR	Average revenue
ARV	Annual rental value
AUDA	Ahmedabad Urban Development Authority
BKC	Bandra Kurla Complex
BRT	Bus rapid transit
CAGR	Compound annual growth rate
CBDs	Central business districts
CC	Congestion charging
CDP	City development plan
CEPAC	Certificate of Potential Additional Construction
CGG	Centre for Good Governance
CGT	Capital gains tax
CIP	Capital improvement plan
CITs	City Improvement Trusts
CPT	Central place theory
DCR	Development control regulations
DDA	Delhi Development Authority
DDP	District development plan
DGT	Development gains tax
DIF	Development impact fee(s)
DMRC	Delhi Metro Rail Corporation
DP	Development plan
DPC	District Planning Committee

DRC	Development Right Certificate
EDC	External development charges
ERP	Electronic road pricing
EWS	Economically Weaker Sections
FAO	Food and Agriculture Organization
FAR	Floor area ratio
FSI	Floor space index
GDP	Gross domestic product
GEM	Generators of economic momentum
GHG	Greenhouse gas
GNCTD	Government of National Capital Territory of Delhi
GoI	Government of India
GST	Goods and Services Tax
GTPUDA	Gujarat Town Planning and Urban Development Act
HDRUAA	Haryana Development and Regulation of Urban Areas Act
HGT	Henry George theorem
HIG	High-income group
HMDA	Hyderabad Metropolitan Development Authority
HME	Home market effect
HPEC	High Powered Expert Committee
HSR	High-speed rail
HUDA	Haryana Urban Development Authority
IAs	Industrial areas
ICT	Information and communications technology
IDSMT	Integrated Development of Small and Medium Towns
IH	Inclusionary housing
IQ	Intelligence quotient
IRs	Investment regions
ITPI	Institute of Town Planners, India
IZ	Inclusionary zoning
JDM	Joint development mechanism
JNNURM	Jawaharlal Nehru National Urban Renewal Mission
LA	Land acquisition
LAC	Land acquisition collector
LDDs	Local development documents

LGT	Land Gains Tax
LIG	Low-income groups
LPS	Land pooling scheme
LRT	Light rail transit
LTT	Land transfer tax
LVC	Land value capture
LVIT	Land value increment tax
LVT	Land value tax
MC	Marginal cost
MDGs	Millennium Development Goals
MDP	Metropolitan Development Plan
MoHUA	Ministry of Housing and Urban Affairs
MI	Material index
MIG	Middle-income group
MLTT	Municipal land transfer tax
MMRDA	Mumbai Metropolitan Region Development Authority
MoUD	Ministry of Urban Development
MPCs	Metropolitan planning committees
MPD	Master Plan of Delhi
MR	Marginal revenue
MRT	Mass rapid transit
MRTS	Mass rapid transit system
MSB	Marginal social benefit
MSC	Marginal social cost
MTCL	Minimum transportation cost location
NCR	National Capital Region
NEG	New economic geography
NIUM	National Institute of Urban Management
NMT	Non-motorized transport
NPCs	National priority cities
NSS	National Sample Survey
NSSO	National Sample Survey Office
NSW	New South Wales
NUPF	National Urban Policy Framework
NUTP	National Urban Transport Policy
NYC	New York City

O&M	Operation and maintenance
ODV	Official declared value
OODC	*Outorga Onerosa do Direito de Construir*
PGT	Planning gains tax
PHPDT	Per hour per direction traffic
PMB	Private marginal benefit
PT	Public transport
R-AH	Residential Affordable Housing
RETT	Real estate transfer tax
RPGT	Real property gains tax
RSS	Regional spatial strategies
SDGs	Sustainable Development Goals
SECC	Socio-Economic and Caste Census
SEWS	Socially and economically weaker sections
SEZ	Special Economic Zone
SIA	Social impact assessment
SMB	Social marginal benefit
SPCs	State priority cities
SPRs	Special priority regions
SSSIs	Sites for Special Scientific Interest
SVT	Site value tax
TCPO	Town and Country Planning Organization
TDR	Transferable development right
TIF	Tax increment financing
TOD	Transit-oriented development
TPS	Town Planning Scheme
TTC	Total transport cost
UA	Urban agglomeration
UDAs	Urban Development Authorities
UDPFI	Urban Development Plan Formulation and Implementation
ULBs	Urban local bodies
UNCCD	United Nations Convention to Combat Desertification
URDPFI	Urban and Regional Development Plans Formulation and Implementation
UT	Urban transport

VCF	Value capture financing
VLT	Vacant land tax
WEB	Wider economic benefits
WEF	World Economic Forum
ZQA	Zoning for Quality and Affordability

Preface

Land economics played a key role in the spatial transformation of developed countries. However, it has not received the importance it deserves from policymakers and planners in developing countries, including India. There is perhaps no branch of economics that is so relevant, yet so neglected. Paradoxically, the subject is not even taught in universities. The disconnect between land use planning and land economics is glaring. This is disturbing as land is an input, output and resource in planned urbanization in developing countries, whose future is 'urban'. Land acts as a platform for cities to generate economic growth and public finance while delivering spatial, economic, social and environmental functions. Unearned urban land rent is a prominent source of inequality in wealth. The lack of access to land is a major cause of poverty in rural areas. However, land policy and management issues are grossly neglected. An integrated approach to sustainable land management (SLM) to attain UN Sustainable Development Goals (SDGs) has not emerged. The synergy between developmental, regulatory and economic instruments is not harnessed. This book delves into the theory and practice of land economics to draw lessons for public policy. The chapters cover concepts and perspectives of land economics, functioning of land markets in developing countries, determinants of location and land use, fallacies of modernist land use planning, sustainable land management design, land-based financing of cities and land, and urban policies in developing countries. The book is driven by the motivation to present a guide on land economics to policymakers and planners, and a reference to teachers and students.

Urban land markets fail for several reasons, including externalities, public goods, monopoly, speculation and rent-seeking. Thus, governments intervene in markets in both developed and developing countries. However, seven decades of land use-led planning through master plans in India suggest that cities are subject to double jeopardy: market failure and government failure. These plans have resulted in scarcity of serviced land and floor space for economic growth and affordable housing. Urban planning has led to sprawl, environmental degradation, social exclusion, corruption and deadweight welfare losses. Rooted in modernist planning theories, the master planning model has narrowly focused on land use, neglecting the more important aspects of land such as density, accessibility, affordability and land rents in locations. It fails to recognize land as a heterogenous good with spatial, economic, environmental and social characteristics. The peculiar nature of land and complexities of land markets suggest that the survey-analysis-plan technique, propagated by planners, is fraught with methodological problems. This technique limits land to its horizontal dimensions, while projecting economic activities and their land use requirements 20–25 years ahead. Land economics, on the contrary, regards land as a multidimensional good, characterized by physical attributes, use permissible under zoning regulations, density permissible under development rules, accessibility to infrastructure, especially transportation, linkages to externalities, 'surplus' land rents, etc.

Indian cities are under-planned and over-regulated. They are under-planned due to neglect of core infrastructure, especially transport, to support and attract growth. By neglecting investment in transport, they have not been able to exploit the synergy between transport, land use, density, development, social inclusion and financing strategy based on a value creation, capture and recycling framework. Cities are over-regulated due to restrictive zoning and density regimes. The master plans undermine the role of market forces in growth while disregarding the limitations of regulatory instruments. They constrain decision-making by firms, households and developers regarding location, land use, land assembly and development. The adverse effects of over-regulation of land markets are exacerbated by under-investment in transport due to abysmal urban finances. The broader view of land suggests that long-term projections of economic activities, forming the basis of rigid land use proposals by master planners, are bound to be erroneous. Further, rigid land use controls at multiple levels are simply unwarranted. They seriously distort the signals transmitted by markets and curtail the degrees of freedom with economic agents.

Drawing lessons from land economics and related disciplines, this book advocates shifting from a top-down, technocratic, prescriptive, rigid, land use-based and comprehensive planning to decentralized, people-driven, responsive, flexible, transport-led and strategic planning paradigm. It suggests that India must liberalize master planning that remains untouched by economic liberalization reforms from the 1990s. The country must also proactively invest in regional and urban transport infrastructure, including mass rapid transit and high-speed rail to re-engineer cities and regions. These projects lead to wider economic benefits, not captured by standard cost–benefit analysis. This book advocates a two-tier planning approach instead of land use controls at regional, city, zone, local and plot levels. The first tier aims at a regional strategic or structural plan, focused on the conservation of national, state and regional heritage and environmental resources and core regional infrastructure networks. The second tier envisages a series of land pooling schemes at local level led by transit-oriented development (TOD), incentivized by government and driven by developers, including people. It aims to integrate transportation, land use, density, development, conservation, inclusion and value capture financing. The book calls for promoting development rather than controlling it. It suggests implementing urbanization as a project with intergovernmental partnerships, using planning and value-increment financing as a resource and regarding landowners–farmers as partners in urban development process. It presents a number of innovative practices in land and urban management and suggests broad directions for reforms in urban planning, financing and governance.

The present volume would not have been possible without the contribution from many practitioners and scholars. I have tried to combine my research with my own experience as municipal commissioner of Visakhapatnam and Hyderabad metropolitan cities, vice-chairman of Hyderabad Urban Development Authority, mission director, Jawaharlal Nehru National Urban Renewal Mission, Government of India and chief secretary to Government of Andhra Pradesh. Research matters in the knowledge-driven economy. Incorporation of the principles and practices of land economics and related discipline would significantly improve the efficacy of urban planning as an instrument to promote economically efficient, socially equitable, environmentally sustainable and financially viable cities.

I am grateful to Professor Jeffrey Williamson of Harvard University, Professor Jerry Rothenberg of Massachusetts Institute of Technology and Professors John Harris, Kevin Lang and Michael Riordan of Boston University who taught me the fundamentals of spatial economics. I thank Dr Isher Judge Ahluwalia, Professors O. P. Mathur and Abhay Pethe for contributing to my understanding of key urban development issues in India. I also thank Dr Alok Kumar Mishra, who teaches land economics, urban economics and transport economics along with me at the University of Hyderabad, for valuable suggestions. I acknowledge the support provided by Mr Arvind Kumar, Director General and Bhaskara, Ravi Rohan, Aditya and Kiran from National Institute of Urban Management (NIUM), Hyderabad and Shri Rajendra Nimje, Director General and Shabbeer, Ramakrishna and Ramana from Centre for Good Governance (CGG), Hyderabad. I specially thank my students of land economics for their inputs and encouragement.

Land Economics
Concepts, Perspectives and Overview

Land: Conceptual Framework

Land includes 'the material and the forces which Nature gives freely for man's aid, in land and water, in air and light and heat' (Marshall 1890, Book IV Chapter 1, p. 138). The United Nations Convention to Combat Desertification (UNCCD) refers to land as 'the terrestrial bioproductive system that comprises soil, vegetation, other biota, and the ecological and hydrological processes that operate within the system' (United Nations Convention to Combat Desertification [UNCCD] 1994). The Food and Agriculture Organization (FAO), while referring to documentation for the UNCCD, defines land as

> ...a delineable area of the earth's terrestrial surface, encompassing all attributes of the biosphere immediately above or below this surface including those of the near-surface climate, the soil and terrain forms, the surface hydrology (including shallow lakes, rivers, marshes, swamps), the near surface sedimentary layers, and associated groundwater reserve, the plant and animal populations (biodiversity), the human settlement patterns and physical results of past and present human activities (terracing, water storage or drainage structures, roads, buildings, etc.). (Food and Agriculture Organization of the United Nations [FAO] 1995; UNCCD 1994)

The above definition is broad. However, academic disciplines focus on limited aspects of land. An integrated approach to address the spatial, economic, social and environmental aspects of land management as a tool for sustainable development has not emerged. In particular, there is a disconnect between land use planning, alternatively called town and country planning, spatial planning or urban planning and land economics. Urban planning in developing countries neglects the optimal allocation of scarce land resources among alternative uses such as development and conservation.

Geography considers land as a physical feature of earth and distinguishes between landforms: plains, valleys, mountains, hillocks, plateaus, etc. It explores the interrelationships between land and such factors as soil, mineral resource, topology, elevation, climate, rainfall, vegetation, population and land use. In ecology, land is a key element of the ecosystem. It links physical, biological, chemical, hydrological, atmospheric, climatic and other sub-systems. One of land's key functions is to support human beings, plants, animals and biodiversity. Land is the basis for livelihoods of people, meeting their needs for food, freshwater and other eco-services. Further, land acts as a source and sink for pollution. It is the key to natural resource management and conservation. On a social level, land is recognized as property, a symbol of prestige and a factor defining the relationships between social classes. In economics, the concept of land is much broader than physical earth. It represents all natural resources with inelastic supply. Land is an 'input' in agriculture, industry, housing and infrastructure; an 'output' in the form of real estate and a 'resource' to finance development. Economists regard land as an ideal object of taxation based on principles of public finance. Land is considered as a 'locational space' to carry out economic activities.

Land is a fundamental form of wealth, with use and storage values. While capital is subject to wear and tear, land appreciates in the expectation of benefits from its future uses. Urban and peri-urban land is a prime object of speculative investment in India. The paradigm: *location, location, location* matters. Well-located land in an urban area is a perfect asset for accumulating wealth. Rising urban land values constitute a significant source of unearned income in both developed and developing countries. Disproportionate rise in the value of land for secondary and tertiary uses vis-à-vis agriculture is a common phenomenon in these countries. Land and housing markets are closely connected with the present socio-economic problems in the United Kingdom, such as affordable housing crisis, excessive household debt, falling investment and productivity, despite increase in wealth, financial instability and increasing inequality (Ryan-Collins, Llyod, and Macfarlane 2017).

Piketty (2014) reveals that the stock of wealth represented by housing as a ratio of gross domestic product (GDP) has increased rapidly in developed countries since the mid-20th century. For about 270 years, the ratio of wealth in the form of residential property to GDP in the United Kingdom and France ranged from 60 per cent to 180 per cent. Since the 1980s, the ratio has exploded in both the countries; housing values as a ratio of GDP have soared to 300 per cent. In the United States, residential property values as a percentage of GDP have increased three-fold since the beginning of the 20th century. The Stiglitz–Piketty debate on capital in the 21st century highlights the nexus between land and credit markets, leading to increasing inequality and financial fragility. Land acts as a collateral security for owners and developers to access credit and for banks to lend money. Over the years, bankers have moved from relationship-based to collateral-based lending. This has channelized credit to real estate in preference to growth-augmenting investments. The 'financialization' of real estate has led to sharply increasing land and housing prices relative to disposable income. The 2008–2009 global financial crisis exposed the housing-credit nexus in fuelling a bubble. Cheap credit for housing based on mortgage-backed securities, improper valuation of property assets and excessive leveraging led to collapse of the financial system and stock market crash.

Land and housing are the most valued household assets. National Sample Survey Office (NSSO) 70th Round data in India reveal that urban households held 93 per cent of the value of their total assets in land and buildings in 2013. For rural households, land constituted 73 per cent of the value of assets, with buildings thereon adding another 21 per cent (National Sample Survey Office [NSSO] 2015). The lack of access to land is a major factor behind poverty in India. Dwelling in a central location in a city ensures the poor access to livelihoods, education and health care. They need a 'place to live', a 'place to work' and a 'place to sell' to overcome poverty. The Draft National Land Reform Policy, 2013, released by the Department of

Land Resources, Government of India (GoI) refers to the significance of land to rural households as follows:

> India has the largest number of rural poor as well as landless households in the world. Landlessness is a strong indicator of rural poverty in the country. Land is the most valuable, imperishable possession from which people derive their economic independence, social status and a modest and permanent means of livelihood. But in addition to that, land also assures them of identity and dignity and creates condition and opportunities for realizing social equality. Assured possession and equitable distribution of land is a lasting source of peace and prosperity and will pave the way for social and economic justice in India. (http://www.indiaenvironmentportal.org.in accessed 15 September 2020)

Land is a major source of disparity in wealth in both rural and urban areas. The Socio-Economic and Caste Census (SECC), 2011, conducted by the Ministry of Rural Development, GoI, reveals that 56.4 per cent of rural households do not possess any land (secc.gov.in accessed on 15 October 2020). About 50 per cent of urban households fall under the landless category (NSSO 2006). According to 2011 Census, 33 per cent of households in urban areas either do not have a room or reside in one room. About 25 per cent of urban residents live in slums and squatter settlements; the figure is substantially higher in metropolitan cities like Mumbai and Visakhapatnam (Census 2011). Exorbitant land and housing prices relative to average household disposable income have led to an acute shortage of affordable housing. In rural areas, credit for short-term consumption with land as collateral has deepened poverty of small and marginal farmers. Understanding land economics is essential to formulate policies to reduce poverty and inequality.

Land is a peculiar good—fixed, permanent, irreproducible, heterogeneous and scarce—with physical, economic, environmental and social characteristics. Structures built on land are durable. Backward and forward linkages between economic activities carried out on land lead to important externalities—positive for some agents and nuisance to others. The demand for land is primarily 'derived' from its potential uses. Both private and public sector players operate in land markets to meet their spatial needs. Supply is inelastic in the sense that the total quantity of land in a jurisdiction, for example, municipality, state or country, is fixed. However, the supply of land and floor space for a particular use can be increased by altering the allocation of land and development rights in planning. Price of land is subject to market forces including speculation, externalities and public policies, especially zoning, development control, infrastructure, land taxation and growth. The peculiar features of land are at the root of urban land market failure in developing countries. Government interventions are called for to address externalities, monopolistic conditions, under-provision of public goods and social objectives such as affordable housing to the poor and protection of the environment. Spatial planning is advocated on grounds of separating incompatible uses, reducing pollution and congestion, conserving non-renewable resources, supplying serviced land and floor space for growth-generating activities and promoting liveable cities.

The multidimensional nature of land calls for a 'transdisciplinary' perspective to analyse spatial issues (Hubacek and Bergh 2006). However, such a perspective has not emerged in developing countries. Even the key features of land that impact urbanization, economic growth, affordable housing, conservation and sustainable development did not receive much attention from economists till specialized branches such as urban and regional economics, environmental economics, natural resource economics and new economic geography (NEG) emerged. However, in spite of these developments, land remains grossly neglected in mainstream economics. The conceptual framework of land is fragmented. This is a concern as space is inextricably linked to economic activity and, virtually, all resource allocation in an economy takes place on land. Location, transport, accessibility, affordability, density and land use play a key role in agglomerating productive economic activities and catalysing growth in developing countries. Any misallocation of land is bound to have adverse implications for economic efficiency, apart from environmental sustainability, social equity and financial viability of development.

NEG and urban economics highlight the interactions between externalities, imperfect competition, scale economies, transport costs and factor mobility in the emergence of spatial agglomerations:

market towns, cities, industrial clusters, metropolitan regions and the like. Environmental economics refers to ecological externalities, including those linked to land utilization in the divergence between social and private benefits and costs. Ironically, much before the specialized branches of economics took roots, town and country planning emerged as a separate discipline in several countries. This was in response to the problems of overcrowding, congestion, pollution, slums, poverty and public health hazards in cities following the Industrial Revolution. Town and country planners emphasized spatial planning and timely development of infrastructure to address the negative externalities associated with urbanization. However, spatial planning has not integrated disciplines such as regional and urban economics, NEG and environmental economics. The neglect of land economics in land use planning in developing countries is glaring. Equally glaring is the neglect of land, location, land use, density, diversity, city and region in mainstream economics. This book aims to explore the concepts and perspectives on land in economics and their relevance to public policy, including land use planning, land policy and urbanization strategy.

Developing countries are passing through the 'urban revolution'. This is driven by two fundamental processes of development: structural transformation and spatial transformation. These processes reinforce each other. As a country develops, the contribution of primary sector to GDP declines, while that of secondary and tertiary sectors increases. For these sectors, both scale and location count. Economic activities subject to increasing returns to scale collocate in city regions to benefit from agglomeration and networking externalities. Such regions are shaped by market forces, externalities and public policies, especially development of public transport (PT), public health and disaster resilience infrastructure. A key objective of this book is to draw lessons from land economics and related disciplines to guide land management in developing countries. It is driven by the need for a national urban strategy to meet the challenges of India's demographic and socio-economic transformation—moving from about 33 per cent urbanization with 429 million urban inhabitants in 2015 to nearly 53 per cent urbanization with 877 million in cities and towns in

2050 (United Nations 2019). Though focused on India, the analytical framework adopted by this book applies to developing countries as well. The rest of this chapter deals with treatment of land in economic theory and lessons for developing countries.

Land in Economic Theory

The economic interest in land emanated from its role as an input in agricultural production. Mercantilism, which dominated economic theory and practice in Europe from the 16th to 18th century, recognized land as a source of precious metals such as gold and silver, extracted by labour. Land fed labour to engage in economic activities such as mining and trade, leading to accumulation of wealth (Polanyi 1957, 69). Physiocrats emphasized the unique ability of land to yield a disposable 'surplus' over cost in agricultural production. According to them, this surplus was instrumental in creating further surplus through input-output linkages (Meek 1962, 19). Kenneth Boulding describes the process in terms of 'food chain theory' as follows:

> The farmer produces ... more corn than the farmer and his family alone can eat. This results in a surplus. If this is fed to cattle it produces meat and milk, which improve human nutrition and perhaps enable the farmer to produce more food... Food and leather 'fed' to miners produce iron ore. Food and iron ore 'fed' to a smelter produce iron. Food and iron 'fed' to a blacksmith produce tools or, 'fed' to a machinist, machines. The tools and machines fed back to the farmer produce more food. (Boulding 1992, 320).

Classical Economics

Classical economics, which emerged at the beginning of the Industrial Revolution, considered the value of a good intrinsic to it, linked to cost of production. It referred to the role of technological progress and capital in production of output. It also acknowledged the importance of land as an 'original and inexhaustible gift of nature' and a factor of production. Adam Smith, writing at the early phases of industrialization, regarded the produce of land as the principal source of revenue and wealth of a nation (Smith, 1776, 1909, 627). In his theory of value, the services from land were costless vis-à-vis capital invested thereon, and so the price paid for land use was akin to 'monopoly rent'. Smith's theory of land rent anticipated later approaches to the subject, for example, rent arising due to factors such as differential fertility, location advantage and access to transport. In the late 18th century, another concept of rent, namely 'scarcity rent', was articulated by Anderson. This is a 'premium' to the soil with higher fertility as compared to land with lower productive capacity (Barlowe 1986, 138).

Malthus (1798) argued that exponential growth in population accompanied by diminishing returns to food grain production due to scarcity of land would eventually lead to misery of the masses. He regarded land rent as a genuine addition to wealth. Ricardo (1817/1951) combined the concepts of monopoly rent and scarcity rent. He held that land rent arose from 'differential' fertility or 'diversity' of land, implying that if lands were having uniform quality, no rent would arise. Further, a limitation to supply of land would lead to scarcity rent. Ricardo argued that as land had no alternative uses, rent to land did not affect the supply price of agricultural goods. An oft-cited remark by Ricardo is:

> Corn is not high because a rent is paid, but a rent is paid because corn is high; and it has been justly observed, that no reduction would take place in the price of corn, although landlords should forego the whole of their rent. (Ricardo 1817/1821, Third Edition: Chapter 2, p. 44)

John Stuart Mill (1848/1909) extended Ricardo's theory of rent to include competing land uses such as agriculture, mining, manufacturing and housing. He applied the concept of rent to production in general. For Mill, the value of land resulted from not only its role as a factor of production but also its access to amenities and services, including scenic beauty that impacted quality of life. Karl Marx did not consider land as a fixed factor on the logic that the yield from land could be enhanced by labour. He described landlords as 'parasitic' and capitalists 'exploitative', observing that land rent was 'a product of society and not of the soil' (Marx 1867/1909).

Henry George, considered as the last classical economist, viewed capital and labour as distinct entities. He regarded capital as a form of labour, produced by labour and complementing it. Land, on the other hand, was gifted by nature and in inelastic supply. It yielded returns to the landowner not due to his or her own enterprise but due to community effort, including public expenditures on infrastructure. George professed that economic progress of society would lead to an increasing scarcity of land for the future generations and accrual of unearned incomes to owners of land at the expense of productive factors like capital and labour. He recommended a tax on rents accruing to land monopolists as an ideal instrument to finance public goods. He also pioneered the 'single tax' movement, arguing that a 100 per cent tax on land rents was adequate to meet the needs of public expenditure (George 1879).

The classical economists presented important concepts of land. The aggregate production function conceptualized by them can be presented as follows:

$$Y = f(L, K, N) \tag{1.1}$$

where Y=aggregate output, L=land, K=capital and N=labour.

The 'classical triad'—L, K and N—recognized three main types of agents in the economy with three different sources of income—landowners getting rents, capitalists earning interests and labourers receiving wages. Most classical economists believed that as fertile land was in limited supply, agricultural production would eventually be subjected to diminishing returns. On the contrary, capital in the form of, say, industrial machines could be replicated and augmented. The classical economists, thus, predicted that there would be limits to growth due to paucity of natural resources, including land.

Neoclassical Economics

Neoclassical economics, pioneered by William Jevons (1865), Carl Menger (1871/1923), Leon Walras (1899) and Alfred Marshall (1920), took the position that the value of a good depends on its demand and supply—not intrinsic attributes. Demand is linked to perceived utility by consumers and supply to profit by producers. Walras presented the theory of general equilibrium; that is, all markets interact with each other and prices and quantities in these markets are determined simultaneously. Unlike the classical school, the neoclassical economists were not worried about the constraints to growth due to scarcity of natural resources, including land. They were concerned with how consumers and producers interact in markets. They adopted the fundamental propositions that consumers maximize utility and producers maximize profit under conditions of perfect competition, perfect divisibility, perfect mobility and perfect information. Further, a basic premise of neoclassical economics is 'substitutability' between man-made capital, for example, fertilizers, and natural capital, for example, land. This led to treating of land as a minor factor of production and neglect of space, location, land use, cities and regions in mainstream neoclassical economics.

By ignoring spatial phenomena such as density, durability and irreversibility of structures and indivisibility of infrastructure, the neoclassical economists did not pay attention to the role of land in rural-urban transformation. This is surprising because when the 'neoclassical revolution' was taking shape, regional and urban planning took roots in the United Kingdom, the United States and other industrializing countries. Planning theory and practice emerged in response to the need for designing space to avoid the evils of haphazardly growing cities that accompanied industrialization. However, economists and urban planners hardly worked together, the former articulating the primacy of the market in spatial transformation and the latter emphasizing the pivotal role of the government through land use planning and development control.

Jevons, who emphasized the importance of capital in industry, even ignored the role of raw materials. In fact, some neoclassical economists argued for subsuming all factors of production under capital. They considered labour as human capital, being the product of investment in education, skill and training. Further, they argued that there were no special features of land that called for its treatment as a separate factor of production. However, Marshall, who added 'organization'—division of labour and management—to the 'input triad', land, labour and capital, did consider land as a distinct factor. He stated that the supply of land is much more inelastic than the supply of capital goods and land differs from other factors of production in that it generates a 'surplus'. Marshall observed:

> ...there is this difference between land and other agents of production that from a social point of view land yields a permanent surplus, while perishable things made by man do not. (Marshall 1920, Appendix K, pp. 831–32)

Marshall also presented the concept of 'quasi-rent' to a factor when supply fails to match demand due to a structural bottleneck such as fixed production capacity. This economic surplus arises in the short run due to unexpected market condition leading to a disequilibrium situation. Joan Robinson argued that rent as a surplus was not confined to land alone. Rent could accrue to a part of any particular factor of production over and above the transfer price, that is, the minimum earning necessary to attract the factor to discharge its function (Robinson 1934, 102). Thus, the neoclassical school broadened the sources of rent. This undermined the special importance accorded by classical economists to land for generating a surplus. The result was that land lost its uniqueness as a factor of production. The seminal paper by Solow (1956) 'A Contribution to the Theory of Economic Growth' described the production function as:

$$Y = f(K, N) \qquad (1.2)$$

where Y=aggregate output, K=capital and N=labour.

Later neoclassical economists even chose to eliminate labour and describe the production function as follows (see Lucas 1988; Romer 1986):

$$Y = f(K) \qquad (1.3)$$

where Y=aggregate output, K=capital.

The above formulation treats human capital as a part of the broader concept of physical capital.

The reasons why the mainstream neoclassical school accorded less importance to land compared to other factors of production are narrated by Heady as follows:

> Land, as a factor of production, has no unique characteristics which should cause it to be set aside by itself in economic analysis. The principles defining the optimum use of land are those drawn from the more general production economics principle .... Land perhaps takes on unique importance only in respect to its use and allocation over time. Even here the tools of analysis and basic economic principles are identical with those which apply to any other production or resource use problems over time. (Heady 1952, 763)

Neoclassical economics assigned a limited role to land as an input. It did not recognize land as an output and a resource in rural-urban transformation.

Specialized Branches of Economics

Specialized branches of economics that dwell on land include agricultural economics, natural resource economics, environmental economics, ecological economics, real estate economics, regional and urban economics, NEG and transport economics. These branches have been confined to selective aspects of land as an economic good.

Agricultural Economics

Agricultural economics, established in the 1920s, aims at applying the tools of economics to agricultural inputs' management, production and marketing. It treats farming as a business and agriculture as an industry. It combines theories of firm and industrial organization. Agricultural economics does not regard the productivity potential of land as fixed. Such potential can be enhanced by more effective use of modern agricultural inputs and better cultivation practices. The discipline is concerned more with the management of agriculture than the role of land. In the past, agricultural economists did regard land as an input in production. However, they did not focus on this aspect as land was of little economic value unless used in conjunction with other inputs such as seed, irrigation, fertilizers and pesticides. They also did not pay attention to the relationship between land and credit in accentuating rural indebtedness and inequality. Practical considerations of agricultural productivity have driven the field to empirical investigation using econometric methods.

Studies by agricultural economists in India have focused on such subjects as agricultural business analysis, efficient resource allocation, food demand and supply, input demand analysis, farm mechanization, water management, cropping pattern, pesticide and insecticide application, marketing efficiency, supply chain management, agricultural pricing and food security. Research on rural land has focused on land and water utilization, rural land market, soil testing, soil conservation and agricultural indebtedness. However, rural land use in growing urban regions, ever-expanding city boundaries to annex rural areas, conversion of rural land to urban use and acquisition of fertile agricultural land for urban development have not received importance. There is practically no dialogue between agricultural economists, urban economists and town and country planners to address the concerns of food security, sustainable agriculture and planned urban development. The Department of Land Resources, Ministry of Rural Development, GoI has created a division dealing with land regulation and land economics. However, land economics has not received due attention from policymakers. This is perhaps due to the lack of conceptual clarity on land as an economic good. As Schultz observes:

> The quantity of land, as it is commonly described, is such a heterogeneous aggregate as to have little or no economic meaning, and very little has been done in applying economics to land ... Whereas the task is a difficult one, all too little has been done to measure land as an economic variable. (Schultz 1953, quoted by Castle et al. 1980, 419)

Environmental Economics

Environmental economics, established in the 1960s, deals with local and global environmental issues such as air and water pollution, land degradation, groundwater depletion, traffic congestion, waste management, greenhouse gas (GHG) emission, global warming and climate change. Its central concern is 'market failure' due to externalities and public goods characteristics of environmental resources: 'non-excludability' and 'non-rivalry'. These factors lead to divergence between private and social costs and benefits. Other key issues dealt with by environmental economics are intergenerational equity in the usage of environmental goods, economic valuation of environmental damages and environmental impact analysis of projects. Environmental economics also studies the economic implications of national, regional and local environmental policies, including their social benefits and costs. Such policies include clean water and clean air regulations, protection of common property resources, pollution quotas, polluters pay instruments, property rights assignment, etc. The Coase theorem states that when there is market failure due to externalities, bargaining between perpetrators and victims would lead to a mutually beneficial and socially optimal outcome under conditions of low transaction costs and well-defined property rights. The result holds irrespective of which group has the initial property rights (Coase 1960). The Coase theorem emphasizes market-based and incentive-driven regulation rather than being blindly led by controls. Land is a key factor in property rights.

Environmental economics focuses on resource allocation in environmental goods, including land. It identifies land with soil, filter for water, vegetation, wildlife as well as a source and sink for pollution. It regards land use changes as a key factor in degradation of environment and loss of biodiversity. The discipline also deals with other natural resources such as raw materials, minerals, forest products, fisheries and common property resources. Most environmental economists consider natural resource economics as a subfield of environmental economics. However, some favour to treat the former as a separate discipline with focus on allocation of nature-given resources for production and consumption. Similarly, some consider ecological economics as much broader than environmental economics. They regard the economy as a sub-system of the ecological system and conservation of natural capital as the central concern. Ecological economics uses a multidisciplinary approach and cross-cutting tools sourced from natural and social sciences such as ecology, economics, anthropology, sociology, archaeology, psychology and history.

An overarching theme in environmental, natural resource and ecological economics is 'sustainable development' aimed at balancing present and future use of environmental resources. Sustainable land management (SLM) is advocated as one of the key strategies to attain sustainable development. SLM is defined by FAO as:

> ...the use and management of land resources—soil, water, animals and plants—for the production of goods to meet changing human needs, while ensuring the long-term productivity potential of these resources and maintenance of environmental functions. (FAO, Sustainable Land Management http://www.fao.org/land-water/land/sustainable-land-management/en/ accessed 31 March 2020)

Land constitutes a critical intersection between economic and ecological systems. SLM aims at achieving socio-economic objectives subject to environmental priorities and constraints. The literature on SLM is focused on rural land management. Researchers have not paid much attention to issues such as rural-urban land interface, peri-urban land use, carrying capacity–based regional planning and building rights.

Real Estate Economics

Real estate economics deals with markets for land and structures, including residential, commercial and industrial properties. It applies economic analysis to study real estate, including property markets—demand, supply and price, location, land use, development, redevelopment, real estate investment and finance, construction industry, property management, land and building regulations, etc. Multiple actors operate in real estate markets—property owners and renters, surveyors, valuers, developers, renovators, real estate agents, town planners, urban designers, architects, structural engineers, financial and legal advisers, public and private lenders, regulators, policymakers, etc. In real estate economics, land is not only an input but also a product and a resource. The discipline is closely connected with urban land economics, dealing with the role of land in urbanization, location of secondary and tertiary economic activities, formation of clusters, operation of land markets, land use planning, land and property taxation, etc. It is also related to housing economics, regarded by some as a part of real estate economics. Further, with the increasing importance of real estate finance, the field has come closer to financial economics.

Real estate economics is closely connected with regional and urban economics. A central theme common to both is location. In least cost theory of industrial location, Weber (1909) contends that firms choose location to minimize the combined costs of transporting raw materials to factory and finished products to markets. In his central place theory (CPT), Christaller (1933) argues that various facilities locate according to a hierarchical pattern. A number of lower order central places, regularly spaced over the region, provide products required more frequently by the consumers; a fewer number of higher order central places offer goods bought less frequently. Lösch (1940) contends that firms choose location to maximize profit. His location theory incorporates profit maximizing behaviour by monopolistically competitive firms and welfare maximizing behaviour by households. The economic agents take transport costs into account, impacting market area, spatial distribution of demand and revenue from sale of output. von Thünen (1826) is credited to present the first theoretically elegant model of rural land use. He suggests that the relative costs of transporting farm produce to a central market determine agricultural land use patterns around the market town. The more productive activities compete for land closer to the market. von Thünen's theory has been extended to explain land use patterns in urban areas (Alonso 1964; Fujita 1989; Mills 1967, 1972; Muth 1969).

Regional and Urban Economics

'Regional economics is the study of the neglected spatial order of the economy' (Nourse 1968). Urban economics, a branch of regional economics, deals with the economics of cities and metropolitan areas. Regional and urban economics originated in response to the neglect of spatial dimensions of economic activity in mainstream economics. In fact, standard textbooks in economics hardly refer to land, space, density, distance, transport, cities and regions while the subjects have been extensively covered by geography. As Heilburn observes:

Traditional economic theory omits any reference to the dimensions of space by treating all economic activity as if it took place at a single point. It refers to consumers and producers, firms and industries, but not to distance or contiguity, separation or neighborhood. The fact that population and economic activity are arranged in a spatial as well as a functional order is simply ignored. (Heilburn and McGuire 1987)

Regional and urban economics applies the analytical tools of economics to study spatial and economic issues of cities and regions.

Location, land use and spatial structure of economic activities are key themes in regional and urban economics. The discipline dwells on some fundamental questions: Why do economic activities agglomerate spatially? Why do cities form, grow or decline? How are economic activities organized in cities? Why do innovation and economic growth localize in large city regions? Orthodox economics fails to answer these questions. It cannot explain the riddle of uneven development due to its preoccupation with 'perfect competition', 'constant returns to scale', 'homogeneous land' and 'perfect divisibility'. As Koopmans observes:

> ...without recognizing indivisibilities—in the human person, in residences, plants, equipment and in transportation—urban location problems down to the smallest village cannot be understood. (Koopmans 1957, 157)

Mainstream economics assumes a spaceless economy in which firms, households and governments choose one and only one location. The competitive model is ill-suited to deal with spatial phenomena, characterized by heterogeneous land, indivisibilities, externalities, imperfect competition, scale economies and transport costs. The spatial impossibility theorem states that in an economy with a finite number of locations, a finite number of households and firms, homogeneous land and transport cost, there exists no competitive equilibrium involving shipment between locations. In such an economy with 'backyard capitalism', production and consumption would occur at an arbitrarily small level to avoid transport costs (Starrett 1978).

Regional and urban economics focus on economic relationships and processes that influence the structure and functions of city regions. It recognizes that urban problems have in-built spatio-economic dimensions and cannot be meaningfully analysed without understanding the complex regional-metropolitan environment in which they occur. The collocation of firms, households and institutions in urban regions leads to external economies and diseconomies of density. It generates productivity benefits and cost savings due to internal economies of scale, external economies of agglomeration and networking and lower transport costs. It also results in diseconomies of density, adversely impacting spatial, economic and environmental outcomes. Regional and urban economics provide analytical tools to investigate urban problems such as overcrowding, incompatible land uses, traffic congestion, pollution, poverty, slums, sprawl, infrastructure bottlenecks, exorbitant land prices and precarious city finances.

Location and land use are central concerns of regional and urban economics. Land is a composite good with spatial, economic, environmental and social dimensions. It is significantly impacted by development rights permitted under planning regulations. The peculiar characteristics of urban land and development rights make urban land markets inherently imperfect. First, land use decisions introduce non-convexity in consumers' preferences and production technologies. Second, clustering in cities leads to positive and negative outcomes that are not priced. Density and use of common property resources lead to important externalities. Face-to-face communication is a key reason why economic agents cluster in cities. This introduces an element of non-price competition. Third, the existence of distance between locations implies that the producers of local goods—public and private—can enjoy monopoly power. Fourth, many spatio-economic phenomena such as rural-urban migration and sprawl are dynamic. They cannot be meaningfully studied with the tools of static analysis. Durable structure and lumpy infrastructure lead to fixed costs, scale economies and dynamic interactions among economic variables. However, urban land use theory and capital theory are not integrated to analyse such issues (Fujita 1989).

The term 'agglomeration' was introduced by Weber to explain industrial clustering (Weber 1909). Agglomeration economies occur in a city region due to spatial concentration of economic activity. The absence of physical distance reduces the costs of transporting inputs, outputs, people, information, ideas and knowledge. Firms locate near industries that are suppliers or customers. They perform better when located near other firms. Workers cluster near firms that provide jobs or a variety of goods and services. They perform better in the midst of other workers. The externalities of collocation impact firms in two ways. A bigger population may mean a bigger local market, increased scale of production and decreased average cost. As plant size increases, it leads to more sophisticated and specialized equipment use, complex production schedule, efficient division of labour and logistics, smoother recruitment and training of workers and better utilization of by-products. In addition to internal economies of scale, external economies are reaped by firms because a large number of them operate in the same area. The production cost of a particular firm may decrease when outputs of other firms increase. Firms benefit from backward and forward linkages, knowledge spillovers, sharing of inputs, infrastructure and risks, access to specialized labour pool, diversity, innovation and competition (Jacobs 1970; Marshall 1890; Porter 1990).

Agglomeration economies arise on supply side. Linkages between manufacturing industries and services and high costs of collaboration when situated away from each other are key factors behind such externalities. Network economies arise on demand side due to increased use, integration and merger of networks, including transport, communication, supply chain and knowledge. Metcalfe's law asserts that the power of a network varies with the square of the number of users, implying that the average cost of using a network reduces as its size increases. Agglomeration and network externalities facilitate productivity growth and reduce transaction costs. Density and distance matter. A 10 per cent increase in agglomeration is found to be associated with a 0.7–1 per cent increase in labour productivity in developed countries; bulk of the increase occurs within the first 20 min of commuting to work (Brueckner 2011; Cheshire, Nathan, and Overman 2014; Combes et al. 2012; Duranton and Puga 2004; Duranton, Henderson, and Strange 2015; Fujita 1989; Fujita and Thisse 2002; Glaeser 2011; Henderson 1974; Mohanty 2014; Mohanty and Mishra 2018; Puga 2010; Rosenthal and Strange 2004). The relationship between urban productivity and growth seems to be more pronounced in developing countries. When individual income is regressed on area density, the coefficient is 0.05 for the United States, 0.08 for India and 0.20 for China (Chauvin et al. 2016).

Urban economists classify agglomeration economies into localization and urbanization. Localization economies arise from the local concentration of a particular activity. Such benefits, known as 'specialization' economies arise due to (a) scale economies in intermediate inputs such as specialized services from accounting firms, marketing experts and business strategists; (b) labour market economies due to pooled availability of specialized workers, making 'spin-offs' and transfers smooth; and (c) communication economies through exchange of information, ideas and knowledge. Urbanization economies occur when the production cost of an individual firm falls as the total output of the urban area rises. These economies differ from localization economies in two ways. First, urbanization economies result from the scale of the entire urban economy, not simply the scale of an industry. Second, these economies generate benefits to all firms in the urban area, not just firms engaged in a particular activity. Diverse cities create urbanization economies by catalysing inter-industry knowledge spillovers, thicker labour markets, human capital accumulation and innovation (Jacobs 1970, 1984; Lucas 1988).

As a country shifts away from primary to secondary and tertiary sectors, it traverses into a new arena of agglomeration. Production moves from decreasing or constant returns to scale to increasing returns. Firms and households pursue non-farm activities wherein both scale and location count. Empirical studies suggest that agglomeration economies are weak in agriculture and pronounced in precision manufacturing and business services. They are strong in high-technology activities, public utilities and knowledge-intensive services such as banking, insurance and finance. Production of manufacturing and services tends to be more efficient when carried out in a denser cluster of entrepreneurs and workers. These activities use modest land in production. Manufacturing needs relatively more land than services. Most services require sizable built-up area, efficiently allocated by cities. Firms cluster to benefit from linkages between economic activities, larger markets, scale economies and reduced transport costs. Producers share common suppliers and benefit from on-job and off-job learning by workers and gains from access public goods supplied by local governments such as transport, water supply, waste management, electricity and other public services. These public goods are often subject to scale economies (Mohanty 2014; Mohanty and Mishra 2014).

The external economies of agglomeration are not without limits. When the concentration of economic activity in an area exceeds a threshold, external diseconomies creep in. The negative effects of density raise the real cost of production of firms, reduce the real standard of living of workers and subject them to the perils of pandemics like COVID-19. Agglomeration diseconomies manifest in overcrowding, skyrocketing land price, overburdened infrastructure, affordable housing shortage, decreased public service quality, increased public service cost, longer commuting time, traffic congestion, pollution and slums. They also lead to adverse impacts on agricultural productivity, rural livelihoods, energy security, environment and climate change. Further, cities, especially slums and squatter settlements, are subjected to devastating outcomes in the event of floods, cyclones and other calamites. The adverse effects of spatial concentration are closely related to infrastructure, density and land use in cities. They call for government interventions, which take the shape of developmental, regulatory and economic instruments. The latter include infrastructure investment, land use zoning, development control regulation (DCR) and land taxation.

New Economic Geography

Economic geography dwells on 'where' and 'why' economic activity occurs. It points to two opposing forces impacting location of economic actors: centripetal or agglomeration and centrifugal or dispersion. In his *Principe de Géographie humaine*, Vidal de la Blache (1921) notes that all societies are confronted with the same dilemma; people must get together to benefit from division of labour, but many factors make their assembly difficult. Losch portrays economic landscape as an outcome of a trade-off between increasing returns in production and transportation costs (Lösch 1940). Harris (1954) and Pred (1966) argue that without the presence of substantial scale economies at the plant level, producers would have no incentive to spatially agglomerate. In his NEG model, Krugman (1991a, 1991b) refers to interactions between indivisibilities, imperfect competition, scale economies, externalities and transport costs in the evolution of regional agglomerations.

Traditional economic geography dwells on 'first nature geography' (climate, topology, access natural resource, proximity to a port, etc.) to explain the location of economic activity. NEG emphasizes 'second nature geography' (location of economic actors relative to one another in the pursuit of economic activity) and self-reinforcing nature of the spatial economy. It suggests that the spectacular phenomena of cities, metropolitan areas, industrial regions, technology hubs, financial districts and the like cannot be explained without reference to increasing returns, externalities and transport costs. The core building blocks of NEG are market structure characterized by imperfect competition, product differentiation due to consumers' preference for variety and positive transportation costs. Together, they give rise to important externalities, influencing the choice of location by firms and households. Combined with factor mobility or intermediate inputs, these forces generate 'cumulative and circular causation' processes, resulting in core-periphery patterns (Fujita and Mori 1997; Fujita, Krugman, and Venables 1999; Helpman 1998; Krugman 1991a, 1991b; Krugman and Venables 1995; Venables 1996).

Krugman (1991a, 1991b) interprets Marshallian externalities in a novel way. He refers to generalized rather than industry-specific externalities. With reference to Scitovsky's distinction between 'technological' and 'pecuniary' externalities, Krugman argues that it is the pecuniary externalities from the demand or supply side that matter when scale economies are present. Consumers want to be close to producers to benefit from a variety of goods while minimizing transport costs. Producers want to be near consumers or firms with vertical linkages to reap scale benefits while catering to a larger demand. However, a place with a concentration of firms, whatever the cause, tends to have a larger market with many consumers and intermediate goods suppliers. Krugman observes:

> Because of the costs of transacting across distance, the preferred locations of each individual producer are those where demand is large or supply of inputs is particularly convenient – which in general are the locations chosen by other producers. (Krugman 1991b, 98)

NEG refers to demand and supply side circular causation processes in the spatial economy. It argues that when scale economies are substantial and transport costs low, regions with established manufacturing attract firms and growth away from regions with less fortunate initial conditions. Thus, a process of 'circular causation', described by Myrdal, and 'positive feedback' between production and demand, referred to by Arthur, sets in motion (Arthur 1990; Krugman 1991a; Myrdal 1957). If production or trade is propelled by scale economies, then agglomerations with greater concentration of production yield larger profits to firms due to positive externalities. They will, therefore, draw more producers and workers. Thus, externalities together with production and trade lead to the emergence of more specialized regions through a 'self-organizing process'. Mainstream economics did not have a tool to deal with scale economies and imperfect competition, leading to elimination of 'space' from economic analysis. This resulted in economic geography playing 'at best a marginal role in economic theory' (Krugman 1991a, 483).

Transport Economics

Transport economics studies the movement of people and goods over space and time. It deals with allocation of resources in the transport sector. It highlights the importance of transport in shaping location, land use, cities, regions and economic growth. In orthodox economics, the demand for transport is derived from the level of economic activity. Firms and households minimize transport costs while choosing that level. This is, however, too naive an assumption as changes in transport-related benefits and costs alter the competitive advantages to locations. They influence returns to scale to firms, inducing changes in location, land use and mix of economic activity (Mishra 2019a; Mohanty 2019). Weber (1909), Christaller (1933) and Lösch (1940) highlight the importance of transport costs in location of firms and households. Urban economics and NEG refer to interplay of centripetal forces due to agglomeration economies and accessibility vis-à-vis centrifugal forces due to congestion diseconomies, increased land and housing prices and shortage of immobile factors (Alonso 1964; Fujita 1989; Fujita and Thisse 2002; Henderson 1988; Krugman 1991a, 1991b; Krugman and Venables 1995; Mills 1972; Muth 1969; Venables 1996). Mainstream economics, assuming perfect competition, perfect mobility, perfect divisibility, constant returns to scale and absence of externalities, ignores the role of transport in the spatial organization of cities and regions.

Transport influences economic activities through direct, indirect and induced impacts. Direct impacts take place within the transport market—through transport suppliers and users. Indirect impacts arise outside the transport market—in goods, labour, land and other markets. Induced impacts occur through wider local, regional and national effects. Traditional benefit-cost analysis of transportation projects focuses on travel time savings. The value placed on such savings is estimated based on the opportunity cost of time lost in reaching valued destinations. However, 'time savings are the base metal of the system, but impact on GDP is the gold' (Mackie, Graham and Laird 2011, 513). Major transport investments lead to 'accessibility premiums' to locations and 'wider economic benefits (WEBs)' to the economy. They expand labour markets, catalyse agglomeration economies, mitigate congestion diseconomies, increase returns to density and networking and facilitate economic growth. Decreased transport costs also lead to increased outputs and reduced prices in monopolistically competitive markets. Additionally, a part of the increase in GDP translates to increased income taxes—'tax wedge' effect—that can finance public goods. Major transport investments impact city form, attract productive activities, enable the poor to access employment and housing opportunities, lead to beneficial effects on the environment and contribute to climate change agenda. They generate 'location rents' and facilitate value capture financing (VCF) of infrastructure (Graham 2007; Mishra 2019a; Mohanty 2019; Venables 2007).

Land and Inequality: New Perspectives

In his *Capital in the Twenty First Century*, based on analysis of historic data for several countries, Piketty (2014) finds that the rate return to capital (r) exceeds the rate of economic growth (g), that is, $r>g$. This implies that the owners of capital do better than other actors in the economy. The capitalists, already rich with accumulated capital, get richer compared to the rest. This led to Piketty arguing that unless appropriate actions are taken by government, wealth will concentrate in the hands of a few through the channels of savings and investment, accentuating inequality. Commenting on Piketty's work, Stiglitz expresses the view that Piketty did not distinguish between capital (which does not include land) and wealth (which includes land). He states that much of the rise in wealth has occurred due to increase in the value of land, especially urban land. However, the increase in wealth driven by land value does not mean that there is more land and, therefore, an increase in the productivity of labour. On the contrary, a rise in wealth due to a rise in land price does not lead to an increase in investment in productive economic activities. Indeed, the society's future prospects may be getting worsened with a decrease in the amount of capital goods.

Stiglitz argues that a rise in land values and rents, including monopoly rents, creates distortions that are detrimental to economic activity. He also informs that in addition to unearned incomes through the land market, people in privileged positions are also able to extract rents indirectly; for example, those with political or bureaucratic influences misuse their positions and resort to rent-seeking. Stiglitz cites the influences exercised by bankers who use their power to create credit and gain superprofits. Bankers lend to those who offer land or built-up property as collateral and use mortgages to derive a share of rents. The borrowers gain from the credit system to buy land assets. However, landowners, as monopolists, do not add value to national income. By using money to buy land for speculation, rather than productive capital to be used by labour, they do not contribute to productivity. The increase in value of land crowds out capital accumulation; the capital stock declines, even though wealth increases. A desirable way to address land market distortions and inequality due to unearned increases in land values is to tax land value increments and capital gains (Stiglitz 2015).

Insights from the Stiglitz–Piketty debate suggest that wealth accumulated through rents to urban land is a major source of inequality. However, neoclassical economics neglected the role of multiple forms of rent in accentuating inequality. Recognizing the merits of taxation of rents to reduce distortions in the economy, Stiglitz (2012) writes in his book *The Price of Inequality*:

> A basic principle of economics holds that it is highly efficient to tax rents because such taxes don't cause any distortions. A tax on land rents does not make the land go away. Indeed, the great nineteenth-century progressive Henry George argued that government should rely solely on such a tax. Today, of course, we realize that rents can take many forms – they can be collected not just on land, but on the value of natural resources like oil, gas, minerals, and coal. There are other sources of rents, such as those derived from the exercise of monopoly power. A stiff tax on all such rents would not only reduce inequality but also reduce incentives to engage in the kind of rent-seeking activities that distort our economy and our democracy (2012, 212–13)

Three major sources of land rents in cities in developing countries are overlooked by mainstream economists. The first is spatial planning, considered inevitable by planners to develop 'orderly' cities and mitigate negative externalities. It prescribes zoning for land uses: residential single-family home, residential high-density apartment complex, industrial, commercial, institutional, conservation, etc. Planning also assigns different development rights to land parcels through density norms regulated by floor space index (FSI) or floor area ratio (FAR), defined as permitted built-up area divided by plot area. The planning system leads to huge unearned increments in the value of land to some lucky landowners due to assignment of higher value use and/or higher FSI. The second is the development of regional and urban infrastructure: highways, public transit, high-speed rail (HSR), water supply, sewerage, storm drainage, parks, playgrounds and the like. These facilities create windfall benefits to owners of land in the infrastructure-impact zones due to enhanced 'accessibility' and 'serviceability'. The third is public and private sector action for economic growth, leading to benefits to areas impacted by productive economic activities. The benefit principle of public finance, coupled with the evidence that urban land is a prime source of inequality in wealth, makes a strong case for taxing various forms of land rents—at least the windfalls that do not owe to the landowners' efforts.

Land Economics: An Overview

The concepts and perspectives on land in economics have evolved over centuries. However, there is a considerable lack of clarity on land as a 'spatial', 'economic', 'environmental' and 'social' good in developing countries. This is rooted in the disregard for space, location, land use, distance, density, transport, cities and regions in mainstream economics. It is linked to the neglect of land economics in land use planning. Land economics passed through its golden era under classical economics, was ignored by neoclassical economics and has received a fragmented treatment in specialized branches of economics. It is slated to witness a revival following the new perspective presented by the Stiglitz–Piketty debate on the role of urban land in rising inequality. Land economics and policy are of crucial significance to developing countries. These countries will traverse through the 'urban revolution' for many decades. Land will be a key instrument to attain sustainable development. In land economics, land represents all factors characterized by immobility. It is associated with multiple forms of rent, including monopoly rent, scarcity rent, natural resource rent, location rent, agglomeration rent, spatial planning and infrastructure-induced rent and the like. Considered as 'unearned income' or a 'surplus', these rents are ideal for financing urban infrastructure. Land policy and urbanization strategy in developing countries would immensely benefit from the concepts, perspectives and tools of land economics.

As an economy shifts from agriculture to manufacturing and services, city regions become the chosen locations of firms and households. Unlike rural areas, where demand for land arises primarily from agriculture, in urban areas, it is mostly 'derived' from the floor space needs of secondary and tertiary production. Other sources of demand include housing, infrastructure and recreation. Supply of land for urbanization includes private and public land in urban, peri-urban and urbanizing rural areas and new towns. Infrastructure, especially transportation, is critical to servicing land for urban uses and mitigating negative externalities. Subject to the constraints of infrastructure, the floor space available for a particular use at a location is controlled by zoning and FSI regulations. While poorly designed planning controls lead to deadweight welfare losses, density and land management become increasingly important for sustainable development as urbanization escalates. Land economics emphasizes that 'location' and 'land use' decisions of entrepreneurs and workers in the spatial economy depend on interactions between market forces, externalities and public policies, not on spatial planning alone.

The classical economists articulated important concepts relating to land. The value of a product, including land, depends on its intrinsic attributes. Land is a key factor of production, is unique, is fixed in supply and is with zero cost of production. Economic rent to land is an unearned increment and an ideal object of taxation. Ricardo associated the concept of economic rent to land with the 'original and indestructible powers of the soil' (Ricardo 1817/1951, 67). He also distinguished between 'intensive' and 'extensive' margins of cultivation in rural land. However, he did not apply the same distinction to urban land. The Ricardian theory of rent made no reference to land use at the 'intensive' margin (i.e., constructing vertically) and 'extensive' margin (i.e., extending horizontally through expansion of city limits). Apparently, the classical economists did not visualize the pace of urbanization and its impact on land. However, the perspectives presented by them built the foundation of land economics.

The standard neoclassical position on land is as follows. The value of a product, including land, depends on its demand and supply. Consumers maximize utility and producers, profit. Market structure is characterized by perfect competition, constant returns to scale, perfect divisibility, perfect mobility and perfect information. Land is a relatively unimportant factor in production as man-made capital can be substituted for natural capital. Moreover, rent is not specific to land alone. The neoclassical production function, thus, includes only two factors: capital and labour. In general, mainstream neoclassical economists failed to recognize the importance of space, location, land use, density, scale economies, cities and regions in economic growth. Their basic assumptions regarding land are not appropriate for developing countries in urban transition, such as India. Land is the single most important input for planned development of city regions in these countries, whose future is 'urban'. Production in these regions is subject to externalities and scale economies. Urban land markets are monopolistic. Monopoly rent and other forms of rent are key features of urban land.

Neoclassical economists neglected land not only as a production factor but also as a positional good, impacted by spatial planning, infrastructure accessibility and environmental externalities. They could not visualize concepts such as 'carrying capacity' of ecosystem, 'accessibility premium' to locations and 'WEBs' to economy. They failed to assess the impacts of government interventions in land market through land use zoning and density regulations and public infrastructure investment, leading to huge private gains. Ironically, land classified as 'commercial' under the master plan commands a much higher value than under 'residential' or 'recreational'. Similarly, land parcels with higher FSI assigned by master plan command much higher price than those with lower FSI. Transport and other infrastructure facilities also lead to differential increases in land prices in locations. Neoclassical economics did not recognize such location-linked windfalls, which could ideally be taxed to finance infrastructure. In fact, it did not acknowledge the uniqueness of land in generating rents, responsible for speculation and skyrocketing land prices in cities of developing countries, and weeding the poor out of urban land markets. By neglecting 'location rents', neoclassical economics fails to explain the rising inequality in wealth within and between nations.

Agricultural economics considers land as an input in production but emphasizes that farm output depends on many factors, including seed, fertilizer, pesticide, irrigation, etc. While the assumption that other factors can substitute land has limitations, agricultural economics has emerged as an empirical discipline. It does not pay attention to issues of inevitable rural-urban transition. Environmental economics deals with divergences between private and social benefits and costs in the use of environmental resources, including land. However, it does not pay much attention to interactions between location, land use, density, development and ecological factors. Urban economics deals with the internal structure of cities: how land is distributed between urban economic activities and why cities have one or more central business districts (CBDs). Till the emergence of NEG, urban economics took CBDs and cities as given. It explained intra-urban land use, land rents, housing prices and transport costs following von Thünen's theory of land use. This camouflages the role of scale economies in the growth of cities. In urban economics, the 'urban systems' theory treats scale economies as localized production externalities (Henderson 1974, 1988). However, it virtually presents such externalities as a 'black box'. NEG strives to explain agglomeration in space based on microeconomic foundations. It refers to interactions between monopolistic competition, scale economies, externalities, transport costs, factor mobility and intermediate inputs. However, it neglects the role of government in making land markets work.

Land economics is fragmented between and hidden in disciplines. No branch of economics has addressed land in all its dimensions. While there is a need to establish land economics as a separate discipline, the evolution of economic thought on the subject presents some valuable concepts and perspectives that can guide land and urban policies in developing countries:

- Land is a peculiar good with spatial, economic, social and environmental characteristics, including immobility, inelasticity, durability and scarcity. It has multiple dimensions, that is, horizontal and vertical, access to infrastructure, links to important externalities, etc. It is an input, output and a resource, and a legitimate object of taxation. Every parcel of land being unique, land markets are heterogeneous.
- Demand for urban land is primarily 'derived' from the needs of secondary and tertiary economic activities for 'floor space', controlled by FSI norms fixed by planners. Supply of land and floor space depend on real estate markets that are significantly influenced by speculative land 'hold-outs', zoning and density regulations and connectivity infrastructure.

- Urban land markets fail due to reasons such as heterogenous characteristics of land; externalities of collocation, density, land use and spatial contiguity; monopolistic conditions; large-scale speculation; and under-provision of public goods and merit goods. They call for government interventions to address market failure. Interventions in countries occur through regulatory, developmental and economic instruments.
- Location and land use by firms, households, developers and other actors in the spatial economy depend on interactions between market forces, externalities and government policies impacting land, transport, labour and goods markets, public goods provision and economic growth drivers. Spatial planning stipulations constitute only one of the factors in such interactions.
- Transport and land use have symbiotic relationships. Transport investments impact land use by reducing travel time and costs, expanding labour market, promoting competition, enhancing access to economic mass, catalysing agglomeration economies, mitigating congestion diseconomies and generating economy-wide benefits. Transport–land use integration is perhaps the single most important tool available to policymakers and planners for SLM in urban areas in developing countries.
- Land rent is an unearned income, in the nature of a 'surplus', a key source of inequality in wealth and an ideal resource to finance infrastructure development in city regions. It is the key to designing a value creation, capture and recycling strategy to self-finance sustainable urban development in developing countries.

Spatio-economic outcomes in a city region reflect the operation of multiple forces that impact accessibility, affordability, density, land use, land value, housing price, conservation, inclusion and other factors in locations. They communicate signals to firms, households and developers, influencing investment and production decisions. Numerous economic agents choose location and develop and use land to optimize their objective function subject to constraints. However, independent decisions by economic agents regarding interdependent activities lead to externalities and market failure, calling for government intervention in land markets. Other reasons for intervention include prevention of speculation in land, provision of public goods, environmental conservation, social inclusion and implementation of planned urban development. Key instruments adopted by government authorities include zoning, density and development control, land acquisition (LA), infrastructure provision and land taxation. Land management issues in developing countries are complex and need to be addressed based on a holistic approach to allocation of scarce land resources. However, such an approach has not emerged—neither in policy nor in practice. In particular, urban planning and development through master plans have not incorporated the fundamentals of land economics.

Government of India (GoI) attempted an urban land policy in 1965. However, the initiative was abandoned and has not been revived till date. Most recently, the National Urban Policy Framework (NUPF), 2018, has outlined 10 guiding principles of urban policy in India along with a 'new' approach to land use planning. However, it does not make any concrete suggestions for land and urban policy reforms. It leaves urbanization strategy to state governments. This is a concern as urban sector reforms are intricately connected with the structure of India's fiscal federalism that neglects the 'third tier'. Further, metropolitan agglomerations are national engines of growth and the Constitution (74th Amendment) Act, 1992, envisages a key role for the central government in metropolitan planning and development. Importantly, urbanization presents a one-time opportunity and must be harnessed as a resource to accelerate growth and attain Sustainable Development Goals (SDGs). India must address the emerging land management issues, deriving lessons from various disciplines, including specialized branches of economics and international practice.

As history reveals, governments played a critical role in the rise of great cities of the world. They implemented strategic planning and development initiatives, working in tandem with market forces (Angel 2012; Fuller and Romer 2015; Kennedy 2011); for example, the 1667 Building Code of London after the great fire, the renovation of Paris from 1853 to 1870 by Baron Haussmann, the 1811 'grid plan' of Manhattan and the 1916 comprehensive zoning ordinance of New York City (NYC) laid solid foundations for orderly development in cities spanning over a fairly long period of time. During the 19th century, the built-up area of Manhattan increased seven-fold along the 1811 grid plan. This plan, along with major transportation investments and transport–land use integration, enabled NYC to become an economic colossus. Spatial planning and timely investment in transportation infrastructure, in conjunction with market forces, shaped the structure and functions of great cities of the world (Mohanty 2019). Governments in developing countries must make use of developmental, regulatory and economic instruments to position their cities as agents of socio-economic transformation.

Cities evolve due to the actions and interactions of numerous actors in the marketplace. When urban policies, including planning and infrastructure development, enable land markets to work without deleterious effects, they create conditions for economic growth. They lead to density and agglomeration economies, while minimizing congestion diseconomies. Density is a key resource for sustainable development as it prevents indiscriminate conversion of agricultural land to urban use, promotes energy security, facilitates affordable housing to the masses and enables VCF of infrastructure. However, density must be combined with investment in transportation infrastructure and carrying capacity–based land use planning to mitigate external diseconomies. Experiences of cities around the world suggest that ill-conceived and poorly managed density, FSI and zoning regulations exacerbate the failure of land markets. They subject cities to double jeopardy: market failure and government failure. The contagion effects of Covid-19 pandemic demonstrate that density without commensurate investment in public health and PT infrastructure, affordable housing and public services can lead to serious social, economic and environmental costs.

Land economics, the subject of this book, is crucially important for developing countries, which are in the midst of spatial and structural transformation. Rural-urban transition in these countries is bound to span over many decades. A key role of urbanization strategy is to promote economically efficient, socially equitable, environmentally sustainable, financially viable and disaster-resilient cities that act as catalysts of rural development and poverty reduction. This is a daunting task as objectives are conflicting, constraints are many and instruments to implement are few. It calls for designing urban planning and land development, financing and management strategies based on a clear understanding of how land markets work and how public policies can incentivize them to deliver outcomes. Referring to theory and practice, the book delves into the determinants of 'location' and 'land use', which master planning aims to artificially regulate based on an outdated, command and control-based approach. Such approach has been abandoned by the developed countries of origin.

The master planning model in developing countries is rooted in modernist urban planning theories. Originating from the Town and Country Planning Act of 1947 in the United Kingdom, it is top-down and land use-led. It aims at controlling land development and use, while assigning a secondary role to transport. Master planning pays scant attention to land as a composite economic good, namely land in physical dimensions + development right + accessibility to infrastructure, especially transportation + land use + land value + links to key externalities. Thus, master planning has not been able to harness the available resources and instruments to manage density, accessibility and affordability in locations, mobility in labour market, and design of land, transport and urban development, etc. It overlooks the fact that decisions of multiple actors in the spatial economy regarding 'location' and 'land use' are influenced by dynamic factors such as investment, technology, input-mix, production, economic growth and public policies. This book aims at incorporating land economics into urban planning, land policy and urbanization strategy in developing countries. It calls for restructuring master planning and undertaking broader reforms in urban planning, financing and governance. It also suggests implementing urbanization as a 'project' based on a value creation, capture and recycling framework to exploit the synergy between transportation, land use and local economic development. The project needs supporting policy and legal-institutional frameworks to promote SLM.

The remaining parts of the book are organized as follows: Chapter 2 describes the peculiar characteristics of land and land markets in developing countries. It explores the causes of urban land market failure and refers to instruments to address the same. Chapter 3 dwells on theories of location; Chapter 4 presents theories of land use. In these chapters, we discuss key models from literature, examine the determinants of location and land use and draw lessons for development strategy. Chapter 5 focuses on land use planning and regulations with special reference to India. We evaluate the existing master planning model and provide directions for a new paradigm. Chapter 6 is devoted to SLM as an instrument to promote sustainable development, integrating transportation, land use, density, inclusion, conservation and financing strategy. We refer to national and international practices with scope for pan-India application. Chapter 7 deals with financing land development, connectivity infrastructure and other public facilities. We refer to theory and practice to suggest a self-financing approach to planned urban development by leveraging benefit taxation and land-based instruments, including taxes on land rents. Chapter 8 discusses key issues in land and urban policies in developing countries. We refer to India's attempt to develop urban land policy in the 1960s. We also refer to NUPF, 2018, and evaluate the so-called new thinking. We suggest revisiting urban planning and development approaches to incorporate key principles and lessons from land economics and related disciplines of urban economics, transport economics and NEG to attain SDGs. Many of the tools and suggestions presented in this book apply to developing countries around the world, not simply India.

Characteristics of Land

Functioning of Land Markets in Developing Countries

Characteristics of Land

Land is a peculiar good, with spatial, economic, environmental and social characteristics. It is geographically fixed, immobile, irreproducible, permanent, heterogeneous, scarce and a fundamental asset. Every parcel of land has a unique location. While rural land is mostly used for agriculture, land in an urban area has many alternative uses. Urban land is a perfect asset for speculation, provided it can be owned at all (Ryan-Collins, Llyod and Macfarlane 2017). The quantity of land per se is finite. However, that for particular urban uses can be increased by expanding city boundaries and converting rural land to urban. Ironically, it is not land per se but floor space that matters for manufacturing and services in urban areas. Floor space for these activities can be augmented by increasing FSI. However, the right to develop land is not entirely a private right. Zoning and development regulations affect the exercise of such rights. Locational fixity, density, use, durability of structure and accessibility to infrastructure subject land to externalities. These factors lead to divergences between social and private benefits and costs, warranting government intervention. Governments also intervene in land markets to acquire land for infrastructure and affordable housing. Further, land use zoning and allocation of FSI, provision of infrastructure and investment in growth-augmenting activities lead to unearned increments to land, making it an ideal object for taxation to finance urban development (Mohanty 2014, 2016, 2019).

Land and urban economics refer to attributes of land. However, there is no comprehensive analysis of land as a composite good in developing countries. There is little research on how the peculiar features of land affect the operation of land markets, how land use policies interact with market forces and why such policies may or may not succeed. The key characteristics of land are as follows.

Locational Fixity

Land is locationally fixed and permanent. It is considered as a gift of nature, endowed with original and indestructible powers. It is not a product of human effort. The location of a land parcel, its geographical features such as physical dimensions, soil, topology, distance from employment centres, markets, schools, highways, public transit and the like are important considerations in location and land use decisions of firms, households and developers.

Immobility

Land is immobile. It cannot be moved from one market to another. Due to this, land is impacted by externalities. In cities, the value of land is closely connected with it being immovable, attracting 'highest and best' use, and commanding rents. A tax on land is considered an ideal resource as it cannot be evaded and passed on to non-beneficiaries of public expenditures on infrastructure and services.

Uniqueness

Land is heterogeneous. Agricultural lands in the same area differ in soil, fertility and suitability for crops. Every parcel of urban land has a unique location with distinguishing geographic, historic, ecological, institutional and economic features. No two pieces of land are alike; it is also not possible to create identical parcels of land. The key dimensions of land—'horizontal', 'vertical', 'accessibility' to infrastructure—and linkage to externalities differ between locations.

Horizontal Dimension

Subdivision of land into parcels for agriculture, industry or single-family homes and extension of city limits to accommodate new urban uses provide examples of 'horizontal' dimension of land. Poor management of horizontal land leads to sprawl, uneconomic expansion in infrastructure networks, longer commuting time, wastage of energy and adverse impacts on agricultural production. Due to these considerations, the subdivision of land is subjected to planning regulations by governments.

Vertical Dimension

Use of land in a multi-storied building complex is an example of the 'vertical' dimension of land. When cities lack connectivity infrastructure and safeguards to protect the environment, high rise structures can lead to traffic congestion, air pollution, noise and deterioration in public services. Due to these reasons, the vertical dimension of land is regulated by development control rules framed by governments, including those related to density, FSI, building height, structural soundness, fire safety norms, etc. FSI determines the buildable area that can be constructed on a plot.

Accessibility Dimension

This dimension is related to land's 'accessibility' to infrastructure facilities such as highway, mass rapid transit (MRT), water supply, sewerage, storm drainage, fire protection, etc. It is also linked to proximity to public and private facilities such as offices, shopping centres, recreational spaces and conservation spaces. Closely associated with accessibility is the concept of 'serviceability', referring to the extent land is serviced by essential public facilities and services.

Inelastic Supply

Land is a scarce resource, inelastic in supply. Availability of land for a particular use cannot be increased or decreased promptly in response to changes in demand. Physical constraints and lack of access to infrastructure contribute to scarcity of land and floor space for uses in various locations. User preference for a particular land or activity does not automatically lead to a supply response. In an urban area, the quantity of land for any use is subject to the limitation set by the master plan. However, the supply of land for that use can be augmented by reducing the allocation to other uses or extending urban boundaries, following legal and administrative procedures.

Derived Demand

The demand for land is 'derived' from its potential uses. Land is an input in agriculture and urbanization. Bulk of the demand for land in an urban area depends on the floor space needs of economic activities—for residences, offices, factories, shops, infrastructure facilities, parks, playgrounds, schools, colleges, hospitals, etc. The floor space that can be generated from a particular land parcel for a particular use depends on the norms set under land use zoning and DCRs.

Durability of Structure

Buildings constructed on land tend to be durable. While a stretch of land remains forever, services offered by structures built thereon may deteriorate with the continuous use by owners or occupiers and atmospheric effects. The utility of a building depends on its location and the kind, quantity and quality of services it is able to receive due to proximity to infrastructure. Durability of structure and infrastructure has crucial implications for divergence between user value and market value of property.

Property Rights

The right of an individual to own or use land or property is exclusive, not absolute. So also, is the right to exclude others from its use or to offer its use by others. Ownership can be separated from a land physically or legally. Land ownership can be divided by establishing horizontal or vertical boundaries. Property rights or interests can be freehold or leasehold. In general, the owner has the right to use, lease, subdivide, mortgage and sell land, while the government has the right to taxation, regulation and eminent domain. The institution of a robust legal framework that governs property titling and transactions, securing land records, etc. is important for land markets to work. Tenure insecurity arises when property rights are ill-defined or not enforced due to poor information system, lack of personnel and weak institutional capacity.

Development Rights

The right to develop land is separated from the right to own land under town planning laws in India, following the British law. Unlike horizontal land in rural areas, urban land has both horizontal and vertical dimensions. The vertical dimension is regulated by FSI. Further, land is subject to other controls such as plot size, ground coverage, setbacks, height of building, fire safety requirement, access to infrastructure, etc. Institution of land use and FSI norms under the master plan and changes in such norms affect the exercise of development rights. Cities like Mumbai provide for 'transferable development rights (TDRs)'. This involves the transfer of right to develop or build from one location to another subject to certain conditions.

Impact of Externalities

Land is a positional good, impacted by externalities due to factors such as physical and functional linkages between economic activities, land use, density, spatial contiguity and access to infrastructure networks, public facilities and a clean environment. The use of a land parcel affects the value of adjoining plots. The actions of individual landowners are not priced, so also public goods like open spaces, leading to market failure. Externalities can be positive or negative. Firms located in proximity benefit from common suppliers of intermediate goods, knowledge spillovers, thick labour markets and sharing of infrastructure facilities. Households residing in proximity benefit from social networking. However, the collocation of firms and households in cities subjects them to congestion, pollution and hazards of communicable diseases.

Planning and Regulations

Land in urban areas is subjected to planning and regulations for reasons such as addressing market failure, controlling monopoly, mitigating negative externalities, providing core infrastructure facilities needed by firms for growth and making land and floor space available for affordable housing. Master plans of cities prescribe zoning for residential, industrial, commercial, institutional, recreational and other land uses. They assign FSI to land parcels in various zones and uses. Land use regulations affect the development, use and value of land in locations. Apart from land use regulations, LA, land pooling and other mechanisms for land assembly adopted by private and public developers to assemble land also affect the operation of land markets.

Land Rent as a 'Surplus'

Being immobile and inelastic in supply, land commands various forms of rent such as monopoly rent, scarcity rent and agglomeration rent. Spatial planning, zoning, infrastructure development and economic growth policies of government lead to unearned increments in values of land at vantage locations. In public economics, land is considered an ideal instrument to finance infrastructure on 'beneficiaries pay' principle. Land value tax (LVT)—an ad valorem tax on land—is advocated to raise local government revenues, while also acting against speculators withholding land from planned development process.

Economic Value of Land

As land is permanent, its value is determined by current use as well as future uses. Land is an asset apart from being a consumption service provider. The expectation of people regarding the future value of land makes them resort to speculative 'holdout' and withdrawal from the market. Thus, apart from current use value, land has storage value.

Further, the value of land in an area reflects its locational features, including ease of access to infrastructure, proximity to public facilities such as school or park, level and composition of economic activity and spatial planning norms appliable. Due to these factors, while the value of capital assets depreciates, the value of urban land tends to increase over time. Speculation in land market, stringent controls over land use and FSI and lack of connectivity infrastructure are responsible for skyrocketing land values in cities of developing countries.

Land as Collateral for Credit

Land and buildings are preferred collaterals for securing credit. This is due to ease of determination of identification, ownership and value as well as 'appropriability' of property—ability of lenders to dispose or liquidate assets in the event of an unacceptable default. The rise of mortgage financing has led to 'financialization' of land, housing and commercial real estate. Bank financing of higher land prices leads to increasing share of credit to land relative to capital and labour, adversely impacting business investment and growth. Distortions in land and credit markets due to structural, regulatory and informational factors, including title issues and legal disputes, also adversely affect the borrowers to secure credit and lenders to sanction loans. The Stiglitz–Piketty debate on capital in the 21st century highlights the role of urban land as a source of rising inequality, acting in conjunction with imperfect credit markets.

Land Markets in Developing Countries

A market is an arrangement in which sellers and buyers come together to fix a price at which goods can be exchanged. It coordinates the independent decisions of numerous producers-sellers and consumers-buyers. Markets send signals regarding consumer preferences for goods and services and their relative scarcities through the price mechanism. There is no single market for land as it is heterogenous, fixed, immobile and unique. Moreover, the market for real estate is essentially a market for rights to property or interests therein, including floor space. The markets for land and floor space are impacted by other markets such as transport, labour and goods and services. They are subject to externalities and government interventions through spatial planning; investment in infrastructure to service land; and regulations to control land use, development, building right, etc. A key challenge for policymakers in developing countries is to make land markets work for inclusive growth and sustainable development.

Demand for land in an urban area is primarily 'derived' from the floor space and public service needs of human activities. It depends on economic, social and environmental functions of the city. Secondary and tertiary economic activities collocate in cities to benefit from agglomeration externalities. They need land and floor space served by infrastructure, especially transport, water supply, sewerage, drainage and waste management. The demand for urban land is characterized by high income elasticity; a 10 per cent increase in income makes people spend 20 per cent more on housing and open space (Cheshire and Sheppard 1998). The demand for floor space varies between locations within a city, depending on historic, geographic and economic factors that determine the potential for agglomeration externalities. Locations within a city such as CBD, financial district, a technology hub or a manufacturing cluster demand a relatively large extent of floor space, leading to increased value of land. Excessive pressure on such locations leads to spillover effects and increased price of land in other areas in the region, spotty development, slums, sprawl and automobile-dependent urbanization. It also results in excessive pressure on existing infrastructure and adverse consequences for food security due to conversion of agricultural land to urban uses. Haphazard urban growth has serious implications for the environment in terms of consumption of non-renewable resources, GHG emission, carbon footprint and carrying capacity of the ecosystem. A major social impact of sprawl is the segregation between the rich and the poor, which leads to exclusionary urbanization.

The supply of floor space for various uses in an urban area depends on the availability of appropriately zoned land and built-up property, FSI/density permitted under DCRs, access to infrastructure, especially transport and conditions of real estate market. Urban land in developing countries is entangled in a web of obscure title, complex tenurial right, cumbersome transaction procedure, high stamp duty, poor record-keeping and prolonged litigation. It is subject to multiple laws and regulations covering aspects such as acquisition, transfer, taxation, planning and development of land. Stringent restrictions on land use, density, FSI and conversion of rural land to urban use are, to a large extent, responsible for the exorbitant land and housing prices and office rents in Indian cities. These restrictions, along with rampant speculation in land markets and chronic under-investment in transportation infrastructure, have led to scarcity of serviced land and floor space in locations with potential for agglomeration economies. They have also led to a shortage of affordable housing not only for the poor and low-income groups (LIGs) but also the middle class.

Investor perception studies regarding 'ease of doing business' in developing countries bring out the key concerns in procurement and development of land for starting a new industry or expanding an existing industry. Table 2.1 presents key land-related issues faced by investors and the factors determining outcomes in the process of operation of land markets and government regulations to correct for market failure.

Why Land Markets Fail

Market failure occurs when the pursuit of private interests by firms and households does not ensure an 'efficient' use of the society's resources or a 'fair' distribution of the society's goods and services. The concept is central to welfare economics, which presents two fundamental theorems. The first welfare theorem states that under certain conditions, a perfectly competitive market leads to a socially optimal outcome. In other words, a perfectly competitive equilibrium is Pareto optimal. This means that given real income distribution and legal property rights, it is not possible to increase the aggregate welfare without reducing the welfare of at least one individual. Alternatively, no reallocation of resources or redistribution of goods and services can make one individual better off without making another worse off. The second welfare theorem states that under certain conditions, every Pareto optimal outcome, whatever be its distributional properties, can be attained through the market by transferring money between agents

Table 2.1 Land Market Issues Confronting Investors in Developing Countries

Issue	Key Concerns	Factors Determining Outcomes
Access to land	• Is land of desired dimensions and quality available? • What will be the purchase price of or lease rent for land? • What will be the time required to take legal possession of land?	• Ownership—state, local, community or private; • Ownership and use restrictions; • Planning and zoning requirements, including development control norms applicable; • Cost of registration of land/property and • Land and property taxes payable.
Property rights	• Is the land or property right secure? • What are the rights of the owners and users versus the rights of the state? • Is the property mortgaged to any party? • Can the property be used as a collateral for securing credit?	• Property titling process; • State of land and property records' management and updating; • Property registration procedures and cost; • Transfer of property rights; • Rules for pledging property as collateral to secure credit; • Jurisdiction of courts in property matters; and • Court litigation, if any.
Land use and development	• For what purposes can the land be used? • What are the planning and development control norms: approach road width, ground coverage, setbacks, open space requirement, FSI, etc.?	• Zoning and land use regulations; • Other regulations such as fire and traffic safety; • Procedures for land conversion and change of land use; • Environmental Impact Assessment (EIA) requirement, if any; • Building construction permit—fees to be paid and time required to obtain such permit and • Utilities—infrastructure and services available; connection costs and time required.
Consistency of treatment	• Are all the competing investors treated equally?	• State of public sector governance—transparency, accountability, rule of law, etc.

Source: World Bank (2005).

in a lumpsum fashion or through an appropriate redistribution of initial endowments. An important condition for the theorems to hold is as follows: both consumer preferences and production possibility sets are convex.

Key assumptions for a perfectly competitive market include the following: a large number of buyers and sellers, none having any power to influence price and each behaving as a price taker; free entry and free exit; each firm produces and sells non-differentiated or homogeneous goods; all goods have prices; households and firms have perfect information about products and prices; factors of production are perfectly mobile; no scale economies exist and there are no externalities. Economists argue that a perfectly competitive market leads to an efficient outcome as the society is able to optimally use its scarce resources to satisfy the social needs. The term 'efficiency' in economics has different connotations as follows.

Allocative Efficiency

Resources are allocated for the production of goods and services that the society desires most. This is achieved when consumers place value on a good or service equal to the cost of additional resources used up in its production, or price = marginal cost (MC).

Productive Efficiency

Production of goods and services takes place at the lowest average cost, given the mix of inputs. It is not possible to produce more of one commodity without reducing the production of at least another commodity.

Technical Efficiency

Production of goods and services occurs with use of the minimum amount of resources. To put differently, maximum output is produced from a given combination of inputs with the choice of technology.

Social Efficiency

The society takes into account externalities and evaluates decisions regarding production or consumption of goods and services by private actors in terms of social benefits and costs. This is achieved when marginal social benefit (MSB) of production or consumption equals marginal social cost (MSC).

Markets fail when the outcomes they produce do not meet the criteria for efficiency. Common factors responsible for market failure are public goods—with missing markets; local public goods—with provision confined to local jurisdictions; externalities; merit goods—with incomplete markets; monopoly power; informational asymmetries; factor immobility; insecure property rights; and unfair distribution of resources. Some of these are described below.

Public Goods

Public goods present a case of missing markets. They are characterized by non-rivalry and non-excludability. Non-rivalry means that the quantity of the good supplied does not reduce as more people consume the same. Non-excludability means that it is impossible or very costly to exclude anyone from consumption. Examples of public goods include defence, clean air, street lighting and flood control. Markets do not provide public goods due to 'free ridership' problem as non-payers cannot be excluded from consumption.

Local Public Goods

Local public goods are public goods whose supply is limited to a geographical area. They include roads, water supply, sewerage, drainage, fire services, local public schools, etc. Members of the local jurisdiction share the cost of local public services. An increase in number of members and service provided may lead to reduction in average cost of service due to returns to scale or in per capita tax payable due to returns to sharing. Most local public goods are congestible.

Externalities

Externalities arise when producing or consuming a good by a person affects the well-being of an unrelated party, without benefits or costs being reflected in market price. Public goods and merit goods lead to positive externalities; public nuisances and demerit goods result in negative externalities. When positive externalities are present, say due to improved public health or education, social marginal benefit (SMB) of production exceeds private marginal benefit (PMB). In the case of negative externalities, say due to pollution from a factory or traffic congestion, social marginal cost (SMC) exceeds private marginal cost (PMC). Figure 2.1 illustrates the divergence between social and private costs due to negative externalities on the supply side. The market demand curve, represented by PMB, is downward-sloping, indicating that demand increases as price falls. Market supply curve, represented by PMC, is upward-sloping, indicating that PMC goes up as production increases. The SMC curve is above PMC in view of congestion externalities. Q_E presents the market equilibrium demand and supply, determined by intersection of PMB and PMC curves at A; AB

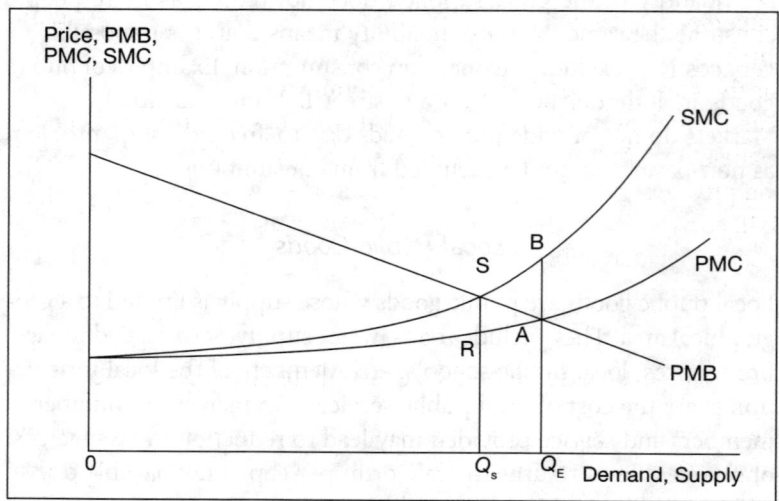

Figure 2.1 *Negative Externality on Supply Side: Divergence between Market and Social Outcomes*

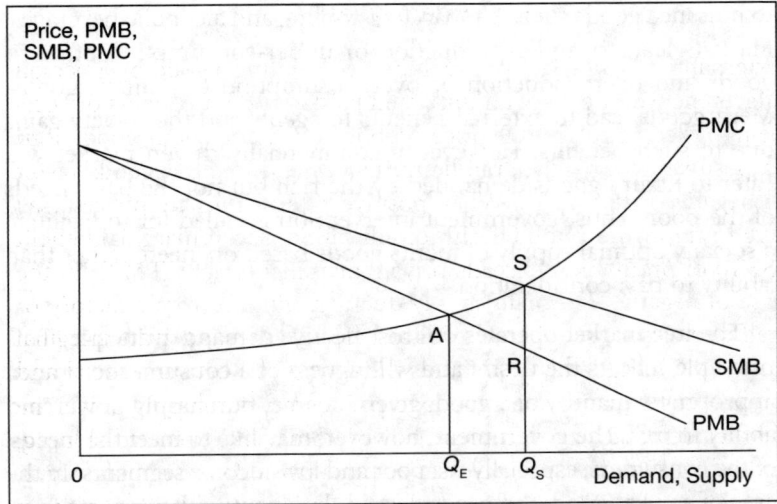

Figure 2.2 *Positive Externality on Demand Side: Divergence between Market and Social Outcomes*

represents the externality damage. Q_S represents the socially optimal outcome, determined by S, where the SMC curve intersects the PMB curve. As may be seen, $Q_S < Q_E$. A Pigovian tax equal to SR is needed for the market to reach the socially optimal outcome, Q_S, and eliminate the deadweight welfare loss to the society equal to Harberger's triangle ASB. Figure 2.2 presents a case of divergence between social and private benefits due to positive externalities on demand side. The SMB curve is above the PMB curve due to external economies. In this case, a Pigovian subsidy is required for the market players to reach social optimum.

Merit Goods: Needs Versus Effective Demand

Merit goods present a case of incomplete markets, characterized by information failure. People underestimate the benefits of merit goods such as education, health care, epidemic control or affordable housing to the poor. Similarly, they underestimate the costs of disbenefits due to nuisance goods such as tobacco, gambling and alcoholic beverages. Markets lead to under-production or under-consumption of merit goods and overproduction or overconsumption of demerit goods. Merit goods lead to external benefits to agents and the society gains due to such benefits. However, a commercially driven market will cater to luxury goods demanded by the rich but not the basic needs of the poor. Thus, government intervention is called for to facilitate a socially optimal supply of merits goods based on 'need' rather than 'ability to pay' consideration.

The free market operates on the 'effective demand' principle. This principle reflects the desire and willingness of a consumer to buy an appropriate quantity of a good, given income, purchasing power and ability to pay. The government, however, may like to meet the 'needs' of the consumers, especially the poor and low-income segments. In the case of a merit good, the needs exceed the quantity that private individuals can effectively pay for. In Figure 2.3, the market equilibrium for a merit good, say, affordable housing to the poor, is determined by the point E where the demand curve DD and the supply curve SS_1

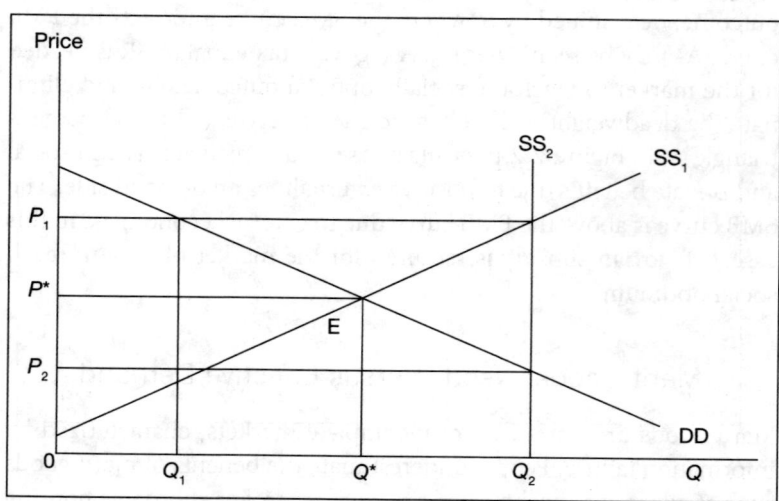

Figure 2.3 *Merit Goods: Needs versus Effective Demand*

intersect. This gives the equilibrium quantity-price combination (Q^*, P^*). If the society decides to satisfy the needs of the people equal to $OQ_2 > OQ^*$, the market will provide that quantity only if price is OP_1. However, charging such a price will limit the market demand to OQ_1. Only when the price is OP_2, will the market demand be OQ_2. Thus, if the government desires that the market provides OQ_2 based on considerations of social equity, it must be willing to provide a subsidy equal to P_1P_2 per unit to the producer.

Monopoly Power

A seller or a buyer or a few of them with monopoly power control the market. Dominance due to factors such as natural monopoly, patent or scale economies, may eliminate competition and lead to predatory pricing. The monopolist sets price at a higher level and supplies output at a lower level than under perfect competition. Under-production leads to underutilization of capacity and lower employment. Figure 2.4 compares monopoly and competitive market equilibrium outcomes.

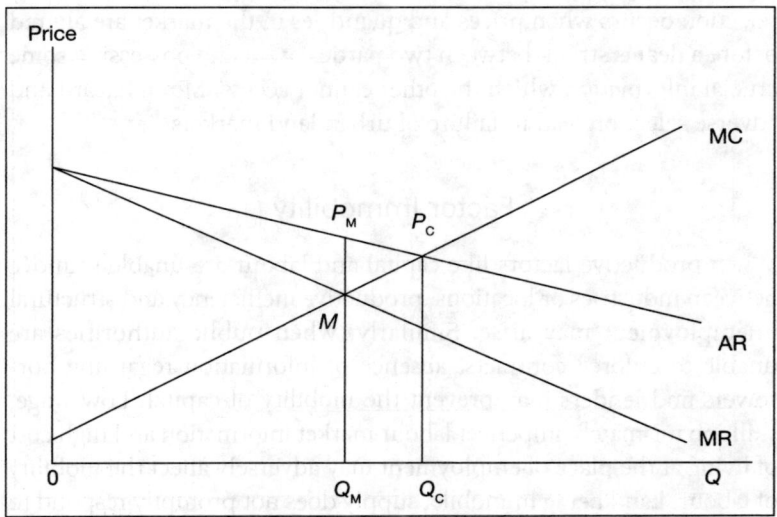

Figure 2.4 *Competitive versus Monopoly Equilibrium Outcomes*

The combination of quantity supplied and price charged by monopolist is (Q_M, P_M)—determined by the equilibrium condition: MC=marginal revenue (MR). The competitive market equilibrium is represented by (Q_C, P_C)—determined by the equilibrium condition: MC=price=average revenue (AR). Price under monopoly=$Q_M P_M > Q_C P_C$=price under competition; quantity under monopoly=$OQ_M < OQ_C$=quantity under perfect competition. The triangle $MP_M P_C$ represents the deadweight welfare loss to the society under monopoly.

Imperfect Information

When producers lack knowledge about consumer preferences and demand, they may be producing too much or too little. Similarly, when consumers are not in a position to have information about the quality of products and prices, they may be paying too much or too little. Asymmetric information between transacting parties leads to moral hazard and adverse selection problems. Moral hazard arises when a party, after striking a deal with another, takes unwarranted risk knowing well that the other party would bear the cost of such risk. Adverse selection occurs when prices and quantities in the market are altered before a deal is struck between two parties, with one possessing some crucial information which the other cannot access. Moral hazard and adverse selection lead to failure of urban land markets.

Factor Immobility

When productive factors like capital and labour are unable to move between industries or locations, productive inefficiency and structural unemployment may arise. Similarly, when public authorities are unable to enforce contracts, absence of information regarding borrowers and lenders may prevent the mobility of capital. Low wage, skill-job mismatch, imperfect labour market information and high cost of living at the place of employment may adversely affect the mobility of labour. Land being immobile, supply does not promptly respond to changes in demand by economic activities, leading to demand-supply mismatch and market failure.

Unclear Property Rights

When property rights are ill-defined or inadequately protected and ground rules for transaction in property are opaque, land and property markets do not function properly. Unclear rights to own, use, sell, transfer, mortgage or develop property; lack of a robust titling system; informal markets; and inability of institutions to formalize informal tenures and titles lead to inefficiency in the operation of real estate markets. Property is a source of security to the owner who should be able to use it as a collateral to secure credit for construction or other purposes. Insecure tenure in slums in developing countries keep large extents of valuable land out of planned urban development, depriving the dwellers of basic amenities on the ground of being residents of 'illegal' colonies.

Inequitable Distribution

Markets lead to an unfair distribution of wealth, income and purchasing power in the absence of corrective policies. The world's 2,153 billionaires reportedly have more wealth than 4.6 billion people who account for 60 per cent of the global population. The wealth of India's richest 1 per cent is more than four times the wealth owned by 953 million people who constitute the bottom 70 per cent of the population (Oxfam 2020). The free market leads to various forms of rents, owing to institutional barriers to mobility of factors of production. Urban land markets lead to huge windfalls to a lucky group of landowners who benefit from spatial planning including zoning, public investments and external economies.

Speculation in Land

Speculation is a key reason for land market failure in developing countries. As urban activities spillover peri-urban areas, speculators keep their land out of the market so that developers bypass the same and travel farther to purchase land. The extra distance creates additional social costs by increasing burden on infrastructure, sprawl and commuting time. Similarly, if landowners know that a high value development, for example, a technology hub is planned near their land, they 'hold out' property to charge extortionary prices later. More money is made by keeping land idle than selling or developing. This prompts developers to conceal plans and engage proxy purchasers to buy contiguous lands. The objective is to increase plot size so as to undertake high-density development and reap scale economies. Oliver Marriot in his book *The Property Boom* refers to a London developer trying to quietly purchase 300 odd separate properties on Euston Road between Warren Street and Great Portland Street underground stations in the late 1950s. Property prices paid varied wildly; for two adjacent cottages valued at £10,000 each, the developer paid £18,000 and £45,000, respectively (Marriot 1967, 161, 162).

Land Markets and Governments

Land markets in urban areas fail in both developed and developing countries. Urban economic activities and land uses interact. The use to which a land is put affects its locational attractiveness and, hence, land values in adjoining areas. The commercial use of a plot may increase the value of lands nearby, while lowering that for residential and other uses. Non-commercial use in an area may dampen land values in the locality but uplift values for commercial use in other locations. However, actions of landowners and users are not priced, so also, public goods. Thus, land markets also fail in developed countries and land use restrictions are imposed to avoid uncompensated interferences with neighbouring plots, ensure supply of adequate infrastructure, facilitate competition, control pollution, mitigate congestion and safeguard heritage and environment resources. In developing countries, the reasons cited for government interventions in urban land markets are many. They extend from correction for market failure due to externalities, under-provision of public goods and monopolistic land market conditions to enabling cities to discharge their economic, social and environmental functions. Further, land taxation is advocated to discourage land hoarding and to recoup the unearned increments accruing to private landowners due to public investments.

Externalities and Market Failure

The clustering of and networking between firms and households lead to important externalities: agglomeration and congestion. These externalities arise due to spatial and functional linkages between economic activities, density, spatial contiguity, intensity of development and access to infrastructure, especially transportation. Positive externalities manifest in opportunities for learning by workers and entrepreneurs; matching of employers and employees; and sharing of inputs, infrastructure and risks. Negative externalities reflect in overcrowding, congestion, pollution, incompatible land uses, sprawl, slums, poverty and hazards of communicable diseases. Externalities cause market failure, leading to divergences between market equilibrium and socially optimal outcomes. Public goods also cause externalities and market failure due to free-ridership effects. Most urban planners consider correcting negative externalities as a primary reason for government intervention in land markets through land use planning and DCRs (Mohanty 2014, 2019).

Economic Functions of the City

City regions drive knowledge-led and network-powered growth. Serviced land is essential for creating floor space to accommodate economic growth. However, the competitive market lacks the incentive to invest in infrastructure to service land in tune with the demands of productive economic activities. Driven by profit motive, the private sector is reluctant to invest in costly infrastructure facilities such as highways, public transit, water supply, sewerage and storm water drainage. While these facilities require large upfront investments, they are subjected to free ridership effects. A part of their benefits spills over the boundaries of the jurisdiction providing services and are freely captured by non-residents. Additionally, the benefits of lumpy infrastructure projects spread over generations and so the current residents are reluctant to meet their full costs. Government intervention in land markets through infrastructure development in anticipation of economic growth is necessary to enable cities to effectively discharge their economic functions as drivers of economic growth, for employment generation and for resource mobilization for rural and urban development.

Environmental Functions of City

Cities lead to changes in land cover and use, the singe-most important factor affecting health of the ecosystem globally. Urban land uses account for two-thirds of global energy consumption and more than 70 per cent of global carbon dioxide (CO_2) emissions. Transport and construction are the largest contributors to environmental pollution. The competitive market does not lead to socially optimal land development and use due to externalities. It leads to overuse of non-renewable resources, air pollution, congestion and spillover effects of land-based activities. Urban land markets, left to themselves, result in the 'tragedy of the commons', incompatible land uses and non-adherence to public health and public safety standards. A key role of the government is to minimize the adverse effects of land use changes on the society's environmental resources through instruments such as carrying capacity–based planning, timely development of infrastructure, transport–land use integration, trip reduction zoning, carbon tax, 'polluters pay', 'congesters pay' charges, etc. Further, the government has the onerous duty to conserve the environment for posterity through protection of rivers, lakes, water bodies, forests, heritage precincts, places of outstanding beauty, environmental hotspots, etc.

Social Functions of the City

Cities attract poor people in search of employment. However, urban land and housing prices soar due to speculation and constraints on supply of land and floor space as a result of restrictive regulations. Urban land markets exclude the poor and LIGs. They force these segments to seek shelter in slums, making them vulnerable to eviction by authorities and hazards of natural and man-made disasters. However, cities need a mix of workers with varying skills to function as large and efficient labour markets. On this ground alone, there is a strong case for government to cater to affordable housing, workplace, vending, transportation and other public service needs of the urban poor, including rural-urban migrants and commuters. Brazil amended its constitution to enable cities to perform their 'social functions', according 'right to the city' to the disadvantaged sections of society and addressing their basic needs for shelter and public services.

Recouping Unearned Increments

Over the course of history, arguments have been advanced by scholars to appropriate unearned increments in land values due to public investments for the benefit of the society at large. Henry George (1879) advocated a 100 per cent tax on land rents to meet public spending needs on economic and moral grounds. Economists also refer to the benefit principle of public finance for taxing land value increments due to spatial planning, public investments in infrastructure and policy initiatives to promote growth.

Choice of Policy Instruments

Developed countries combine developmental, regulatory and economic instruments to make urban land markets work. However, developing countries like India routinely prefer regulatory tools. They ignore economic instruments while neglecting development of infrastructure. In general, urban planners and economists differ in the choice of instruments to correct for land market failure. Planners contend that unregulated land markets lead to inefficient urban form, under-supply of infrastructure, suboptimal land use, under-provision of affordable housing and overexploitation of environmental resources. They emphasize the need for spatial planning and regulatory controls to address deficiencies in the free market system. Such instruments include allocation of land and development rights for various uses; enforcement of land use, density, FSI and infrastructure norms; and direct interventions through acquisition of land for planned urban development. Most economists, however, favour the institution of ground rules regarding property rights and adoption of fiscal instruments such as taxes, charges, subsidies and pricing of development rights to make land markets work. Richard Arnott observes:

> Economists and planners are often at loggerheads. Economists see the strengths of markets; planners see their weaknesses. When a market fails in some respect, economists favor pricing solutions, while planners favor regulatory solutions. Economists tend to be pragmatists; planners tend to be idealists. Economists generally respect consumers' tastes, while planners often challenge them. Though the philosophical differences between economists and planners are difficult to reconcile, a more productive dialogue between the two groups is possible if each better understands the language and the logic of other. (Arnott 2012, 51)

While Arnott's view is based on economic theory, urban planning regulations have flourished in developed countries for more than a century and are very much in action in developing countries. Policymakers agree that spatial planning, including zoning regulations, is inevitable for sustainable development. However, such instruments can be more effective, if combined with economic instruments.

Regulatory Instruments

Traditionally, town and country planners have advocated government intervention in land markets to (a) mitigate negative externalities of density, spatial contiguity, obnoxious land uses, traffic congestion, air pollution, public health hazards and the like; (b) build city and regional infrastructure networks; and (c) utilize scarce land resources to serve public interest. They argue that without standards for land subdivision and building construction, independent actions by firms and households will produce suboptimal outcomes. It will not be possible to quantify such actions to recover costs of public services. Additionally, direct interventions in land markets are essential to provide city services and promote 'orderly' urban development so that services can be extended without difficulties. In the past, urban planners favoured public assembly of land and development of infrastructure together to stimulate efficient urban form and land use pattern.

Modern urban planning emerged in the latter part of 19th century in response to the appalling conditions of overcrowded and 'killer' cities in Western Europe, created by the Industrial Revolution. It aimed at securing planned urban growth with land use and land development instruments to serve public interest, while avoiding negative externalities. One of the foremost advocates of town planning in the United Kingdom in the 1930s, Sr G. Gibbon summarized the arguments for planning as follows:

> Briefly, planning should secure that development of land which is likely to be best for the general good, with fair treatment of private interests and including in "development" all uses of land, reservation of open spaces among others. It should lay down such provisions for the use of land as would be made by a person of enlightenment and public spirit if he owned all the land. (Gibbon 1937, 13)

Urban planning was regarded as a technical activity, concerned with land use planning and designing of urban settlements in the best interest of the society. It envisaged two types of land use controls. The first land use control includes spatial plans, zoning codes and land use regulations that establish the legal-institutional framework within which land uses for market-led development must occur. The key legal tools in this regard are master plan mandating development norms and patterns; zoning to control the classification and intensity of land use; planning permission to regulate development; installation of core infrastructure to service land; and land taxation to act against idle landholding by speculators. The second land use control comprises direct actions by public authorities to undertake land development to ensure planned land uses. The two categories of controls, though interrelated, may have conflicting objectives.

Master Planning

Master planning originated in the UK Town and Country Planning Act of 1947. This Act legislated that 'all' land use in the future must be in accordance with the plans prepared by local authorities. It prescribed that no material development could occur without permission from local authority; ownership alone could not confer the right to develop land. This originated the planning permission system. The Act also assigned overarching powers to local authorities to undertake compulsory acquisition of land for implementing the approved land use plans. Further, it stipulated that all development value, defined as difference between assumed value of land with planning permission to develop and existing use value vested in the state.

The master plan, covering a horizon of about 20 years, presents a detailed view of the built-up form of the designated urban area in its ideal end-state. It comprises a report, land use maps and an implementation framework. It prescribes: (a) allocation of land for various uses, (b) regulation of land development and FSI and (c) plan for core infrastructure networks. Plan implementation envisages the tools of legal protection to the plan, zoning, subdivision and building regulations, capital budgeting, infrastructure development and urban renewal. Other instruments include land assembly, taxation, particularly land and property taxes, and capacity building. Cities in developing countries, including India, have adopted the master planning model. Paradoxically, while the model has undergone drastic changes in developed countries in response to changes in the economy and the society, it thrives in India without much change. The reasons for this include professional training of planners at the top of the planning profession influenced by high Western standards; inappropriate legislative basis for planning; and vested interests of administrators, planners, politicians and consultants.

The experience in the United Kingdom following the Town and Country Planning Act of 1947 revealed that elaborate norms and information requirements prescribed by planners choked the planning process. This adversely impacted development and prompted a movement towards much less detailed planning. The performance of the 1947 Act was dismal. However, its prescription that no development could occur without planning permission has come to stay. This has, in essence, nationalized the development right on land. The Planning Advisory Group Report, 1965, in the UK advocated the concept of development plan (DP), comprising structure and local plans to replace the detailed master plan. This was legalized in the Town and Country Planning Act of 1968. The structural plans were envisaged to be strategic DPs presenting a broad framework of policies and strategies looking forward up to 20 years. Local plans were to be prepared in accordance with structure plans. The UK Planning and Compulsory Purchase Act, 2004, prescribed for replacing structural plans by regional spatial strategies (RSS) and local development documents (LDD). The Localism Act, 2011, decentralized decision-making regarding planning to communities and neighbourhoods. Thus, British town planning has moved away from an interventionist regime to a democratic and decentralized paradigm.

Land Use Zoning

Land use zoning originated before master planning took roots. Subsequently, it has become a central component of the master plan. Zoning aims at balancing residential, commercial, industrial, institutional, recreational and other land uses needed for socially desirable urbanization, correcting for externalities due to density, spatial contiguity, not-in-my-backyard (NIMBY) syndrome, pollution, congestion, noise, conversion of agricultural land to urban uses, etc. It also allocates land for infrastructure and community use. Spatial planners contend that the joint development of a large number of sites leads to more optimal land use and scale economies than if owners acted independently. Further, activities on adjacent sites impact on one another in positive and negative ways, but transaction costs to arrive at private agreements between landowners can be exorbitant. Conservation of natural and heritage resources also warrants government intervention. Often zoning is advocated to promote affordable housing for the poor and local economic development. It provides norms for conforming and non-conforming land uses, density, FSI, housing, including light and ventilation, fire safety, infrastructure, etc. Zoning rules are supplemented by (a) subdivision regulations, prescribing street layouts, lot sizes, land allocation for public use, taxes and charges towards infrastructure and services, etc. and (b) building codes, setting standards of construction.

The practice of zoning was widespread in Europe by the end of the 19th century. It gained momentum in the United States in the early 20th century. NYC developed the first zoning ordinance in 1916. It established regulations for height and setback controls on buildings and for separation of incompatible uses to prevent industry from encroaching into the office and department store district of Manhattan. The United States Department of Commerce issued Standard State Zoning Enabling Act in draft form in 1922 and in final form in 1926. This enabled local governments to establish planning districts to mitigate negative externalities, ensure public health, safety and convenience, etc. In 2026, the US Supreme Court in the case of *Village of Euclid, Ohio vs. Ambler Realty Company* upheld the constitutional validity of zoning on the grounds of protecting public health, welfare and safety. Following this landmark judgement, zoning was extensively adopted by cities across the United States by 1930. The paradigm has percolated to every part of the world, including India.

Planning Permission

The Housing and Town Planning Act of 1909 in the United Kingdom was the first major piece of legislation to empower local authorities to 'restrict' private development not in conformity with town planning principles. It advocated Town Planning Scheme (TPS) without mandating the same. The Town and Country Planning Act of 1947 advanced the general proposition that all land use in the future should be in accordance with the plans prepared by local authority. Further, any material development required permission from such authority. The Act also empowered local authorities to acquire land to implement the master plans. If a particular parcel of land could not be excluded from the benefits of development but the landowners were unwilling to contribute to the same, then the local authority could resort to compulsory acquisition of land.

Town planning norms for development in layouts cover width of approach and internal roads, distribution of land among various uses, provision of infrastructure, dimensions of open spaces, reservation of land for LIGs, etc. Building norms include minimum size of plot, plot coverage ratio, width of access road, setbacks, FSI, height of building, all around open spaces, fire safety requirements, allocation of space for service personnel, etc. The landowner or developer must apply for permit to the designated planning authority to take up development, redevelopment, renewal or construction, by providing all necessary documentation and paying the prescribed fees. Some regulations also prescribe for 'completion' or 'occupancy 'certificate' from the local authority before putting the premises to use.

Direct Intervention

Direct intervention by government in land market was advocated by the UK Town and Country Planning Act, 1947, to implement the approved land use plans. This legal provision has been adopted by planning laws in developing countries like India. Some scholars argue that direct intervention in land market is required to enable the government to appropriate the 'surplus' accruing to land for the social good. They contend that unearned increments to land arise due to community actions such as spatial planning and public investments in infrastructure. In the past, public authorities in developing countries supplied government-owned or acquired land to public and private developers to undertake planned urban development, including affordable housing. The developers were required to install public facilities such as roads, water supply, sewerage, drainage, schools, hospitals, parks and playgrounds. A portion of developed land was handed over to government for sale to raise resources for installation of external infrastructure. Alternatively, the cost of connectivity infrastructure was recouped through external development charges (EDC). Governments also implemented TPS based on the concept of land pooling and negotiated purchase of land from private landowners to undertake land development based on public-private partnership.

Several cities around the world have resorted to slum rehabilitation programmes with in situ upgradation of slums or relocation. In general, relocation programmes are opposed by slumdwellers on the ground of being deprived of access to employment opportunities. Mumbai and Pune have implemented slum redevelopment scheme in partnership with private developers. This involves demolition of slums and free-of-cost accommodation to eligible slumdwellers in high rise structures built on a part of the land. The other part is used by the developer to construct apartments for sale in the market to recoup the cost of free houses to slumdwellers. However, the schemes are complex due to vexatious land ownership, occupation and tenurial issues, political economy factors and difficulties in accommodating the dislocated slumdwellers during the construction period.

Economic Instruments

The efficacy of regulatory interventions in land markets depends on several factors, including cause of market failure, design of instruments, local government capacity to implement regulation, complementary policies and vested interests. When the markets for land and floor space are heavily constrained by low FSI and large-scale land hoarding by speculators, land use–related instruments may not succeed in increasing floor space for economic activities. Similarly, reservation of land or floor space for the poor and LIGs in land development and housing projects may not be able to address the shortage in affordable housing when real estate markets are extreme and exclude such sections on considerations of 'effective demand', disregarding their 'needs'. Economists also argue that stringent regulations lead to adverse incentives to subvert them. They promote rent-seeking and channelize effort to get a large share of the pie rather than increasing the pie (Stiglitz 2012, 2015). They diminish the pace of release of developable land in the market and discourage the construction of floor space, as landowners suspect the motives of regulators. Further, the capacity of urban planners to implement regulations is limited in developing countries. Economists advocate pecuniary instruments, operating through the price mechanism, to supplement regulatory interventions.

The experiences of developed countries suggest that overambitious, ill-designed and poorly implemented spatial planning controls lead to high social costs. Such controls eliminate the valuable signals transmitted by demand and supply channels in the spatial economy to guide resource allocation. They dampen private sector initiative to procure and develop land for growth-generating activities and affordable housing. A central issue in urban policy in developing countries is to make land markets avoid, correct or offset weaknesses, simultaneously minimizing the deleterious effects of regulatory controls. The choice of the mix of instruments for intervention in urban land markets is crucial. In their textbook *Public Sector Economics*, Boadway and Wildasin (1984) provide the following rules based on the known principles of public finance:

> ...while typically the remedy for market failure due to public goods is for public sector to provide the goods, the remedy for externalities is often to provide incentives to the private sector to produce the correct amount." (61)

As regards provision of public goods, it is obvious that cities in developing countries have failed to make adequate investments in core infrastructure such as highways, arterial and radial roads, public transit, water supply, sewerage, drainage, gas, broad band connectivity, public health and disaster resilience. This is attributed to failure of master plans to present a coherent plan financing strategy, non-exploitation of land and property taxes by municipalities and constraints of fiscal federalism that neglects the 'third tier'. As regards the correction of externalities, it is obvious that instead of economic instruments such as LVT, carbon tax, congestion charging (CC), pricing of development rights and incentives to drive private developers to produce socio-economic and environmental outcomes, state and city governments in India have chosen to focus on physical intervention in land markets through land use, density and FSI regulations and compulsory acquisition of land to implement the urban plan. Decades of under-investment in transportation infrastructure, along with command and control–based land use planning at multiple levels, have exacerbated the failure of land markets. Paradoxically, economic instruments have not been exploited by cities in developing countries to supplement regulatory tools. Some economic instruments that could be adopted by Indian cities to supplement planning and regulatory tools are discussed below.

Land Value Taxation

LVT and its variants, including vacant land tax (VLT), are ideal accompaniments to regulatory interventions in urban land markets to promote desired uses. They act against hoarding and withdrawal of land parcels from development. They dissuade speculation in land and moderate land price by removing the speculative element in value.

Land-based taxes are also among the most appropriate sources to mobilize government revenues (George 1879). They subscribe to the benefit principle of public finance. Spatial planning and investment by public authorities in infrastructure and economic growth benefit the landowners more compared to what they contribute. Even a mere announcement by the government that certain areas in the periphery of a large city would be included in the master plan could lead to large increases in land values in those areas. Similar is the case with major infrastructure projects such as highways, public transit, HSR, water supply, sewerage and drainage.

Economists contend that a well-designed LVT leads to bids of land such that they balance economic forces. Lower land values exert downward pressure on housing costs and rents. They make homes and business premises cheaper. Lower rents also lead to higher net wages, stimulating savings and consumption. LVT, thus, facilitates investment in production. It prevents a disproportionate amount of capital, often linked to a large debt, from being tied up with idle property. Georgists argue that income and sales tax regimes suppress economic activity and encourage bubbles. LVT, on the contrary, promotes productive economic activities and acts as a market stabilizer. It reduces the chances of erratic property booms and busts. While the merits of LVT prominently figure in urban policy documents and debates around the world, developing countries, including India, have not made a serious attempt to implement LVT or incorporate the principles of LVT in land and property taxes. VLT, though permissible under municipal laws in India, remains unexploited due to political and bureaucratic factors.

Benefit Taxes and Charges

Spatial planning, infrastructure and growth lead to direct and indirect benefits to numerous agents in the economy; for example, land use and FSI assigned by the city master plan result in windfall benefits to a lucky group of owners of land at vantage locations. Similarly, transportation infrastructure investments lead to WEBs by enhancing access to 'economic mass'. These benefits capitalize into revenue bases of all levels of government through user charges, benefit charges, benefit taxes, general taxes, etc. They facilitate resource mobilization based on the principle that those who gain from public services must pay towards costs. As a corollary, those who create disbenefits to the society must pay for the mitigation of damages. 'Users pay', 'beneficiaries pay', 'polluters pay', 'congesters pay', 'exacerbaters pay' and 'growth pays' are fundamental principles of urban public finance to promote efficiency in resource allocation.

Cities create externalities of collocation, density and networking, which benefit multiple actors in the economy, including central, state and local governments. In particular, these externalities capitalize into agglomeration-linked benefit charge and tax bases. Economic principles suggest that cities must have access to such revenues to internalize externalities and correct for market failure. Land-related benefit charges include betterment levies, FSI charges, special assessments, community infrastructure levies, etc. They also cover 'congesters pay' charges in the form of Pigovian tolls or surrogate instruments such as motor vehicles tax, fuel tax, truck weight fee, and transport tax. They act against urban expansion based on personalized automobiles and promote the use of PT. Land-related benefit taxes include taxes on land rents, monopoly rents, scarcity rents and agglomeration rents, LVT, VLT, water and sewer benefit taxes and the like. Property tax is a benefit tax for collective civic services. Income tax, sales tax and Goods and Services Tax (GST) are general benefit taxes for living, working and shopping in the city (Bahl, Linn and Wetzel 2013). Ironically, central and state governments in India benefit significantly from the development of metropolitan regions which account for the bulk of their revenues. A strong economic case exists for escrowing a part of the benefit taxes and charges accruing to them to facilitate debt financing of urban infrastructure projects which augment their tax bases.

Pricing of Development Rights

Environmental economics principles suggest that higher value land uses in a city should not occur in a laissez faire way but in a rationed fashion so as to maximize the overall efficiency of urban development. In a way, this rationing of 'development rights' by public authorities is akin to rationing of water extraction, fishing and forestry rights, wherein unrestricted operation by private market players results in net social disbenefit due to market failure. Higher value land uses—urban versus rural, industrial, commercial, retail and hospitality use versus residential, high density versus low density, etc.— also lead to windfall gains to a select group of landowners. Further, constraints imposed on land uses lead to monopoly and scarcity rents. Thus, cities globally resort to the sale or lease of development rights in areas served by public infrastructure projects to raise resources to finance them. Pennance (1967) and Hagman and Misczynski (1978) pioneered the idea of auctioning the right to develop. They presented a view that once a landowner has received planning permission, the right to exercise such permission could be put up to auction. Brazil has successfully used the notions of auctionable and purchasable development rights. Hyderabad and Bengaluru have introduced the tools of premium FSI that can be availed on payment of special fees.

Location and Land Use Incentives

Cities compete to attract the location of investments that generate growth, employment, housing and public finance. They resort to innovative land management tools such as incentive zoning, premium FSI, density bonus and fiscal incentives to supplement regulatory instruments. Planning-linked gains are often negotiated under town planning laws, for example, 'planning obligations' under Section 106 under the UK Town and Country Planning Act, 1990. The case for such tools rests on the logic that no matter how adept the planners are, the dynamics of a growing region cannot be captured by mechanical projections of economic activities and their land use requirements. Ahmedabad city has developed 76-km long Sardar Patel Ring Road and demarcated 1 km area around it as Residential Affordable Housing (R-AH) zone, permitting FSI of 4 for the construction of residential units of 36–80 m^2 of built-up area. The city has successfully combined transport, land use and density to promote affordable housing under its inclusionary zoning (IZ) initiative. Planning incentives and dispensations under the income tax and GST rules have attracted developers to implement several affordable housing projects. A rigid urban planning model could not have achieved the results. The rise of Bengaluru and Hyderabad as information technology hubs could not have been possible without changes in zoning and development regulations in tune with the demands of economic growth.

Making Land Markets Function

Urban land markets fail for many reasons. A key challenge to land policy and management in developing countries is to make urban land markets work to promote economic growth, deliver affordable housing and workplaces to the poor, conserve environmental resources and support rural development and poverty alleviation. The tasks are daunting as spatio-economic outcomes in a city region depend on interactions between multiple market and non-market forces in a dynamic setting. Land, transport, labour and goods markets, agglomeration, networking and knowledge externalities and spatial planning, infrastructure development and economic growth policies interact in complex ways.

Land markets do not work when ground rules regarding definition, recording, protection and exercise of property rights are not clear. Appropriate governance institutions need to be put in place to enforce such rights. Externalities, monopoly and public goods also lead to malfunctioning of land markets. Countries around the globe, thus, regulate land markets; they also adopt developmental and economic instruments. Further, public authorities own, control and acquire land to meet future requirements of public uses such as highways, MRT, hospitals, schools, public offices, water supply, sewerage and drainage systems. In developing countries, land records have traditionally been in public domain. Governments in these countries also intervene in land markets to secure planned urban development, apart from mitigating negative externalities. Planners argue that the joint development of land parcels yields better spatio-economic outcomes than when developed in isolation. It facilitates infrastructure planning, high-density development and scale economies.

Urban land markets in developing countries are imperfect and fragmented. They are subject to pervasive externalities and informational asymmetries. Unaccounted money is channelled to these markets through speculative deals. Returns to idle landholding by the wealthy far exceed those from selling or developing. The poor and LIGs are weeded out of urban land markets. Further, land use is a major contributor to environmental degradation and climate change. While the issues of urban land are formidable, instruments to address market failure are limited. In this regard, economists advocate the structuring of instruments based on diagnosis of market failure. They present broad guidelines: increasing competition, incentivizing market players to attain socially optimal outcomes and providing public goods and merit goods in tune with the demands of economic growth and urbanization. However, the master planning approach has favoured regulatory controls, ignoring economic instruments such as land taxation, CC, pricing of development rights and fiscal incentives. According primacy to land use, it has neglected infrastructure development, especially regional and urban transport (UT). Further, zoning and density controls prescribed by master plans are not aligned to the 'context' and 'initial conditions' of cities.

Geography, history and economics of city regions define their contexts. They shape land use, density, development and land value patterns in locations, leading to differential in-built advantages. Setting 'initial conditions', they present opportunities, constraints and signals to firms, households and developers. The paradigm *location, location, location* makes some places more attractive for growth-generating businesses than others. Such locations include CBD, mass transit hubs and industrial growth nodes. They combine accessibility, density and economic mass, catalysing scale, scope, agglomeration and networking economies. When government actions reinforce the strength of locations, say due to public transit investment and policies to promote transport–land use integration, they create conditions for competitiveness of firms. These considerations underscore the importance of structuring urban development projects, taking contextual factors into account, prioritizing objectives, identifying constraints, planning resources and designing implementation instruments.

The master plans in developing countries like India follow the 'comprehensive' planning approach. They are deterministic. Planning methodology typically follows the 'survey-analysis-plan' technique advocated by Patrick Geddes, regarded as the father of modern urban planning. It involves data collection, analysis of past trends and projections of economic activities and their land use requirements in the future, 20–25 years ahead. While master planning adopts a narrow view of land, land economics regards it as a composite and heterogeneous good, that is, land with physical dimensions+land use permissible under zoning code+FSI or density permissible under development regulations+accessibility to transportation and other infrastructure that depends on public investment+linkages to externalities that arise from the collocation of many economic actors and provision of public goods+land value and rent that depend on demand and supply, infrastructure access, present and future use potential and other factors. Land economics questions both the object and methodology of comprehensive planning. It regards such detailed planning unnecessary.

Master plans in developing countries, while embarking on utopian objectives, have relied narrowly on regulatory controls to attain them. Ignoring ecosystem carrying capacity, financing and implementation constraints, they have neglected developmental and economic instruments. Master plans have assigned land use and FSI to locations without considering their accessibility, affordability, density, land value, land rent, housing price and other characteristics. Master planning has accorded a secondary role to transport, undermining its role in enhancing mobility, promoting density, catalysing external economies of agglomeration and networking, mitigating congestion, balancing employment and housing and facilitating economic growth. Obsessed with land use and density controls, master plans have not exploited the synergy between regulatory, developmental and economic instruments in providing 'accessible' and 'affordable' locations to firms, households and developers to pursue chosen economic activities. Ironically, there is no evaluation of the social benefits and costs of master planning in developing countries, including India.

The importance of combining regulatory, developmental and economic instruments in design of planning and development strategies can be gauged from the example of affordable housing shortage. Such shortage signals that the supply of land and floor space is constrained, given market forces and public policies. While the urban poor and LIGs cannot afford the exorbitant land and housing prices in cities, the formal master plans have not allocated space to these segments. These factors, combined with chronic lack of investment in transportation infrastructure, have led to an acute scarcity of space even for the middle class. In this context, a combination of liberalization of land use and FSI to ease land and housing constraints, investment in PT to service locations, implementation of policies to promote TOD and transport–land use integration, allocation of space to the LIGs around transit nodes and corridors, a steep VLT to penalize speculative land holdouts and VCF of transportation infrastructure could be appropriate.

A fundamental premise of urban economics is that cities evolve due to actions of numerous firms, households and developers in their pursuit of economic activity: investing, producing, transacting, consuming, transporting, working, commuting, learning and innovating. These agents choose 'location' and 'land use' while optimizing objective function subject to constraints: spatial, economic, environmental, social, etc. Subjecting them to many mechanical controls is bound to dampen enterprise and initiative. People must have enough flexibility in optimizing their welfare, while adding to economic growth. Planners must appreciate that sustainable development objectives are conflicting, constraints of conservation and inclusion are binding and instruments to attain spatio-economic outcomes are limited. Thus, interventions in the functioning of urban land markets must be designed carefully; they must not be based on an 'one size fits all' approach. Land economics prescribes incentivizing developers to make serviced land and floor space available for growth while contributing to inclusion and conservation, investing in public goods in anticipation of growth and levying a graduated tax on vacant land, steeply increasing with the period land is held idle to prevent speculative 'holdouts'. Policymakers and planners must study the determinants of 'location' and 'land use' in designing policies and instruments to make land markets work for inclusive growth and sustainable development.

Determinants of Location

Theory, Practice and Lessons for Development Strategy

Location, Location, Location

A key paradigm in economic geography and spatial economics is *location, location, location*. This applies to most economic activities, particularly real estate. If one has to identify a single determinant of attractiveness or value of a residential, commercial or industrial property in an urban area, it is 'location'. Whether it is proximity to CBD or an employment centre, access to a public transit network or market for goods and distance to a natural landscape or a place of scenic beauty, location summarizes the strengths and weaknesses of a place to carry out business, work, live, transact or recreate. The productivity of secondary and tertiary sector firms in a spatial economy is significantly dependent on location and land use. As land is fixed, immobile and unique in terms of locational characteristics, no two locations are the same. The choice of location by an economic agent involves trade-offs. Moreover, location often involves lumpy investment and relocation is costly. These considerations make the location choice a crucial long-term decision for firms and households. Economic geography, human geography, regional and urban economics and NEG explore the reasons why firms and households choose specific locations. They are particularly concerned with the question why economic activities collocate in large city regions in spite of the diseconomies of clustering.

The world is not flat. Distance and density matter. Distance is important as transport cost affects not only market prices but also location and land use. Both first nature geography (topology, climate, access to natural resource, waterway, etc.) and second nature geography (location of economic agents relative to one another) are important for the location of firms and households. Not all locations provide the same benefits and opportunities to producers in terms of access to raw materials, intermediate inputs, skilled labour, infrastructure, technology and market area. The uneven distribution of natural resources, productive factors such as capital and skill and markets for finished goods guide industries in locating their activities. Profit-maximizing producers compare revenues and costs in alternative locations, offering varying facilities and services. Similarly, utility-maximizing consumers evaluate the benefits and costs of locations to maximize net benefits. They take into account the uneven distribution of economic activity, labour market opportunity and access to housing, infrastructure, amenities and other factors affecting quality of life.

Productive activities subject to scale economies concentrate spatially. Economic growth localizes in a limited number of large city regions to benefit from collocation and networking. These externalities lead to agglomeration economies, manifesting in productivity benefits and cost savings. Large city regions are homes to such external economies. They compete with each other to attract capital, creative entrepreneurs and skilled workers. The world's top 750 cities accounted for 57 per cent of global GDP and their share would rise to 61 per cent by 2030 (Oxford Economics 2017). In 2016, the 300 largest metropolitan economies in the world, containing 24 per cent of global population, contributed nearly 50 per cent of global GDP. These economies, which include nine from India, also concentrated and accelerated economic growth between 2014 and 2016. They explained 67 per cent of real GDP growth and 36 per cent of employment growth in the world, while accounting for just 22 per cent of increase in population. Furthermore, these 300 largest metropolitan areas witnessed a faster pace of economic expansion as compared to the global economy. They experienced a compound annual growth rate (CAGR) of 3.3 per cent in real GDP over the period 2014–2016 as against 2.6 per cent globally. GDP per capita in these areas grew at 2.2 per cent annually compared to 1.5 per cent worldwide (Brookings Institution 2018).

Several theories have emerged in geography, economics and other disciplines to explain the location of economic activity in space. They cover a wide variety of themes such as industry, firm and household location, economies and diseconomies of agglomeration, backward and forward linkages between economic activities, density and spatial contiguity, transportation access and cost, inter-regional and international trade, core-periphery pattern, economic activity-environment nexus, etc. The central questions addressed by location theories include: What do economic activities locate, where and why? These questions apply to the location of firms, industries and households. Theories bring out two important considerations in location choice—transport costs and economies of scale and agglomeration. They also bring out the role of cumulative and circular causation processes on supply and demand sides in influencing the location choices of firms and households.

Location theory flourished in geography throughout the 19th century. However, it was not till the 1950s that the subject received serious attention from economists. This was due to the fact that, traditionally, the analysis economic phenomena did not recognize their spatial dimensions and implications. This is surprising as by end of the 19th century, Alfred Marshall highlighted the importance of externalities in industrial agglomeration and how they generate self-reinforcing processes. He argued that firms locate in an 'industrial district' to exploit the external economies of proximity with other firms. Marshall's 'industrial district argument' runs as follows:

> When an industry has thus chosen a locality for itself, it is likely to stay there long: so great are the advantages which people following the same skilled trade get from near neighborhood to one another. The mysteries of the trade become no mysteries; but are as it were in the air, and children learn many of them unconsciously. Good work is rightly appreciated; inventions and improvements in machinery, in processes and the general organization of the business have their merits promptly discussed: if one man starts a new idea, it is taken up by others and combined with suggestions of their own; and thus, it becomes the source of further new ideas. And presently subsidiary trades grow up in the neighborhood, supplying it with implements and materials, organizing its traffic, and in many ways conducing to the economy of its material....
>
> ...a localized industry gains a great advantage from the fact that it offers a constant market for skill. Employers are apt to resort to any new place where they are likely to find a good choice of workers with special skill

which they require; while men seeking employment naturally go to places where there are many employers who need such skills as theirs and where therefore it is likely to find a good market. (Marshall 1920, 224–25)

Marshallian externalities fall into three groups—called the 'Marshallian triad': (a) knowledge, (b) input and (c) labour market externalities. The clustering of firms in an industry facilitates the exchange of information and ideas; producers and workers benefit from knowledge spillovers. When firms collocate, they attract suppliers of intermediate inputs and ancillary services to locate nearby; producers purchase their requirements more efficiently, share indivisible assets and save in transportation costs. Further, the concentration of many firms in a single location facilitates the emergence of a specialized pool of workers with industry-specific skills. While the Marshallian externalities arise due to specialization, Jane Jacobs refers to the benefits of collocation of diverse industries, leading to inter-industry knowledge spillovers and innovation. Michael Porter points to the advantages of industrial clustering, resulting in competition externalities that encourage learning and excellence. Theories of Marshall, Jacobs and Porter associate the gains from collocation, cooperation and collaboration with the density of the economic mass and proximity between economic agents.

Urban economists divide the economies of agglomeration in a spatial economy into three categories mentioned below.

Economies of Scale

These arise from large-scale production with increased plant size, more sophisticated division of labour, more efficient production with better utilization of capacity, etc. They are economies of scale internal to the firm.

Localization Economies

Arising from the localization of firms in a particular sector, these are external economies—external to the firm, but internal to the industry. They arise from the local concentration of inputs suppliers, industry-specific skilled workers, technical expertise and sharing of common facilities.

Urbanization Economies

These are external economies—external to industry, but internal to the urban area. They result from diversity of economic activities; inter-industry knowledge spillovers; increased size of specialized labour, intermediate input and output markets; and access to regional, national and international infrastructure networks.

While the collocation of economic activity in a region catalyses agglomeration economies, such economies are subject to limits. When spatial concentration exceeds a threshold, it leads to diseconomies manifesting in exorbitant land and housing prices, overcrowding, traffic congestion, noise, pollution, slums, poverty, public health hazards, crime, social malaise, etc. Larger cities tend to increase the time and money costs of travel and the disutility of longer commuting. In this context, transportation cost is of particular interest due to its impact on several markets: transport, goods, labour, land, etc. It augments agglomeration economies in nodes while mitigating congestion diseconomies in trunks. The term 'transportation cost' is used in economics to represent all 'spatial frictions', including bottlenecks in raw material supply to production site, final goods supply to markets and commuting from residences to workplaces. Transport economists talk of the cost of four T's—transport, time, trade and tariff. Apart from cost of shipping, transport cost includes the opportunity cost of time and impacts of congestion, vehicular pollution and psychological stress on commuters. Poor transport infrastructure and high cost of mobility in urban areas in developing countries erode their benefits as unified labour markets and dissuade the location of industry or business.

This chapter is focused on determinants of location. J. H. von Thünen presented a theory of location of agricultural activities around a central market in 1826 (Thünen 1826). This theory was later extended to household location in urban areas by Alonso (1964), Mills (1967, 1972) and Muth (1969). As regards industrial location, it was Alfred Weber who first attempted a 'pure theory' of industrial location

(Weber 1909). Since his 'least cost' location theory, several models have emerged in economic geography and regional economics, dealing with the location of secondary and tertiary activities. A summary of various theories of location is given in Table 3.1, followed by greater details of some popular models.

Table 3.1 Theories of Location: From von Thünen to Krugman

Theory/Model	Salient Features/Determinants of Location
Thünen (1826)	Trade-off between transport costs to sell output in a central market and rents paid to cultivate land determines the location of agricultural activities around the market.
Weber (1909)	Least cost location theory: minimization of input and output transportation costs and comparison of least transportation cost location with other locations offering localization economies.
Hotelling (1929)	Location determined by spatial competition between firms and pricing of products based on geographic location.
Christaller (1933)	CPT: hierarchy of central places based on 'threshold', minimum population to sustain the provision of certain services and 'range' or average distance customers will travel to buy such services.
Pallander (1935)	Modified Weber's model by adding market area analysis, namely division of market between firms and choice of least cost location within the respective market areas.
Lösch (1940)	Profit maximization theory or market area approach based on comparison of production cost and market area that can be monopolized and controlled to maximize sales revenues.
Hoover (1948)	Least cost location with minimization of transport cost and production cost under conditions of perfect factor mobility; production cost takes into account agglomeration economies and diseconomies.
Isard (1956)	Linked location theory to general economic theory; choice of production site from among alternative locations viewed as substituting expenditures among various factors such that the best site is chosen.

Theory/Model	Salient Features/Determinants of Location
Moses (1958)	Determination of location and production together with the application of the principle of substitution of cheaper inputs for costlier inputs in production.
Renner (1951)	Factor-oriented location—based on industrial symbiosis or combination of six factors: capital, transport, raw materials, market, power and labour.
Pred (1966)	Behavioural location theory—emphasizes availability of information and capacity to use the same; decision-makers may not entirely be rational.
Krugman (1991a)	Spatial agglomerations result from interaction between centripetal and centrifugal forces, including imperfect competition, scale economies, externalities and transport costs, leading to cumulative and circular causation processes.

Weber: Cost Minimization Theory

Weber (1909) presented a theory of industrial location in which transportation costs, involving raw material sources, production site and market, are compared with the benefits of localization economies. The theory refers to general and specific, regional and local factors in the choice of location. General factors apply to all industries as against specific factors that are applicable to a particular industry. Weber includes costs of transportation, land rents and labour among general factors. Regional factors that apply to the region as a whole include geographic terrain, transportation system, etc. Local factors include agglomeration forces such as availability of infrastructure, including power, water and cheap labour, and dispersion forces such as land values and taxes. Weber developed a model involving a two-stage analysis. The first stage envisages determining the location that minimizes the sum of input and output transportation costs. The second stage involves comparing localization economies against higher transportation costs that the firm would incur if it chooses another location instead of the one with minimum total transportation cost.

Weber's least cost theory of location is based on the following simplistic assumptions:

1. There is a single profit-maximizing firm producing a good with two raw materials, 1 and 2, whose sources are located at two points in space—at M_1 and M_2, respectively.
2. There is a single market for the good located at a point in space, M_3. Demand for the good is price inelastic and the firm can sell any amount of the good in the market.
3. Perfect competition prevails; prices of inputs 1 and 2, p_1 and p_2, respectively, and of output, p_3 are given. No producer can get monopolistic advantage from the choice of location.
4. The same production technique is used in all possible locations. Production costs are, therefore, invariant.
5. The units of each raw material used in the production of one unit of the good are fixed. There is no substitutability between inputs.

Let us assume that m_1 tons of raw material 1 and m_2 tons of raw material 2 are required to be transported from the respective input sources to the factory to produce m_3 tons of output. Units of m_1 and m_2 needed per unit of m_3 are fixed. Let t_1, t_2 and t_3 be the transport costs per ton-kilometre for raw materials 1 and 2 and final good, respectively. Let d_1 and d_2 be the distance between the respective raw material sources and the factory. Similarly let d_3 be the distance from the factory to the market. Thus, the first stage location problem for the firm is to minimize total transport cost (TTC):

$$\text{Minimize TTC} = t_1 d_1 m_1 + t_2 d_2 m_2 + t_3 d_3 m_3 \qquad (3.1)$$

The cost minimization exercise gives the point of firm location at K in the triangle $M_1 M_2 M_3$, called Weber location–production-triangle, which is presented in Figure 3.1.

The quantities $t_i d_i m_i$ ($i = 1, 2, 3$) are called the 'forces of attraction'. The minimum transportation cost location (MTCL) will be at the interior of triangle $M_1 M_2 M_3$, if none of the forces of attraction exceeds the sum of the other two. If the cost of transporting raw materials 1 and 2, namely $(t_1 d_1 m_1 + t_2 d_2 m_2)$ 1 km farther away from the market is less

Determinants of Location 81

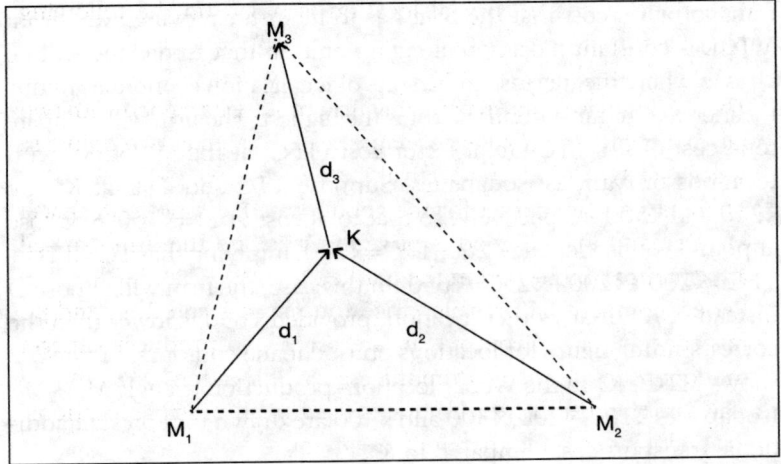

Figure 3.1 *Weber Location–Production Triangle*

than that of transporting final product, namely ($t_3 d_3 m_3$) 1 km extra, that is, the production process is 'weight-gaining', then the firm will locate nearer the market. Weber calls this 'market-oriented' location. If the cost of transporting raw materials 1 km away from the market is more than the cost of transporting final product 1 km extra, that is, the production process is 'weight-loosing', then the firm will locate nearer the raw material sources. Weber calls this 'raw materials-oriented' location. The location of the firm, *ceteris paribus*, will be nearer the source of that raw material in which it is more intensive. Weber developed a concept of material index (MI), defined as weight of inputs divided by weight of output. If MI < 1, location will be market-oriented; if MI > 1, the firm will locate nearer to raw material sources.

As the second stage of location choice, the firm compares the localization economies, for example, cost of labour and intermediate inputs or availability of skills, managerial and technical expertise at MTCL, with those in locations entailing higher transportation cost. A different location will be chosen if localization benefits minus transportation costs exceeds the corresponding figure at MTCL. Weber defines 'isodapane' contour around MTCL along which the additional transportation cost that the firm has to incur for moving away from MTCL is constant. Location along a point on that isodapane will be chosen where the increase in benefits of localization economies minus the increase in transportation cost is the highest. The firm will compare total cost (TC)=TTC+total factor cost (TFC) at the MTCL K^* with locations on various isodapanes. Suppose TTC and TFC at K^* are ₹200 and ₹500, respectively, so that total cost (TC)=₹700. Suppose at point D on isodapane ₹200, TFC=₹250, implying that TC=TTC+TFC=₹200+₹200+₹250=₹650. In this case, the firm will choose D instead of K^* or any other location, provided ₹650 is lower than the corresponding figure for locations on isodapane contours. Figure 3.2 shows MTCL K^* in the Weber location–production triangle $M_1M_2M_3$. Isodapanes ₹100, ₹200, ₹300 and ₹400 are drawn to represent additional transport cost compared to K^*.

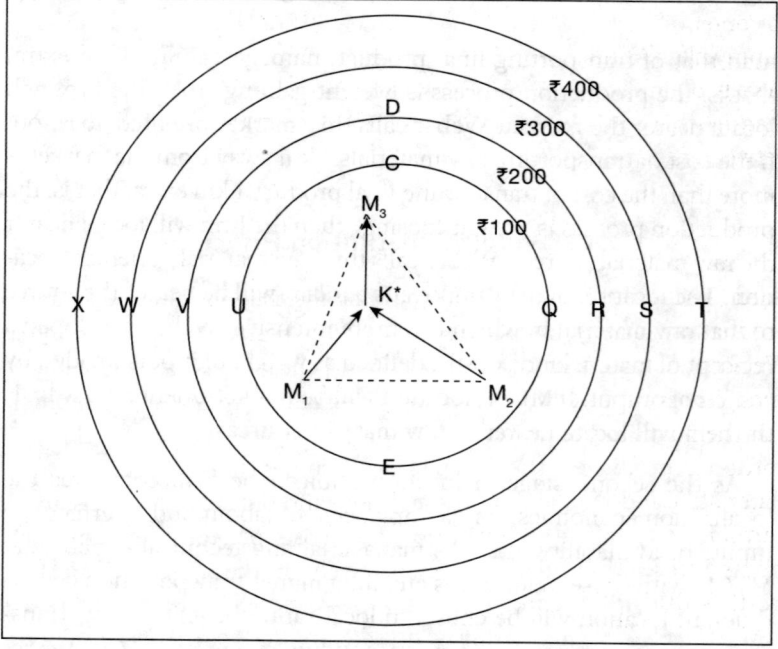

Figure 3.2 *Weber Model: Isodapane Analysis*

Weber's model made a pioneering contribution to location theory in that it gave a rational explanation for the choice of location by industry in terms of trade-off between transportation costs and localization benefits. However, the model has limitations. It is cast in a partial equilibrium framework, which is static and supply oriented. It heavily relies on technical coefficients and ignores demand-side factors such as consumer preferences. The model overemphasizes transport costs and involves subjective considerations such as measurement of localization economies at several locations and comparison of the same with TTCs. The concept of 'isodapane' is geometrically elegant but has little practical value. By assuming raw material sources and output markets as points in space, Weber's model abstracts from the physical size of city or urban region and linkages between economic activities that lead to urbanization economies. Further, it ignores substitutability between inputs. The model's costing formulation for location based on 'MI'—weight of inputs divided by weight of output—does not apply to contemporary manufacturing and high technology firms with global supply chains and low transport and communication costs. However, in spite of limitations, Weber's model built a strong foundation for later theories that consider location by a firm as an outcome of interactions between centripetal and centrifugal forces.

Moses Model: Substitution Principle

Isard (1956) and Moses (1958) combine the theories of location and production. They incorporate substitution behaviour of firms into Weber's analysis, that is, firms substitute cheaper inputs for costlier ones, *ceteris paribus*. Moses relaxes the assumption in Weber's model that the quantities of raw materials (m_1 and m_2) are used in fixed proportion to produce output (m_3). Moses assumes that the prices of raw materials 1 and 2, p_1 and p_2, respectively, and output p_3 are constant. Further, t_1, t_2 and t_3 are fixed transport costs per ton-kilometre for inputs 1 and 2 and final good, respectively. In the triangle $M_1M_2M_3$, arc IJ is drawn to represent constant distance d_3 from the market at M_3. If we constrain the firm to locate on arc IJ, then the distance from the location of the firm to the market will no longer be variable (Figure 3.3).

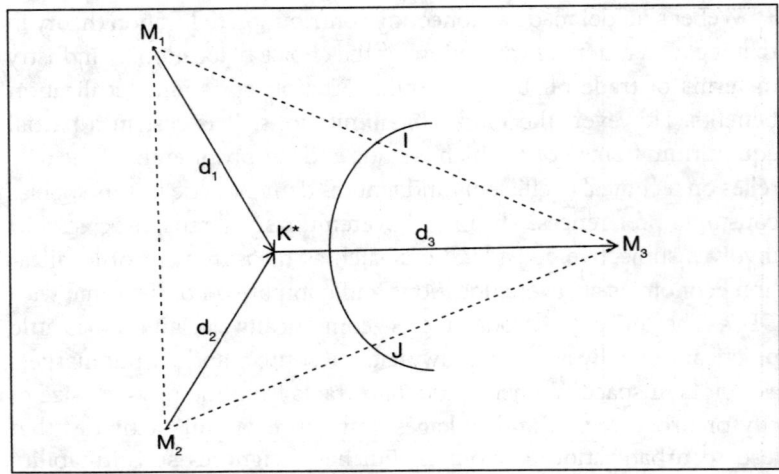

Figure 3.3 *Weber–Moses Location–Production Triangle*

If the firm locates at I, then the delivered price of input 1, that is, $p_1+t_1d_1$, will be minimum as distance d_1 from M_1 to I will be minimum. Similarly, the delivered price of input 2, that is, $p_2+t_2d_2$, will be maximum as distance d_2 from M_2 to I will be maximum. Thus, the ratio $\dfrac{p_1+t_1d_1}{p_2+t_2d_2}$ will be minimum at I. If the firm locates at J, then the delivered price of input 1, that is, $p_1+t_1d_1$, will be maximum as distance d_1 from to M_1 to J will be maximum. Similarly, the delivered price of input 2, that is, $p_2+t_2d_2$, will be minimum as distance from M_2, to J will be minimum. Thus, the ratio $\dfrac{p_1+t_1d_1}{p_2+t_2d_2}$ will be maximum at J.

The budget constraint for the firm at any point on the arc IJ is represented by the expenditure to be incurred on inputs 1 and 2: $m_1(p_1+t_1d_1)+m_2(p_2+t_2d_2)=B$ (assumed). The absolute value of the slope of this budget line is equal to: $\dfrac{dm_2}{dm_1}=\dfrac{p_1+t_1d_1}{p_2+t_2d_2}$. This ratio is nothing but the delivered input price ratio; it is minimum at point I and maximum at point J.

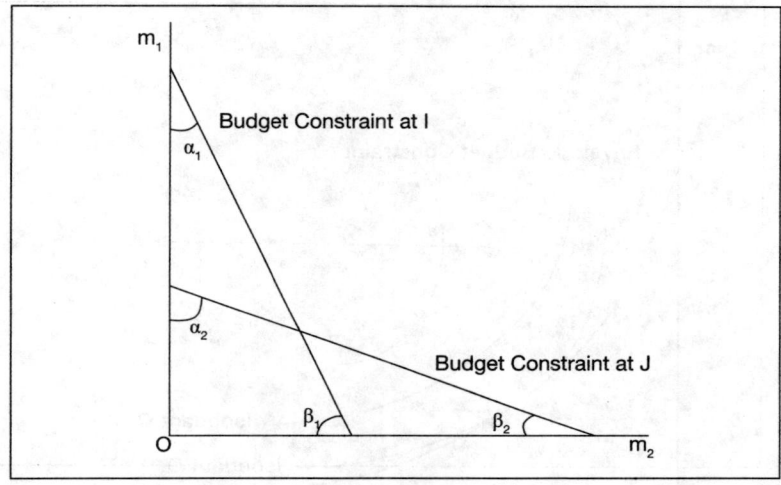

Figure 3.4 *Weber–Moses Model: Input Budget Constraints*

In Figure 3.4, the budget lines for locations I and J are drawn with the same expenditure on inputs—similar to iso-cost line in the theory of production in microeconomics. The budget line for location I subtends an angle α_1 with m_1-axis and β_1 with m_2-axis. Similarly, the budget line for location J subtends an angle α_2 with m_1-axis and β_2 with m_2-axis. The delivered input price ratios can be represented by the tangents of the respective angles, $\tan \alpha_1$ and $\tan \beta_1$, for budget line at I and $\tan \alpha_2$ and $\tan \beta_2$ for budget line at J. I and J are the extreme points on the arc IJ. Plotting all the budget lines for all the possible points of firm location from I to J, we arrive at the envelope budget constraint. This is the outer limit of all the budget lines associated with individual locations along arc IJ. Equilibrium location for the firm occurs at the point where the envelope budget constraint is tangent to the highest attainable isoquant. In Figure 3.5, the optimum combination of inputs m_1^* and m_2^* occurs at E^*, the point at which the envelope budget constraint is tangent to the isoquant Q_2. Note that the optimum location E^* and optimum input mix (m_1^*, m_2^*) are jointly determined.

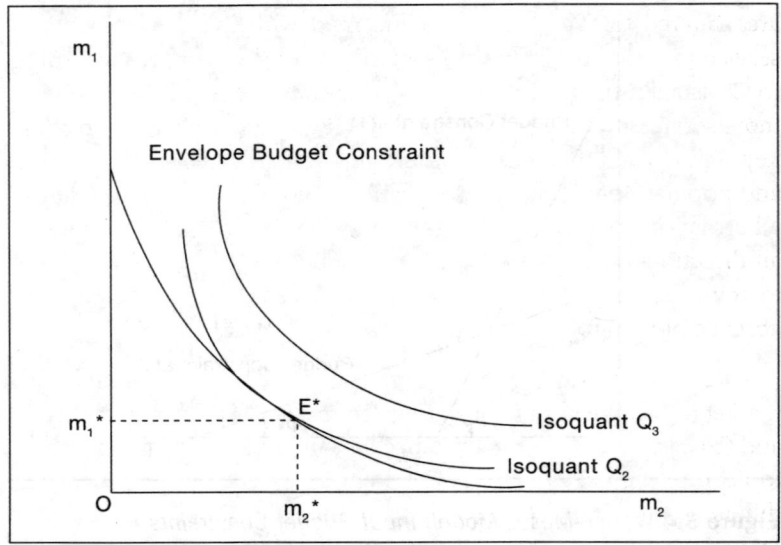

Figure 3.5 *Weber–Moses Model: Location–Production Equilibrium*

Moses model enriched Weber's least cost location theory by combining production theory and location theory. It suggests that firms take location and production decisions simultaneously. However, the model is abstract and has limited applicability for empirical analysis. Moreover, location decisions are often taken by firms well before they take decisions regarding production technology and input mix.

Christaller: Central Place Theory

German geographer Walter Christaller (1933) propagated CPT to explain the spatial distribution, size and number of human settlements. The theory, considered by many geographers as one of geography's 'finest products', is based on the premise that not all types of activities, such as a grocery store, bakery, cinema hall, multiplex and shopping mall, locate in all places. CPT explores the relationships between settlements of different population size, range of economic activities performed, nature of goods and services provided and the market area catered to. The theory is concerned with the determinants of service location in a network of market towns and cities. According to Christaller, the main function of a central place is to supply one or more services to the surrounding market area. CPT is based on some key assumptions: homogeneous terrain, even distribution of resources and population in space, similar patterns of purchasing power across all areas, uniform cost of transport varying linearly with distance in all directions, consumers' preference to buy from the nearest places to minimize transportation cost, perfectly competitive market and absence of monopoly power.

CPT relies on two key basic concepts: (a) 'threshold'—minimum market or income required to sustain the selling of a good or service—and (b) 'range'—maximum distance consumers are prepared to travel to acquire a good or service. Different services choose to locate in different central places on the basis of their threshold population. If this minimum is not reached, then some services or activities will not start in a central place as they will not be viable. Similarly, consumers will not choose a long range to purchase a good or avail a service as the costs of transport and inconvenience will outweigh the benefits. Range has two limits. The upper limit denotes an area beyond which no consumer will be willing to undertake travel to purchase goods or services. The lower limit represents the market area needed by a firm to have minimum demand that will ensure a profit. Using the concept of threshold, Christaller placed the rank order of central places from the lowest to the highest as follows: hamlet, village, town, city and regional capital/metropolis. CPT suggests that a large number of widely distributed smaller central places would provide lower order goods and services to cater to widespread demand. A small number of higher order central places would provide both lower order and higher order goods and services. CPT suggests three principles for hierarchy of central places in a region.

Marketing Principle

The objective of this principle is to serve the maximum number of consumers with the minimum number of central places. If spatial distribution of settlements is entirely based on the range of a good or service, it will lead to evenly spaced central places with hexagonal market area. This means that a settlement of each order will be surrounded by six settlements of the next lower order. Each central place will serve two central places of the next lower order or one-third of the surrounding central places.

Transport Principle

The objective of this principle is to minimize the road length and maximize the connectivity between central places. The distribution of central places will be most favourable when a lower order central place lies half-way on the straight-line road joining the next higher order central place. This suggests that the market area of a higher order central place will include half of the market area of each of the six surrounding lower order central places. If any central place is smaller in size than predicted, it must be due to its lower accessibility and vice versa.

Administrative Principle

The objective of this principle is to provide a hierarchy of controls so that the administration of lower order central places is completely controlled by the next higher order central place. This is achieved when the market area of each of the higher order central places includes the market areas of each of the six neighbouring lower order central places. The implication is that for efficient administration, the six surrounding complementary central places are added to the higher order central place.

CPT provides a log frame to analyse the spatial distribution of central places, including market towns, cities, metropolitan areas, etc. It presents important concepts such as interdependencies between settlements of different sizes, hierarchy of functions and central places, population threshold and market range. These concepts are adopted by town and country planners in developing countries like India in designing cities and urban regions based on land use requirements of central places of different orders. However, CPT is criticized for its unrealistic assumptions such as isotropic terrain, even distribution of resources and purchasing power, perfect markets and absence of consumers' preferences for shopping places. CPT does not consider factors such as spatial variations in population density, income and price elasticity demand. It neglects historic, cultural and environmental dimensions of places. It is also static and cannot explain the dynamics of evolution of regional spatial stricture. Further, CPT undermines the role of government in urban regions and cities through town and country planning and development of infrastructure connecting places. CPT's most conspicuous deficiency is seen in its limited applicability to the analysis of real-world spatial-economic structures of regions. Also, with the emergence of e-commerce and e-delivery of services and the 'platform revolution', the concepts of 'threshold' and 'range' need to be revisited.

Losch: Profit Maximization Theory

August Losch, a German economist propagated the theory of profit-maximizing location based on a 'market area' approach. Unlike perfect competition in Weber's model, Losch assumes a market structure characterized by monopolistic competition. He argues that industry will not necessarily choose the least cost (transportation cost + labour cost) location; rather, it will locate at a place where it can maximize profit. According to him, Weber's cost-minimizing location theory neglects demand by assuming the location of market at a point in space rather than a demand spread over a geographical area. Further, it overlooks the fact that consumers have to incur transport costs in procuring the goods. Transport costs affect not only the location of a firm but also its spatial market size that influences output sold, price charged and distribution of sale. Holding spatial variations in production costs constant, Lösch (1940) argues that the optimum location of a firm occurs where the largest market area is monopolized or controlled to maximize sales revenues. He adopts two key assumptions: (a) firms maximize profit while choosing location and (b) no abnormal profits occur in economic activities over space as they are open to a large number of monopolistically competing firms. In presenting his industrial location model, Losch further assumes the market area to be a homogeneous plain over which identical consumers are evenly distributed, each facing a downward-sloping demand curve.

Losch refers to individual and market spatial demand curves. Individual demand curve shows the amount of good a consumer located at a distance from the factory will demand, given factory price and transport cost. Market demand curve is derived based on the sum of individual demands at various distances by all consumers residing in the market area. For simplicity, the individual spatial demand curve is assumed to be identical for all locations. The firm can sell its good in a circular area surrounding it. As the distance from the factory increases, the transport cost will progressively rise, increasing the delivery price, that is, factory price plus transport cost, and eventually making the market demand for the good zero at the edge of the market area. By rotating the spatial demand curve 360°, the Losch demand cone is generated, defined by zero transport cost at the factory point and maximum transport cost at the edge of the circular market area beyond which there will be no sale. The firm can supply its good to this market area with higher profit as a monopolist or to an extended market area, which will invite entry of other producers. Competition among producers will eliminate supernormal profit and lead to normal profit. Thus, every firm will try to first capture the area where it can act as a monopolist. Losch argues that the landscape will comprise hexagon nets, each hexagon being the market area of a monopolist seller.

To derive the Losch demand cone, we assume a single firm producing a homogenous good and supplying the same to a single customer. The inverse supply and demand functions are represented by the following equations (see Figure 3.6):

$$p^S = a_0 + a_1 Q^S + p^t \tag{3.2}$$

where p^S = supply price, Q^S = quantity supplied, p^t = transport cost (assumed to be fixed) and a_0 and a_1 are positive constants.

$$p^D = b_0 - b_1 Q^D \tag{3.3}$$

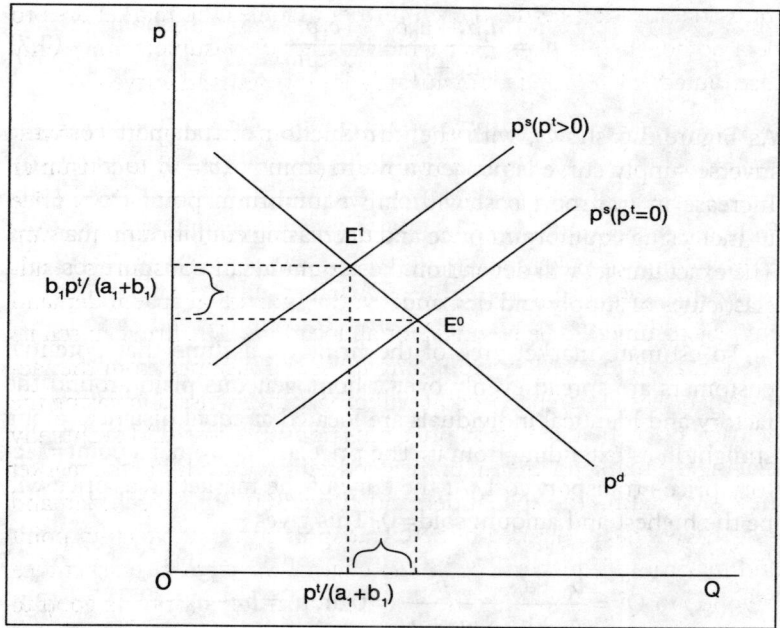

Figure 3.6 *Effect of Increase in Transport Cost on Price and Output*

where p^D = demand price, Q^D = quantity demanded and b_0 and b_1 are positive constants.

The market equilibrium conditions are

$$Q^S = Q^D = Q^e \qquad (3.4)$$

$$p^S = p^D = p^e \qquad (3.5)$$

Combining Equations (3.2)–(3.5) leads to equilibrium quantity and equilibrium price combination (Q^e, p^e), presented by

$$Q^e = \frac{b_0 - a_0}{a_1 + b_1} - \frac{p^t}{a_1 + b_1} \qquad (3.6)$$

$$p^e = \frac{a_1 b_0 + a_0 b_1}{a_1 + b_1} + \frac{b_1 p^t}{a_1 + b_1} \qquad (3.7)$$

As Figure 3.6 shows, with the introduction of transport cost, the inverse supply curve is pushed upward from p^s ($p^t=0$) to p^s ($p^t>0$). Increase in transport cost will shift equilibrium point from E^0 to E^1, increasing equilibrium price and decreasing equilibrium quantity. The exact impact will depend on the magnitude of transport cost and elasticities of supply and demand.

To estimate market area of the firm, we assume that potential customers are spread evenly over a homogeneous plain around the factory and identical individuals are located at equal distances along straight lines extending from it. The price at a customer's point = factory price + transport cost. At the edge of the market area, price will be the highest and amount sold = 0. This gives

$$Q^e = \frac{b_0 - a_0}{a_1 + b_1} - \frac{p^t}{a_1 + b_1} = 0 \text{ or, } p^t = b_0 - a_0 \qquad (3.8)$$

Similarly, at the edge of the factory, transport cost $p^t=0$. This implies

$$Q^e = \frac{b_0 - a_0}{a_1 + b_1} - \frac{p^t}{a_1 + b_1} = \frac{b_0 - a_0}{a_1 + b_1} \qquad (3.9)$$

The amount sold by the factory is derived by calculating the volume of the cone defined by circular base with centre at $p^t=0$, radius $p^t=b_0-a_0$, and bounded by $Q^e = \frac{b_0 - a_0}{a_1 + b_1}$ at the factory and $Q^e=0$ at the boundary of market area. Figure 3.7 shows the Losch demand cone.

Unlike Weber's partial equilibrium approach, Losch's theory presents the first attempt towards a general equilibrium theory of location, taking both supply and demand factors into account. However, the assumptions that the market area is a homogeneous plain, population and resources are uniformly distributed over space, production costs

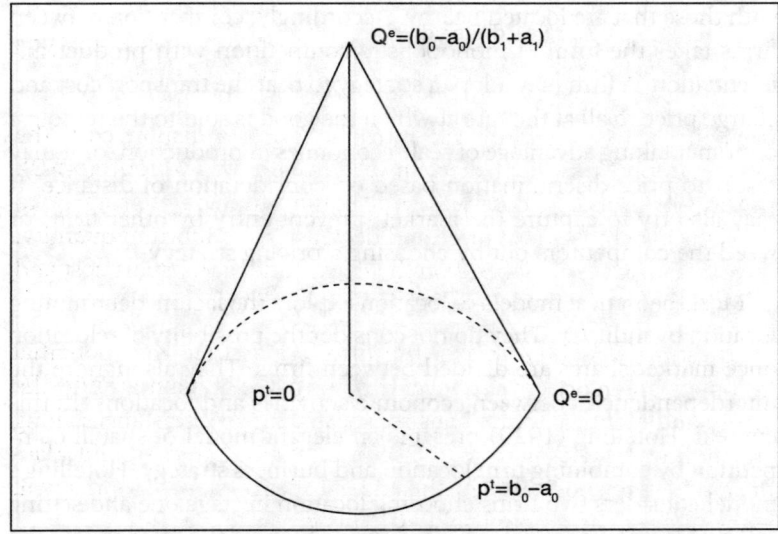

Figure 3.7 *Lösch Demand Cone: Influence of Transport Cost on Market Area*

are spatially invariant, individual spatial demand curves are identical and transport rates are uniform are not realistic. The Losch model is abstract, not useful for analysis of industrial location problems in practice.

Hotelling: Spatial Competition

Theories based on Weber's model explain the location of industry based on a trade-off between agglomeration benefits, comprising localization and urbanization economies and transportation costs. Another set of theories approaches location with the coexistence of scale economies due to agglomeration externalities and transportation costs, leading to the spatial division of market area between firms. Physical distance acts as a barrier to entry into a local market. Thus, a firm in a local area does not compete with all others; it competes only with those that are located nearby. Accordingly, competition between firms takes the form of monopolistic competition with product differentiation. A firm may adopt a strategy to bear the transport cost and charge price to all at the rate at which the good is sold to the remotest customer taking advantage of scale economies in production, or it may resort to price discrimination based on consideration of distance. It may also try to capture the market, prevent entry by other firms or weed the competitors out by choosing a pricing strategy.

Most theoretical models of location explore the factors determining location by industry. They do not consider the possibility of relocation once market shares are divided between firms. They also ignore the interdependencies between economic activities and locations. In this context, Hotelling (1929) presents an elegant model of spatial competition by combining firm location and business strategy. Hotelling's model considers two firms choosing location in stage one and setting selling prices of products in stage two. The model demonstrates the 'principle of minimum differentiation' or the inherent tendency of firms to make similar choices with regard to location or product-characteristic dimensions. As Hotelling observes, there is an 'undue tendency for competitors to imitate each other in quality of goods, in location, and in other essential ways (Hotelling 1929, 41).

Hotelling's model of spatial competition adopts the following simplistic assumptions:

1. Demand for a product is distributed uniformly along a linear market with one unit demanded by each consumer and is price-inelastic.
2. Two firms, for example, 1 and 2, offer the same homogeneous product; market operates under conditions of duopoly.
3. The initial locations of the two firms are given: firm 1 is located at A and firm 2 at B on the linear market.
4. There is no cost of relocation to any firm.
5. The cost of transportation per unit of distance (say, kilometre) is constant, that is, transport cost varies linearly with distance.
6. The cost of transport is borne by the customer.

Given the above assumptions, the cost that a consumer incurs to purchase a product from firm 1 located at A or firm 2 located at B is defined by the equation: delivery price = sale price + transport cost incurred from the customer's location to the firm. In Figure 3.8, the linear road is depicted as OL and the distance from O and L is d; A is to the left of B, $OA = a$ and $LB = b$. We assume that the distance from O to the market boundary of firm 1 at X is x. Let the price charged by firm 1 at A be p_A and that charged by firm 2 at B be p_B. Further, let the transport cost per unit distance for a consumer purchasing from firm at A be t_A and that for a consumer purchasing from firm at B be t_B. Under duopoly, three conditions are required to be satisfied:

1. Consumers located at O must always buy from A, implying that the delivery price at A must always be lower than the delivery price at B, that is,

$$p_A + t_A a < p_B + t_B (d - b) \tag{3.10}$$

2. Consumers located at L must always buy from B, implying that delivery price at B must always be lower than the delivery price at A, that is

$$p_B + t_B b < p_A + t_A (d - a) \tag{3.11}$$

3. There must be an indifferent consumer at X on the boundary dividing the market area between the two firms at A and B. This implies

$$p_A + t_A(x - a) = p_B + t_B(d - x - b) \tag{3.12}$$

The solution the above equation gives the following expressions:

$$x = \frac{p_B - p_A + at_A + (d-b)t_B}{t_A + t_B} \tag{3.13}$$

$$d - x = \frac{p_A - p_B + (d-a)t_A + bt_B}{t_A + t_B} \tag{3.14}$$

Suppose $t_A = t_B = t$ but $p_A \neq p_B$ due to price competition between firms, then we have from Equations (3.13) and (3.14)

$$x = \frac{p_B - p_A + at + (d-b)t}{2t} = \frac{p_B - p_A}{2t} + \frac{d+a-b}{2} \quad (3.15)$$

$$d - x = \frac{p_A - p_B + (d-a)t + bt}{2t} = \frac{p_A - p_B}{2t} + \frac{d-a+b}{2} \quad (3.16)$$

Equations (3.15) and (3.16) imply that $x > d - x$ if $p_A < p_B$; that is, market area for firm 1 will be larger than that for firm B when price charged for the same homogenous good by firm 1 located at A is lower than that by firm 1 located at B. Figure 3.8 portrays the case of $t_A = t_B$ and $p_A < p_B$. As may be seen, market area for firm 1 equal to OX is larger than the market area for firm 2 equal to LX. The inequality $p_A < p_B$ may

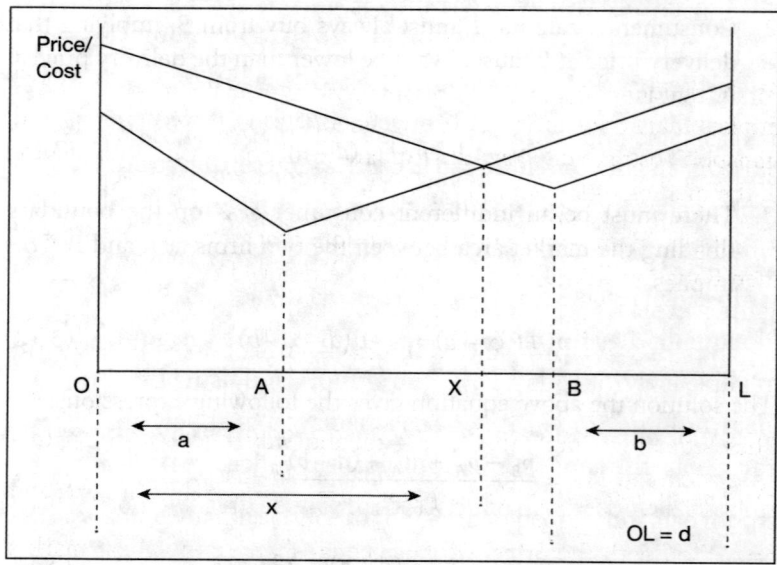

Figure 3.8 *Hotelling's Model of Spatial Competition*

be explained by strong scale economies for firm 1 vis-à-vis firm 2 or differential pricing strategy.

Firms 1 and 2 are initially located at A and B, respectively. Suppose firm 1 at A relocates to the right of A, then its market area will expand and that of firm 2 will shrink. In reaction, firm 2 will relocate to the left of the new location of firm 1 to increase its market area. This will invite further reaction from firm 1. The process will continue until the two firms locate at the centre of the market, each having a share of half of the market. Only this arrangement will give rise to a stable situation. Whereas the free market will lead to a concentration of the two firms at the centre of the market, such an outcome will not be socially optimal as average distance to be travelled by the consumers to purchase the good will be longer than when the firms were at A and B, respectively. Assuming $p_A = p_B = p$ and $t_A = t_B = t$, Equations (3.13) and (3.14) yield the value of x and $d - x$ as follows:

$$x = \frac{(d+a-b)}{2} \text{ and } d - x = \frac{(d-a+b)}{2} \quad (3.17)$$

As the modulus of x equals the modulus of $d - x$, Equation (3.17) implies that when there is no price competition between firms and transport costs are uniform, firms 1 and 2 will both locate at the centre of the market, as shown in Figure 3.9.

Suppose there is no price competition, that is, $p_A = p_B$, but $t_A \neq t_B$, then Equations (3.13) and (3.14) can be reduced to

$$x = \frac{at_A + (d-b)t_B}{t_A + t_B} \text{ and } d - x = \frac{(d-a)t_A + bt_B}{t_A + t_B} \quad (3.18)$$

These equations imply that $x = d - x$ if and only if $at_A + (d-b)t_B = (d-a)t_A + bt_B$ or, $(2a-d)t_A = (2b-d)t_B$ or, $\frac{t_A}{t_B} = \frac{(2b-d)}{(2a-d)}$. Thus, if $t_A = t_B$ and $b = a$, then both the firms will have equal share in the linear market OL, as shown earlier. If $t_A > t_B$ or, $\frac{t_A}{t_B} > 1$, we will have $b > a$ and this will

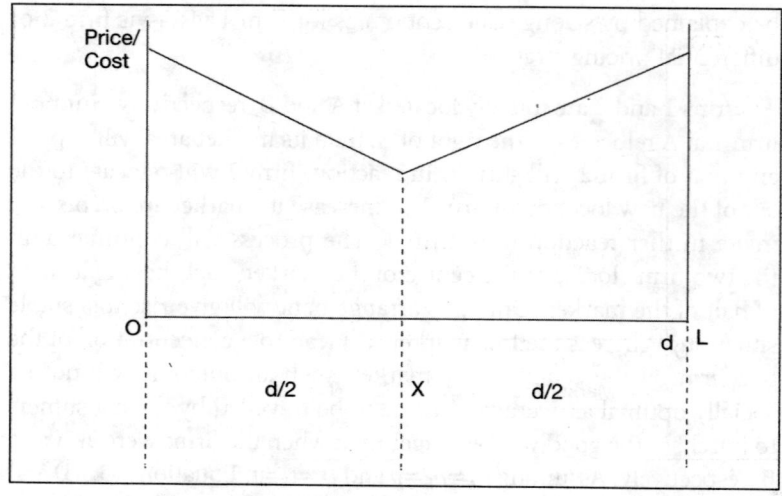

Figure 3.9 *Hotelling's Model: Spatial Competition Equilibrium*

mean $x < d - x$ (see Figure 3.10). Thus, if prices charged by the two firms at the delivery points are the same, that is, $p_A = p_B$ but $t_A > t_B$, A will have a market area smaller than that for firm B due to transportation cost disadvantages. When $p_A = p_B$ but $t_A < t_B$, A will have a market area larger than that for firm B due to cheaper transportation. Figure 3.11 presents the general case with production cost incorporated into the model, apart from product price and transport cost.

Hotelling's model of spatial competition and division of a linear market area is simple and intuitive. It tries to explain the real-world phenomenon why rival firms cluster in space despite the pressure on prices due to competition, for example, retailers, restaurants, ice cream vendors on a beach road in a city, etc. The model has been extended by researchers to non-linear and complex markets. It has also been enhanced to incorporate price competition. When firms collocate, price competition can intensify, but the intensity of such competition can be reduced by resorting to product differentiation. Because of product differentiation, price changes may not lead to dramatic shifts in demand for products of firms. Some criticisms of

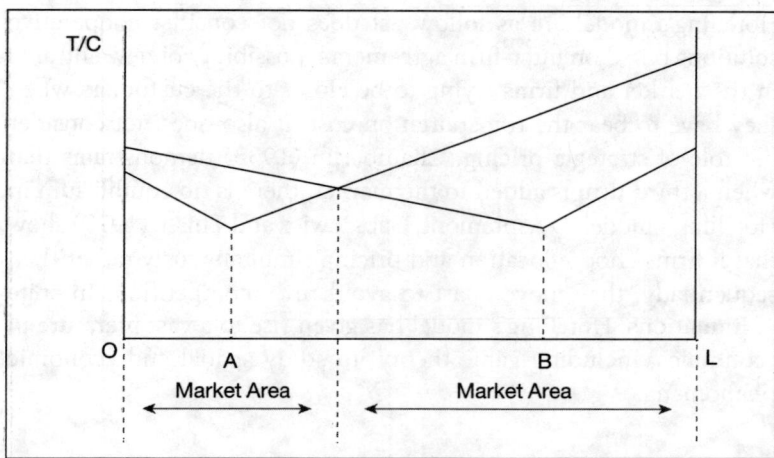

Figure 3.10 *Hotelling's Model: Unequal Market Area Division*

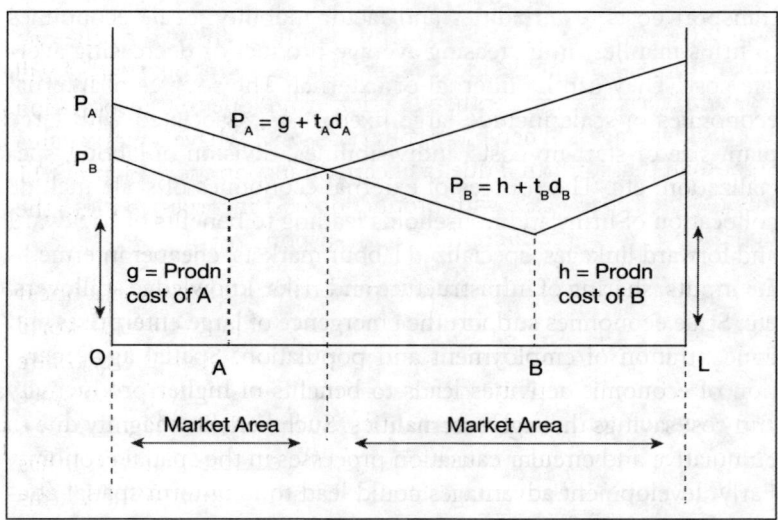

Figure 3.11 *Hotelling's Model: Production Cost Differential and Market Area*

Hotelling's model are as follows: it does not consider cooperative solutions based on inter-firm agreements, possibility of new entrants in the market and firms trying to be closer to the customers when they have to bear the transportation cost. It also does not consider the role of strategic pricing. Chamberlin (1933) demonstrates that when a third firm is added to the market, there is no equilibrium in Hotelling's model. D'Aspremont, Gabszewicz and Thisse (1979) show that if firms choose location and pricing simultaneously rather than sequentially, they move apart to avoid price competition. In spite of limitations, Hotelling's model has given rise to a vast literature in economics, including game theory, to study spatial and economic phenomena.

Krugman: New Economic Geography

Krugman (1991a, 1991b), in his NEG model, explains the location of economic activity in space in terms of interactions between market structure characterized by imperfect competition, scale economies, transport costs, externalities and factor mobility. Scale economies to firms manifest in increasing average product or decreasing average cost. They can be internal or external. The sources of internal economies of scale include large fixed costs, associated with large plant size or start-up costs, indivisibilities, division of labour, specialization, etc. The sources of external economies of scale include collocation of firms and households leading to benefits of backward and forward linkages, specialized labour markets, cheaper intermediate inputs, sharing of infrastructure and risks, knowledge spillovers, etc. Scale economies support the emergence of large enterprises and concentration of employment and population. Spatial agglomeration of economic activities leads to benefits of higher productivity and cost savings through externalities. Such benefits magnify due to cumulative and circular causation processes in the spatial economy. Early development advantages could lead to long-term spatial concentration of economic activities. However, transport costs matter in international and inter-regional trade. When transport costs to supply products to markets are high, there will be a tendency to disperse production.

Let us consider an economy producing a single manufacturing good with production, subject to increasing returns to scale, represented by the following simple function:

$$Q = L^{\lambda} \quad \text{where} \quad \frac{d\frac{Q}{L}}{dL} > 0 \qquad (3.19)$$

where Q=quantity of output, L=labour input

The assumption of increasing returns implies that average product will be increasing as input usage increases (or average cost falling as output increases). From Equation (3.19)

$\frac{Q}{L} = L^{\lambda-1}$ and the first order derivative of this $\frac{d\frac{Q}{L}}{dL} = (\lambda - 1) L^{\lambda-2} > 0$, implying $\lambda > 1$.

Suppose there are 100 similar factories dispersed over a region, with each using the same production technology specified in Equation (3.19) and employing L workers, then the total output $= 100 L^{\lambda}$. If the same technology is used to deploy $100 L$ workers in a single factory, then the total output $= (100 L)^{\lambda} = (100)^{\lambda}(L)^{\lambda} > 100 L^{\lambda}$, as $\lambda > 1$. Thus, the market or a central planner will promote a single factory that employs $100 L$ workers rather than 100 factories, each employing L workers. As $100 L$ workers live around the factory, they give rise to a factory town.

The concentration of production in a factory at one location enables to reap the benefits of scale, but it also means that the transportation cost to ship output to other locations will be higher than that if production was taken up in additional locations, each catering to local demand (Brueckner 2011). Let us assume that the economy has population N and the same is equally divided among five regions, each with $\frac{N}{5}$ residents-workers. The economy produces one single manufacturing good which is subject to increasing returns to scale. Let us further assume that each resident consumes one unit of the output, implying that total consumption equals $N=Q$. Let the cost function be represented by

$$C = C(Q) \quad \text{where} \quad \frac{d\frac{C}{Q}}{dQ} < 0 \qquad (3.20)$$

One may note that in view of scale economies, average cost will decrease as output increases.

Let us consider two cases: (1) production is centralized in one region, one-fifth is consumed in that region and four-fifth is transported to the four other regions—in equal quantity; (2) production is equally divided among all regions so that no transportation of good to any region is necessary. Let T be the shipping cost per unit of the good. The two cases are presented below.

Case 1: Centralized production

In this case, let the average cost of production be $\frac{C(Q)}{Q} = \frac{C(N)}{N} = \theta$.

Then, the total cost = production cost + transport cost

$$= \theta N + \frac{4}{5} TN \qquad (3.21)$$

Case 2: Dispersed production

In this case, let the average cost of production be $\dfrac{C\left(\frac{Q}{5}\right)}{\frac{Q}{5}} = \dfrac{C\left(\frac{N}{5}\right)}{\frac{N}{5}} = \mu$.

Then the total cost = production cost + transport cost

$$= \mu N + 0 = \mu N \qquad (3.22)$$

Under the assumption of increasing returns to scale, average cost will be decreasing as production increases, implying that $\theta < \mu$ or, $\mu - \theta > 0$.

On comparing Equations (3.21) and (3.22), it is observed that centralized production will be more profitable than dispersed production if

$$\theta N + \frac{4}{5}TN < \mu N \text{ or } (\mu - \theta) > \frac{4}{5}T \qquad (3.23)$$

Inequality (Equation [3.23]) will hold if $\mu-\theta$ is large or T is small enough. It may be noted that $\mu-\theta$ is a measure of the strength of scale economies. Thus, centralized production will occur if scale economies are very strong or transport costs are very small. Strong scale economies lead to substantial cost advantage for centralized production and low transport cost means that this advantage is not neutralized by the cost of shipping output. Ironically, when the Industrial Revolution led to economies of large-scale production, that is, $\mu-\theta$ large, and the railroad revolution resulted in a drastic reduction in shipping costs, that is, T small, large industrial agglomerations and cities emerged in the West, which have flourished till date.

Krugman (1991a) presents a two-region model with imperfect competition, scale economies, externalities, transport costs and factor mobility to explain the phenomena of economic agglomerations over space. In order to realize scale economies while minimizing transport costs, manufacturing firms will locate in the region with larger demand, but the location of demand or market itself depends on the distribution of manufacturing. The centripetal force for spatial concentration is, thus, a circular causation. When firms subject to increasing returns locate in region 1, they attract migrant workers from region 2 to reap scale economies by increasing production. When such workers move to region 1 in response to higher nominal wages offered by firms to attract them, they carry with them not only 'own' production but also consumption possibilities. Thus, a self-reinforcing process sets in: firm location, increased production, scale economies, migration of workers, increased demand, bigger market, increased production and scale economies.... The increase in market size due to the influx of workers is similar to home market effect (HME) in international trade theory.

When a large number of firms locate in a region, a large variety of products are produced there and prices fall with increase in output under conditions of imperfect competition. Thus, the workers benefit from access to a large variety of goods, lower price, higher real wage, that is, nominal wage divided by price, lower transport and communication costs, etc. These factors will attract still more workers. Because of scale economies, there is an incentive for firms to locate the production of each variety in one region. However, because of positive transport costs, *ceteris paribus*, it is more profitable to produce in the region offering the larger market and ship output to other regions. This implies the availability of even more varieties of differentiated products in the region. Thus, a circular process involving *forward linkage* (incentives of workers to be close to producers of consumer goods) and *backward linkage* (incentive of producers to locate where the market is large) acts as a centripetal force for spatial agglomeration of economic activity.

NEG suggests that economic agglomerations are shaped by the tension between agglomeration or centripetal and dispersion or centrifugal forces. Main agglomeration forces are as follows: (a) market size: producers prefer larger markets due to consumers' preference for a variety of products (demand linkage); local suppliers of intermediate inputs decrease the costs of other producers due to economies of scale in production (cost linkage); (b) thick labour markets: spatial concentration of economic activity leads to specialized labour pooling and (c) pure external economies such as those through knowledge spillovers. Key dispersion forces include (a) transport costs, (b) immobile factors such as land and other natural capital, (c) barriers to trade, (d) increase in land values and housing rents due to overcrowding and (e) pure external diseconomies such as those due to congestion and pollution. Access to markets and immobile factors is shaped by distance and transportation costs. Greater concentration of economic activity puts pressure on land and housing and leads to overcrowding, congestion and increased land and housing rents. These factors act against agglomeration. The relative strengths of centripetal and centrifugal forces determine the spatial concentration of economic activity (Krugman 1991a, 1991b). Krugman's NEG model is conceptually rich and theoretically elegant. However, it is not amenable to empirical testing.

Determinants of Location: Practice

Weber made a fundamental contribution to location theory with his least cost approach as early as 1909. He aimed at a 'pure theory' to study location across industries and highlighted the role of transport costs and localization economies in location. Following Weber, several theories have emerged in economic geography and regional economics identifying the determinants of location of industries. However, a general theory of location is yet to emerge. Weber's theory, in spite of limitations, remains the only model of location with wider applicability. It still applies to industries with high 'MI'. Other theories of location that made landmark contributions include Christaller—concepts of threshold and range; Losch—sales revenue/profit maximization and monopolization of market area; Hotelling—spatial competition and market share; Moses—joint determination of location and production decisions of economic agents; and Krugman—interactions between centripetal and centrifugal forces. The factors shaping industrial location and spatial agglomeration brought out by economic theories include transport costs; international and external economies of scale including localization and urbanization economies; production structure including substitutability between inputs, costs, sales revenue, profit, spatial competition and market share. NEG models attempt to explain the location of economic activity and formation of spatial agglomerations in terms of microeconomic foundations. They refer to interactions between imperfect competition, scale economies, transport costs, externalities, factor mobility and intermediate inputs, leading to circular and cumulative causation processes, and influencing location patterns.

Most of the theories of industrial location were developed in the background of industrialization in the 19th and first half of the 20th centuries. They have focused on location decisions of individual entrepreneurs or firms rather than corporates. The theories of industrial location have not been empirically tested in developing countries. Every theory has some merits and limitations as the limited empirical studies suggest. However, none includes all the key factors in location under one umbrella in view of the complexities involved. No theory has adopted a dynamic general equilibrium framework wherein location, investment, production and other variables such as costs, prices, demand and supply factors and externalities interact to produce outcomes. While scale economies on the supply side are taken into account, those on the demand side due to networking externalities have not been considered. Importantly, location decisions call for investment decisions which depend on economic and behavioural factors, including perception of investors regarding risks and returns. However, only limited research has been undertaken in developing countries to study the perception of investors regarding where to invest. Such research points to the following factors in location-investment-production decisions, apart from the conventional factors such as availability of raw materials, power, water, other infrastructure and finance and proximity to markets.

Talented Workers

Recruitment and retention of talented workers are important considerations for the success of a business in the long run. To be successful in this knowledge age, firms must be able to attract, develop and support 'the creative class' who conceive and put new ideas into practice, produce innovation and develop technology-intensive industries. This class and their companies choose to cluster in large city regions to reap the benefits of face-to-face communication, collaboration, learning, innovation, productivity growth and scale economies. As Florida writes:

> Ideas flow more freely, are honed more sharply, and can be put into practice more quickly when large numbers of innovators, implementers, and financial backers are in constant contact with one another, both in and out of the office. Creative people cluster not simply because they like to be around one another or they prefer cosmopolitan centers with lots of amenities, though both those things count. They and their companies

also cluster because of the powerful productivity advantages, economies of scale, and knowledge spillovers such density brings. (Florida 2005, 50)

Transport Accessibility

Transport accessibility—to highways, railroads, public transit, airport, etc.—plays an important role in the location of firms and households. Firms choose places keeping in view the need to transport raw materials and finished products. They also consider the commuting costs of workers. Places must be accessible to different categories of workers, including users of PT and personalized vehicles. Workers choose residential location to minimize commuting costs, relative to housing and other costs and wages. Transport catalyses growth by promoting density and agglomeration economies in city centres while expanding labour markets.

Real Estate Costs

Real estate costs, including cost of constructing factories or offices, or alternatively, renting business premises constitute an important component of business costs, next perhaps to the cost of personnel in the case of several firms. Businesses also consider the likely real estate costs to be incurred by workers as housing and transportation costs are weighed against the wages they receive from employers. Large metropolitan agglomerations have high real estate costs, but they provide the benefits of collocation externalities.

Clustering Benefits

Spatial clusters of economic activity enable firms to benefit from sharing of inputs and infrastructure while pursuing competitive and collaborative strategies. As Porter (1990) argues, the geographic concentration of interconnected companies, specialized suppliers, common service providers, firms in related industries and associated institutions (e.g., universities, standards agencies, business chambers, etc.) in a particular field make firms not only compete but also cooperate.

Urban Externalities

Dynamic city regions attract firms and workers due to their external economies of agglomeration and networking. These economies arise from the collocation of firms, households and institutions in close quarters. They are returns to density and connectivity, leading to productivity benefits associated with learning; sharing and matching; and reduced costs of transporting goods, people, ideas, information and knowledge. Empirical studies point to the presence of such external economies in metropolitan city regions of the world, particularly in developing countries.

Taxes and Regulations

Taxes payable to central, state and local governments, availability of tax incentives such as tax holidays, exemptions from payment of key taxes and charges, nature of regulatory requirements, etc. play a key role in attracting location of investment as countries, states and local jurisdictions compete to attract industry, business and growth.

Corporate Strategy

In the case of some companies, corporate strategy and leadership play a decisive role in the choice of location. Some corporates favour a centralization strategy with strengthening of head office and a few other locations. Others support decentralization with firms or offices in many different locations with the delegation of powers. Some others adopt a hub-and-spoke type of strategy with a two-way exchange between centralized production facilities and decentralized input or industrial parts suppliers, etc.

Quality of Governance

Indicators of governance quality for a country, state or region are important considerations for the location of investment or industry in view of their implications for competitiveness of business. These factors include rule of law, enforcement of property rights and contracts, provision of core infrastructure, investment in health and education, leading to availability of a healthy, educated and skilled workforce, proactive action for single window clearance and facilitating ease of doing business, ease of access to credit, etc.

Lessons for Development Strategy

'Location' is the key to understanding why productive economic activities cluster. It is important for designing development strategy, encompassing both urban and rural areas. Innovation and growth do not locate everywhere. They localize in city regions. The transportation, information and communication technology (ICT) and platform revolutions have not undermined the importance of such regions in developing countries. Public health hazards of density, manifesting in contagion effects of communicable diseases, have not reduced the importance of city regions from the Spanish Influenza times—as drivers of economic growth, employment generation in formal and informal sectors and public finance for development. They have only repeatedly exposed the failure of the free-market system to address social objectives and of governments to correct for market failure. Ironically, rural-urban migrants who went home from cities like Hyderabad and Bengaluru following the Covid-19 lockdown in 2020 returned back to the cities within months due to the lack of employment opportunities in villages. Policymakers and planners must appreciate why *location, location, location* matters and why density and land development must be managed rather than being controlled.

As early as the 1950s, development economists like Gunnar Myrdal and Albert Hirschman recognized that industrial development is bound to be uneven, and that economic growth would be pronounced in regions experiencing industrial agglomeration (Hirschman 1958; Myrdal 1957). Both provided fundamental insights into why growth localizes as a result of circular causation processes, leading to increasing returns. Myrdal viewed economic process as 'cumulative because of circular causation', unfolding 'backwash' and 'spread' effects. He stated that 'the effects via migration, capital movements and trade as well as all the effects via the whole gamut of other social relations....'

constitute the media through which spatially uneven development occurs (Myrdal 1957, 30–31). When an industry locates in a region, it unleashes an agglomeration process. As employment grows, demand for the firm's product rises, increasing profits. This attracts labour, capital and intermediate inputs from outside. Enhanced profits also augment investments through increased savings. Backwash effects result when an agglomerating region attracts factors of production from other areas. Counteracting these are spread effects or external diseconomies arising from factors such as increased payments to immobile factors, thereby retarding agglomeration. Hirschman (1958) highlights the role of linkages in industrial growth. A 'backward linkage' arises when the demand for an industry's products facilitates the establishment of an upstream industry experiencing scale economies. A 'forward linkage' results from an interaction between scale and market size; it enables an industry to reduce the costs of potential downstream users of its products. The presence of these linkages leads to a process of unbalanced growth over space.

The theories of development presented by Myrdal and Hirschman had the potential of explaining the dynamics of uneven growth in developing countries. However, in spite of path-breaking ideas unleashed as early as the 1950s, development economics failed to present a formal model of increasing returns to scale associated with collocation of economic activity in space. It even ignored the prevailing wisdom in location theories, starting from Weber (1909). It neglected the geography of investment, production, geonomics and innovation. It goes on to credit Krugman (1991a) for rediscovering Myrdal (1957) and Hirschman (1958) in his simple, yet path-breaking model of NEG to explain the emergence of core-periphery patterns based on microeconomic foundations. Krugman brought into focus the role of centripetal and centrifugal forces operating through cumulative and circular causation processes in fostering regional specialization. He emphasized interactions between imperfect competition, increasing returns, externalities, factor mobility and transport costs in spatial agglomeration of economic activity. While Krugman did not discuss the role of political economy and governance in location decisions of firms and households, such factors can be accommodated in the conceptually rich framework of centripetal and centrifugal forces presented by NEG.

Traditionally, location theories have emphasized the role of economic factors in spatial agglomeration: costs—raw materials, land, labour, capital and transport; infrastructure—water, power, transportation and communication; labour—skills composition and manpower quality; market access—opportunities for selling product, making profit, capturing market area and spatial competition; and benefits—localization and urbanization economies. NEG refers to interactions between economic factors including scale economies and transport costs and cumulative and circular causation processes. Newer theories refer to the role of political and governance factors, including law and order, enforcement of property rights and contracts, etc. Some also dwell on behavioural determinants of location. While the factors identified by conventional location theories still apply to heavy industry, those for high-tech manufacturing and services have undergone significant changes. This is due to globalization, reduction in transportation and communication costs, change in energy consumption patterns, increase in demand for skilled workers and rise of mega urban agglomerations (UAs) as hubs of innovation and growth. Other contributing factors include strides in ICT, rise of knowledge economy and new technology giants, platform revolution, growth of multinational corporations and heightened competition among governments to attract investment and growth. Investment–location–production decisions are overwhelmingly determined by market forces, corporate strategy, investors' preferences and internal decisions of industrial houses, aided by government policies.

In an increasingly globalizing and networked world, if a large business has to thrive, it has to compete regionally, nationally and globally. Studies on FDI inflows to developing countries point to the empirical determinants of foreign investment. These include country-, region- and sector-specific factors such as per capita GDP, external debt, foreign trade openness, exchange rate, capital flows, FDI policy, infrastructure, real labour cost, human capital, market size, agglomeration economies, interest rate, return on investment, regulatory frameworks, quality of governance, rule of law, political risks and dispensations provided by governments. Investor perception surveys on 'why business locates where it is' link the choice of location to availability of men, materials, money, machinery and market, apart from land and proactive governance. They reveal that well-governed city regions instil confidence in investors regarding the smooth conduct of business, apart from providing incentives. The World Bank has also identified the key role of governance-related factors in 'ease of doing business'. The latter is related to factors such as starting a business, employing workers, dealing with construction permits, getting electricity, registering property, getting credit, protecting minority investors, paying taxes, trading across borders, contracting with government, ending contract and resolving insolvency (World Bank 2020).

As globalization proceeds, the location of secondary and tertiary firms is increasingly being determined by market forces, supported by forward-looking government policies and institutions. The World Economic Forum (WEF) identifies 12 pillars of competitiveness to rank countries. These are institutions—legal-administrative framework; infrastructure, including well-developed transportation and communication networks; technological readiness—capacity to leverage ICT; stability of macroeconomic environment; health—healthy workers; education—well-educated and skilled manpower; product market efficiency; labour market efficiency; efficient financial system; size of market to exploit scale economies; business dynamism and clustering efficiency; and technological innovation capacity (WEF 2019). The above pillars, with suitable modifications, apply to states and regional locations. In fact, city regions in both developed and developing countries are competing nationally and internationally to attract investment, entrepreneurship, talent and production based on their locational strength and the conducive climate they offer for business. Policymakers and planners must understand why investment and growth continue to localize in these regions in spite of the diseconomies of density. They also need to recognize the crucial role of governments in developing countries through instruments such as spatial planning, 'just-in-time' investment in infrastructure, especially transportation and public health, disaster risk reduction and fiscal mechanisms to manage the positive and negative effects of externalities.

While theory and practice identify geographic, historical, economic, behavioural, political and governance-related determinants of location, the technocratic master plans of cities in India largely ignore such factors. They are command and control–based, untouched by economic liberalization reforms from the 1990s'. The master plans prescribe land use zoning and density patterns for the plan horizon year, 20–25 years ahead. They expect economic actors to choose location and undertake land use to fit into such patterns. The land use–led plans also undermine the role of infrastructure, especially transportation and determinants of competitiveness. Particular businesses tend to have particular requirements for production, input mix, technology, infrastructure, location, land use, floor space and the like. Thus, blanket land use and density controls based on planners' wisdom constrain the choice of productive economic activities by firms, households and workers. They lead to mismatch between the demands of competitive business and location. Further, they promote rent-seeking and corruption, leading to distortions and deadweight social welfare losses. These considerations suggest that master plan–determined land use zoning for economic activities may not be an efficient way to attract the location of major investments, which depend upon risks and returns. Business climate and incentives are critical for competing in the globalizing economy.

Empirical evidence suggests that the quality of governance at country, state and city levels stands out as one most critically acclaimed enabler of competitiveness. Well-governed city regions around the world act as hubs of innovation and growth; they attract, enable and nurture creative entrepreneurs and skilled workers to compete, cooperate and collaborate. They resort to a spatial planning approach that is flexible enough to respond to the dynamic drivers of investment and growth. They also resort to negotiation with developers through instruments such as 'planning obligations' in the United Kingdom, 'development contribution' in Australia and 'incentive zoning' in the United States. However, city regions in developing countries are plagued by governance deficit and a climate of suspicion and mistrust between planners and developers. They impose elaborate land market regulations that do not serve broader social objectives. The chronic under-investment in infrastructure and acute scarcity of land and floor space for productive economic activities and affordable housing in these countries reflect weak urban and metropolitan governance institutions. These institutions are ill-equipped to discharge their fundamental economic functions to nurture skill and entrepreneurship, create growth, generate employment and mobilize public finance. They fail to address the concerns of infrastructure, public services, public health, social inclusion, environmental conservation and disaster resilience. A fundamental question in developing countries like India is as follows: Who is in charge of the city? The answer is blurred. Urban policy needs to recognize the crucial role of empowered city and metropolitan governments in offering well-governed and competitive 'location' to firms, households and developers to pursue their chosen activities.

Determinants of Land Use

Theory, Practice and Lessons for Land Policy

Land Use: Theoretical Perspectives

Location of economic activity and land use are closely related. They describe the spatial organization of local and regional economies. Land use represents how land is managed to adapt to the needs of households and firms. Like location, land use patterns in a spatial economy are largely shaped by interactions between market forces and government policies. They have crucial implications for spatio-economic outcomes in a local area or region such as production, consumption, economic growth, affordable housing, land value and house rent. Economists and geographers have explored the reasons behind the observed patterns of land use in rural as well as urban areas since the time of von Thünen's seminal work: *The Isolated State* (1826). Thünen propagated a theory of agricultural land uses organized around a central market. Subsequently, the theory was extended by Alonso (1964) to urban land uses and refined by Muth (1969) and Mills (1972). While urban land use patterns are largely shaped by market forces, spatial planning, including zoning and land development regulations, play a crucial role in the evolution of the spatial structure of cities and urban regions.

Rural Land Use: von Thünen's Model

von Thünen (1826) presents a theory of land use in an agricultural economy, linking the market, land use, production, land rent, distance and cost to transport produce. Although the theory is focused on land use in a rural area, its conclusion that more productive activities compete for land closer to the market applies to spatial organization of an urban region. Thünen also propagated a theory of land rent based on proximity to the market—very different from the Ricardian theory. Ricardo associated land rent with differential fertility, determined by intrinsic characteristics of land such as 'original and indestructible power of the soil', topography, microclimate and proximity to natural amenities like a river or lake.

von Thünen's model of land use in an agricultural economy organized around a central market is based on the following simplistic assumptions (see Arnott 2012):

1. A single agricultural good is produced by farmers in a featureless plain.
2. Land is of uniform fertility; farmers take land for cultivation from landlords by paying a rent.
3. The price of the good p is given; competition among farmers leads to zero economic profit in all locations.
4. Land and labour are used in fixed proportion to produce a fixed yield per unit area, say an acre.
5. Transport cost—for shipping produce from field to the central market for sale—varies linearly with distance.

Under the above assumptions, the rent that a farmer would be willing to pay for land at distance d to the central market can be expressed as

$$r(d) = pq - wn - qtd \tag{4.1}$$

where p=price of output sold in the central market, q=quantity of output (in tons) produced per unit area, w=wage rate per worker, n=number of workers deployed for cultivation per unit area, t=transport cost per unit of output-distance (ton-kilometre), d=distance to the central market, pq=revenue per unit area accruing to the farmer, wn=labour cost per unit area and qtd=cost of transporting produce from a unit area to the market incurred by a farmer cultivating land at a distance d to the market. The assumption of zero economic profit implies that if it were possible to cultivate land at some distance from the market, its rent will bid up to the point where it is equal to zero.

Determinants of Land Use

The closest distance d^* to the market at which land rent is zero or the 'extensive margin' of cultivation is determined by the following equation

$$qtd^* = pq - wn \text{ or, } d^* = \frac{1}{t}\left(p - \frac{wn}{q}\right) \qquad (4.2)$$

At the central market $d=0$, which implies that transport cost $=0$ and therefore, rent per unit area is maximum, equal to $pq - wn$. The rent will fall linearly as distance from the market increases till it becomes zero at $d=d^*$. In other words, as d increases from 0 to d^*, land rent falls from $pq - wn$ to 0. The rate of decline in land rent per unit distance is qt, which just offsets the increase in transport costs. Referred to as the 'accessibility premium', qt is the extra amount a farmer would be willing to pay in rent to be one unit distance closer to the market. Beyond d^* farmers will keep land fallow unless the rent payable is negative.

Figure 4.1 depicts the bid rent function indicating the highest rent per unit area that a farmer will be willing to bid to cultivate land at a given distance d from the central market. Bid rent is the amount that

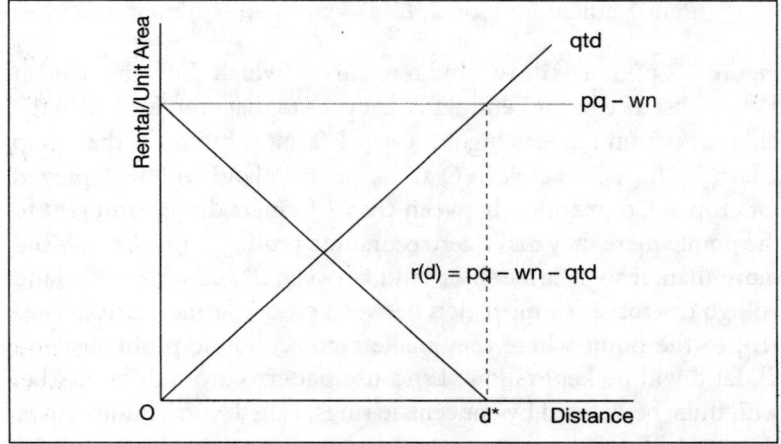

Figure 4.1 *Von Thünen Model: Extensive Margin of Cultivation*

drives economic profit to zero. As can be seen from Figure 4.1, it is zero beyond $d=d^*$

Equation (4.2) leads to the following conclusions, other things being equal:

1. As t decreases, say, due to an improvement in transportation technology, d^* increases.
2. As p increases, say, due to excess of demand over supply on account of market and trade related factors, d^* increases.
3. As q increases, say, due to improvement agricultural technology, d^* increases.
4. As w increases or n increases, d^* decreases.

Suppose that instead of a single crop, two crops are cultivated: 1 and 2. Let the wage rate w be the same for both the crops while other variables p, q, n and t differ between the two crops. Then the bid rent per unit area of land for cultivating crop 1 and crop 2 as a function of distance to the central market, respectively, can be represented by

Rent gradient for crop 1: $b^1(d) = p^1 q^1 - wn^1 - q^1 t^1 d$ \hfill (4.3)

Rent gradient for crop 2: $b^2(d) = p^2 q^2 - wn^2 - q^2 t^2 d$ \hfill (4.4)

Figure 4.2 presents the two bid rent curves, which show that land at a given distance to the central market goes to that crop for which the bid rent per unit area is higher. Crop 1 farmers bid more than crop 2 farmers for land between O and d^1; hence, land will be deployed for crop 1. Competition between crop 1 farmers drives land rent to the point where they make zero economic profit. Crop 2 farmers bid more than crop 1 farmers for land between d^1 and d^2; hence, land will go to crop 2. Competition between crop 2 farmers drives land rent to the point where they make zero economic profit. Beyond d^2, land will be kept fallow. Land use patterns around the market will, thus, be defined by concentric rings, called 'von Thünen rings' (Figure 4.3).

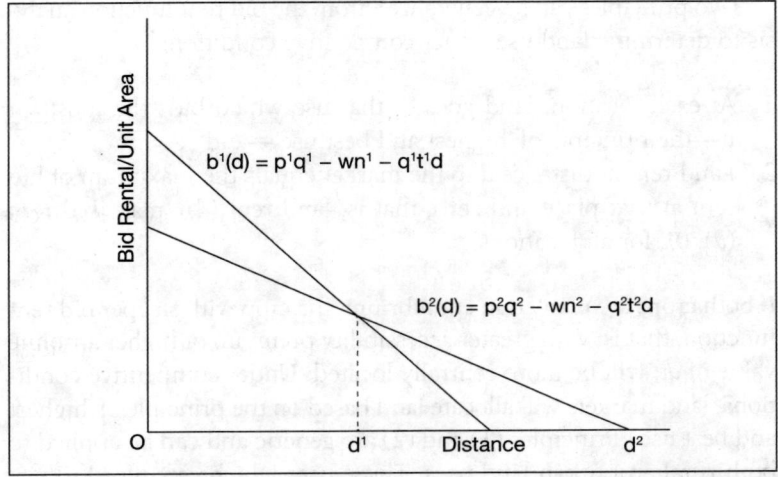

Figure 4.2 *Von Thünen Model: Bid Rent Functions*

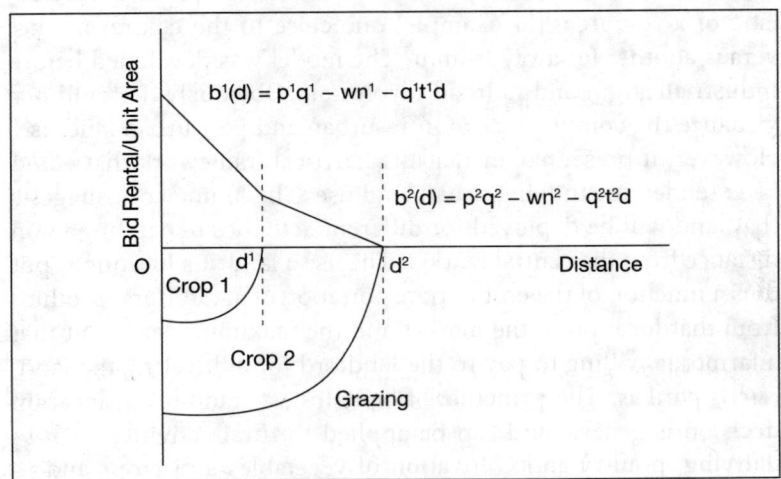

Figure 4.3 *Von Thünen Model: Rural Land Use Patterns*

Two principles can be generalized from the bid rent function analysis to determine land use under competitive conditions:

1. At each location, land goes to that use which bids the most for it—the principle of 'highest and best use'—and
2. Land rent at distance d to the market equals the maximum of bid rent at that place and zero, that is, land rent $(d) = \max\{\text{bid rent }(d), 0\}$, for all locations.

If both crops are planted in equilibrium, the crop with steeper bid rent function, that is, with greater accessibility premium or higher absolute value of qt, will be more centrally located. Under competitive conditions, land markets will allocate land based on the principle of 'highest and best use'. Principles (1) and (2) are generic and can be applied to both rural and urban land uses. Those uses which can afford to pay higher rent will be more centrally located.

von Thünen's model was the first major formulation in spatial economics, linking it to the theory of rent. It presented the concept of economic rent that depends on location or spatial characteristic of a resource, for example, one close to the central market versus another far away from it. The model was developed before industrialization and railroad revolution. Obviously, it could not visualize the complexities of intra-urban and peri-urban land use. However, it presented an elegant analytical framework that could be extended to studying urban land use. This framework suggests that land will be deployed for different activities depending upon distance from the central market. The use a land at a location is put to is a function of the cost of transportation of agricultural produce from that location to the market and the maximum land rent that a farmer is willing to pay to the landlord for cultivating the land, *ceteris paribus*. The principle of benefit-cost trade-off in location decision is generic and can be applied to rural activities such as dairying, poultry and cultivation of vegetables and crops and to urban activities such as retail, commercial, industrial, residential, and institutional.

Determinants of Land Use 121

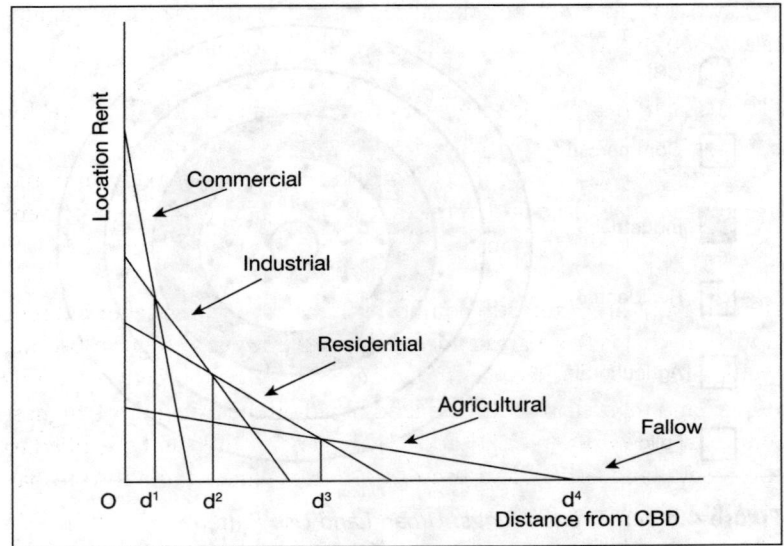

Figure 4.4 *Von Thünen Model: Urban Land Use Patterns*

Figure 4.4 presents an example of the spatial organization of economic activity in an urban region based on the framework of von Thünen model. Note that we replace the central market in the agricultural economy by CBD in the urban economy. Figure 4.5 shows land use patterns around CBD in concentric rings. In the context of residential use, the von Thünen principle can be extended to high-density high-rise buildings, low-rise apartment complexes, single-family homes, farmhouses, no development zone, etc. The bid rent analysis suggests that the more productive activities that can afford to bid higher rent for land use will locate closer to CBD. The benefit of being one unit distance nearer to the city centre, where jobs and commercial activities are located, is reflected in savings in transportation cost. This must be offset by the higher expenditure incurred as land rent or housing cost to ensure spatial indifference. This view is incorporated by Alonso (1964) and later models in urban economics.

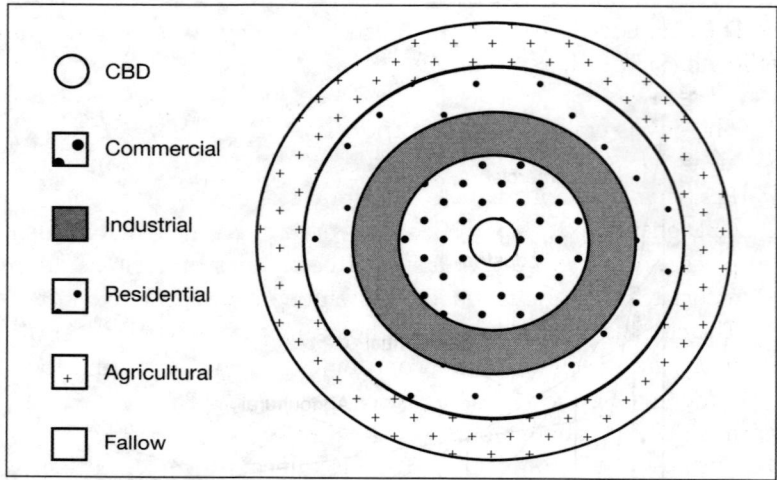

Figure 4.5 *Von Thünen Rings: Urban Land Use Pattern*

Urban Land Use: Alonso–Muth–Mills Model

Alonso (1964), Muth (1969) and Mills (1967, 1972) extend the von Thünen model of agricultural land use to explain the pattern and intensity of land use within urban areas. They present simple, yet powerful models to explain the spatial structure of cities using microeconomic analysis. They adopt the view that differences in commuting cost in an urban area must be offset by differences in the cost-of-living space for a household to be indifferent between locations. Alonso presented a model where individual consumers consume land directly. Muth and Mills chose models that treat land as an intermediate good used to produce housing, which is a final consumption good. These pioneers of urban economics presented the concept of spatial or locational equilibrium. Stated more generally, the concept suggests that when identical individuals choose different places in an urban area for residence, these places must be offering an equivalent bundle of net benefits, taking all relevant factors into account—wages, land and housing rents, housing prices, taxes, transport costs, access to amenities and civic services, etc.

The standard Alonso–Muth–Mills (AMM) model is based on the following simplistic assumptions:

1. The city is circular, monocentric with radius d^* so that the city area $= \pi d^{*2}$. All the jobs are located in CBD—a point in space. Residents commute daily to CBD for working and shopping.
2. CBD offers a fixed wage w (assumed to be higher than that at other places in the city due to external economies of agglomeration associated with the spatial concentration of economic activity).
3. The city has N number of households, spread uniformly over the urban area. Each household contributes one unit labour and commutes to CBD for work. A single consumption good C is produced in CBD with labour alone.
4. The cost of commuting to CBD, T is a linear function of distance d, that is, $T = td$ where t is a positive constant.
5. Each household consumes the private consumption good C and land L. C is the numeraire with price equal to unity. One unit of land translates to one unit of housing so that L can also be interpreted as representing housing.
6. Let $r(d)$ be the amount payable by the consumer towards land rent at a distance d to CBD.
7. All city residents maximize utility subject to budget constraint, represented by the equation: income = expenditure on (consumer good + land rent or housing cost + transport cost).
8. The utility function of the representative resident is subject to standard neoclassical assumptions of convexity—positive but diminishing marginal utility.

Model 1: Consumption of C by the Representative Resident Is Variable, While Consumption of Land L Is Fixed

The condition of spatial equilibrium requires that each household spends the same amount in land rent plus commuting cost so that there is spatial indifference and no incentive to change location. This implies for all d, $r(d)L + td =$ constant, implying

$$r(d) = -\frac{t}{L}d + k \quad \text{where } k \text{ is a constant} \tag{4.5}$$

Taking derivatives of both the sides

$$r'(d) = -\frac{t}{L} \tag{4.6}$$

The same result (Equation [4.6]) can be obtained by solving the optimization problem of the representative resident, which can be stated as

$$\text{Maximize}_{c} U = U(c, L) \text{ subject to } c + r(d)L + td = y \tag{4.7}$$

where U is the utility function of the representative resident subject to standard neoclassical assumptions, c = consumption of the private good with price normalized to unity, L is the consumption of land and y = income or wage received from employer at CBD. As L is fixed, the problem reduces to maximize $c = y - r(d)L - td$ for all residents living at a distance d from CBD. The first-order conditions for this unconstrained optimization problem: $\frac{\partial c}{\partial d} = 0$ gives $r'(d) = -\frac{t}{L}$. This equation suggests that a resident living 1 km further away from CBD, who incurs t more through commuting cost, pays t less in land rent in order to be spatially indifferent; hence $\frac{t}{L}$ less in rent per unit land area. This expression represents the 'accessibility premium'.

As the city area is assumed to be fully occupied by N number of residents, each consuming L units of land, the endowment condition can be stated as follows:

$$\pi d^{*2} = NL, \text{ or } d^* = \sqrt{\frac{NL}{\pi}} \tag{4.8}$$

Substituting d^* for d in Equation (4.5), we have $r(d^*) = -\frac{t}{L}d^* + k$ or, $k = r(d^*) + \frac{t}{L}d^*$ where d^* is determined by (4.8). Replacing k in (4.5),

$r(d) = -\frac{t}{L}d + r(d^*) + \frac{t}{L}d^*$ or, $r(d) = \frac{t}{L}(d^* - d) + r(d^*)$. As the rent at the boundary of the city will be equal to the agricultural rent r_A or, $r(d^*) = r_A$, we have

$$r(d) = r_A + \frac{t}{L}(d^* - d) = r_A + \frac{t}{L}\left(\sqrt{\frac{NL}{\pi}} - d\right) \quad (4.9)$$

Equation (4.9) represents the equilibrium rent function with slope $-\frac{t}{L}$. As can be seen, this function is increasing in t, r_A and N and decreasing in d. The following conclusions can be inferred from our analysis:

1. Land rent adjusts to ensure spatial equilibrium: supply of land = demand for land at all locations.
2. Land goes to that use which bids the most for it.
3. Land uses are ordered away from CBD according to the accessibility premium equal to $\frac{t}{L}$.
4. The household group with steeper bid rent function locates closer to CBD.
5. The absolute value of the slope of the bid rent function at a particular location equals the accessibility premium to land use there.

Figure 4.6 depicts the determination of equilibrium land use in the economy, with spatial limit to the urban area shown. Land use for urban activities such as commercial, industrial, retail, high density residential and single-family homes will extend from O to d^* and land use for rural activities such as agriculture and dairying, from d^* to the right, as shown in Figure 4.6. Under free market conditions, the city boundary will extend to the point d^* where the bid rent for use of land for urban activities will be equal to the agricultural land rent, which is assumed to be fixed for simplicity. Figure 4.7 shows bid rent as a function of distance, called 'rent-distance function' in the literature.

One may note that the rent payable by the representative resident for using land for urban activities beyond d^* will be zero. Therefore, the rent-distance function will be as shown in Figure 4.7, with the

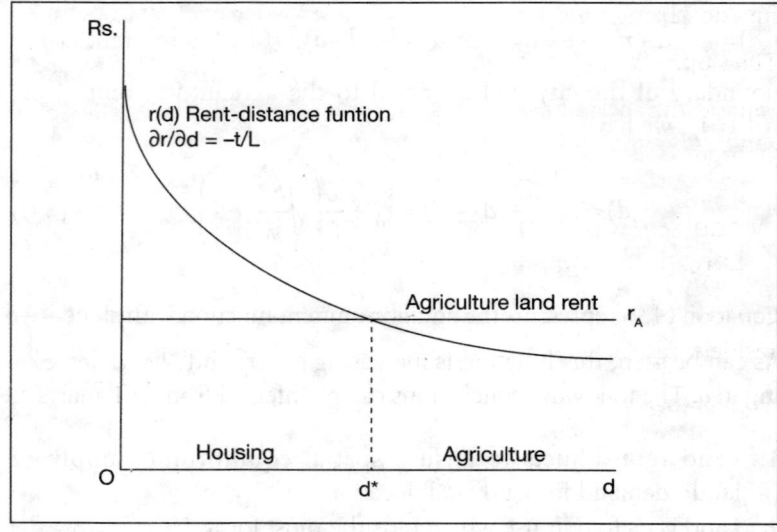

Figure 4.6 *Alonso–Muth–Mills Model: Determination of Urban Boundary*

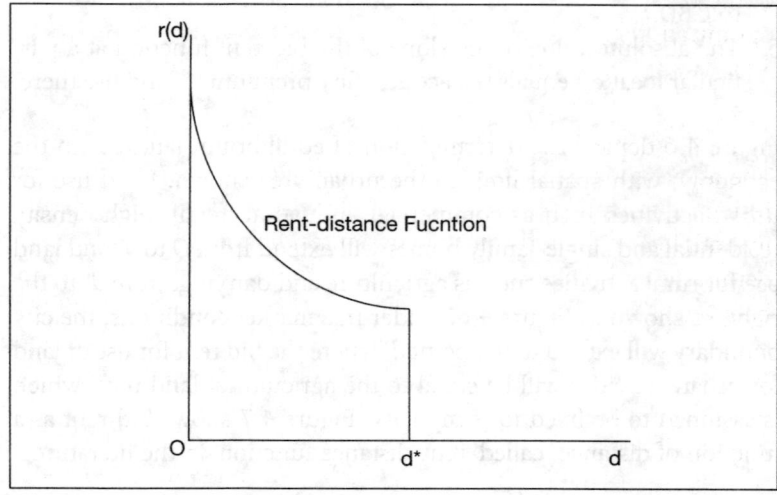

Figure 4.7 *Alonso–Muth–Mills Model: Rent–Distance Function*

function being represented by the distance-axis beyond the point d^*. The slope of the rent-distance function will equal $-\frac{t}{L}$ whose absolute value is the accessibility premium. Under reasonable assumptions, it can be shown that the rent-distance function is convex.

Model 2: Both Consumption of the Private Good C and Land L by the Representative Resident Are Variable

The constrained utility maximization problem of the representative resident can be presented as follows:

$$\underset{c,L}{\text{Maximize}}\ U = U(c, L) \text{ s. t. budget constraint } c + r(d)L + td = y \text{ or,}$$

$$c + r(d)L = y - td$$

where U is the utility function subject to standard neoclassical assumptions of diminishing marginal utility with convex indifference curves. Both consumption c of the good C and consumption of land L are variable. Substituting for c in U, the constrained optimization problem of the representative resident can be replaced by the unconstrained optimization problem: maximizing U as a function of d and L, namely

$$\underset{d,L}{\text{Maximize}}\ U = U(y - r(d)L - td, L) \qquad (4.10)$$

The above expression implies that consumers choose distance from residence to workplace in CBD and plot size so as to maximize utility and, hence, are indifferent between residing in different locations within the city. The first-order conditions for spatial equilibrium can be given as follows:

$$\frac{\partial U}{\partial d} = -r'(d)L - t = 0 \text{ or, } r'(d) = -\frac{t}{L} \text{ and}$$

$$\frac{\partial U}{\partial c}(-r(d)) + \frac{\partial U}{\partial L} = 0 \text{ or, } \frac{dc}{dL} = r(d) \qquad (4.11)$$

Further, the spatial equilibrium or uniform spatial utility condition requires

For all $0 < d \leq d^*$ (city edge),

$$U(y - r(d)L - td, L) = \bar{U} \text{ for some } \bar{U} \quad (4.12)$$

Condition (4.11) is equivalent to the standard result in microeconomics that the consumer will choose consumption of C and L so that the budget line is tangential to the highest attainable indifference curve. Condition (4.12) depicts the spatial equilibrium requirement that consumers are equally well off at all locations, achieving the same level of utility regardless of where they live in the urban area. Otherwise, they will have a tendency to change location. Lower land cost at a distant suburban location serves as a 'compensating differential' that reconciles suburban residents to long, inconvenient and costly commute daily. In order to offset the reduction in net income $y - td$ associated with an increase in d, the land rent $r(d)$ must decrease as d increases so that residents are indifferent between locations. Thus, the rent-distance function will be downward-sloping with slope $-\dfrac{t}{L}$ as in the case of model 1. Further, under reasonable assumptions, it can be shown as a convex function of distance to CBD.

Let us consider distance d^0 and d^1 from CBD or the city centre such that $d^1 > d^0$. Then, $y - td^1 < y - td^0$. The budget constraints for the representative resident at distance d^0 and d^1 from CBD, respectively, are

$$c + r(d^0)L = y - td^0 \text{ and } c + r(d^1)L = y - td^1.$$

The two budget constraints are shown in Figure 4.8, which also presents the spatial equilibrium for the representative resident at distance d^0 and d^1 from CBD, respectively. Note that the budget line for d^1 lies below that for d^0 on the c-axis and point of tangency with the highest attainable indifference curve $U = U(c, L)$ for d^1 lies to the right of that for d^0, implying that land consumption at $d^1 = L^1 >$ land consumption at $d^0 = L^0$. Further, the absolute value of the slope for budget line for

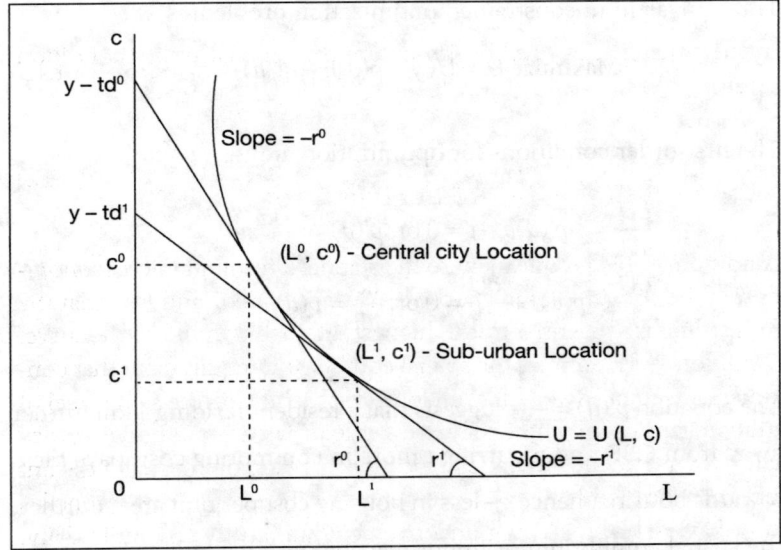

Figure 4.8 *Alonso–Muth–Mills Model: Central versus Suburban Location*

$d^1 = r(d^1)$ (r^1 in the figure) < absolute value of the slope for budget line for $d^0 = r(d^0)$ (r^0 in the figure). These results suggest that equilibrium land consumption increases and equilibrium land rent decreases as one moves away from the central area to a sub-urban location.

Model 3: Both Consumption of C and Housing H by the Representative Resident Are Variable

Let us assume that the price per unit of housing incurred by a representative resident living at distance d from CBD $= p(d)$, $h =$ consumption of housing so that $p(d)h =$ total cost of housing. The constrained optimization problem for the resident is

$$\underset{c,h}{\text{Maximize}}\ U = U(c, h) \text{ s. t. budget constraint } c + p(d)h + td = y \text{ or,}$$

$$c + p(d)h = y - td$$

The equivalent unconstrained optimization problem is

$$\underset{d,h}{\text{Maximize }} U = U(y - p(d)h - td, h) \quad (4.13)$$

The first-order conditions for optimization are

$$\frac{\partial U}{\partial d} = -p'(d)h - t = 0 \text{ or, } p'(d) = -\frac{t}{h} \text{ and}$$
$$\frac{\partial U}{\partial c}(-p(d)) + \frac{\partial U}{\partial h} = 0 \text{ or, } \frac{dc}{dh} = p(d) \quad (4.14)$$

The equation $p'(d) = -\frac{t}{h}$ suggests that a resident residing 1 km further away from CBD and incurring t more in commuting cost, pays t less towards housing; hence, $\frac{t}{h}$ less in housing cost per unit area. Further, the spatial equilibrium or uniform spatial utility condition to ensure locational indifference will require

$$\text{For all } 0 < d \leq d^* \text{(city edge)},$$
$$U(y - p(d)h - td, h) = \overline{U} \text{ for some } \overline{U} \quad (4.15)$$

Figure 4.9 shows the central city and sub-urban equilibrium housing/floor space consumption levels (q) and housing/floor space prices (p). It suggests that equilibrium housing/floor space consumption by the representative resident increases and housing/floor space price decreases as distance from CBD increases. Figure 4.10 shows that housing/floor space price-distance function is downward sloping and convex with slope $-\frac{t}{q}$.

Model 4: Housing (Floor Space) Production

Housing or floor space production can be considered as a function of land, building materials, labour, machinery, etc. For simplicity, we assume

Determinants of Land Use

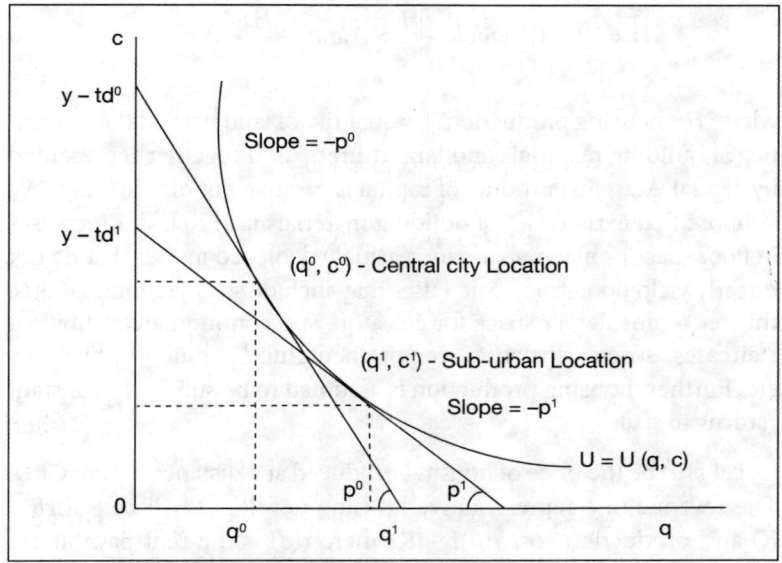

Figure 4.9 *Alonso–Muth–Mills Model: Central versus Suburban Housing*

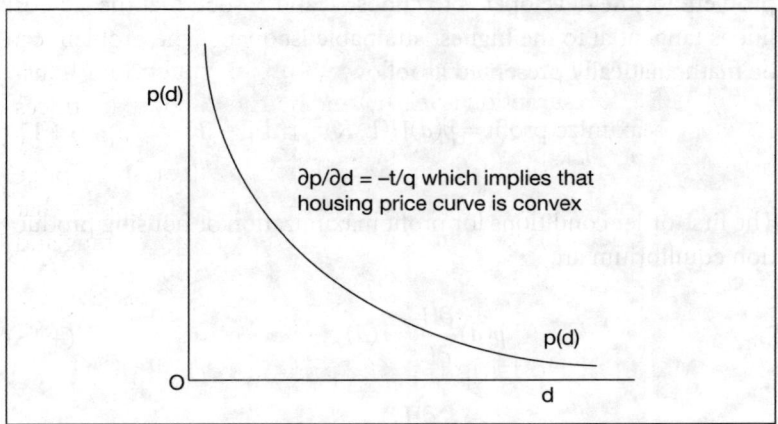

Figure 4.10 *Alonso–Muth–Mills Model: Housing Price Distance Function*

$$H = H(L, K) \text{ where } \frac{\partial H}{\partial K} > 0 \text{ and } \frac{\partial^2 H}{\partial K^2} < 0 \qquad (4.16)$$

where H=housing production, L=quantity of land used and K=quantity of building materials and labour units used together represented by capital. Marginal product of capital is positive but diminishing. We suppose that extra doses of building materials lead to lesser increases in floor space as materials are increasingly deployed in uses that do not directly yield floor space. Such uses may include stronger foundations, thicker beams, larger space for elevators and common areas, fire exit staircases, stricter structural requirements under building byelaws, etc. Further, housing production is assumed to be subject to constant returns to scale.

Let $p(d)$ be the price of housing produced at a distance d from CBD. The revenue of a representative housing developer will be $p(d)H(L, K)$ and production cost $r(d)L+iK$ where $r(d)$ is the rent payable for procuring land at distance d from CBD and i is the cost capital assumed to be fixed, which is determined nationally and independent of the housing location. $H(L, K)$=constant represents a generic isoquant and $r(d)L+iK$=constant represents a generic iso-cost line. The optimization problem for the developer is to choose L and K such that the iso-cost line is tangential to the highest attainable isoquant. The problem can be mathematically presented as follows:

$$\underset{L, K}{\text{Maximize profit}} = p(d)H(L, K) - r(d)L - iK \qquad (4.17)$$

The first-order conditions for profit maximization or housing production equilibrium are

$$p(d)\frac{\partial H}{\partial L} = r(d) \qquad (4.18)$$

$$p(d)\frac{\partial H}{\partial K} = i \qquad (4.19)$$

From Equations (4.18) and (4.19), we have

$$\frac{dK}{dL} = \frac{r(d)}{i} \qquad (4.20)$$

Equation (4.20) represents the condition that the absolute value of the slope of the highest isoquant attainable will be equal to that for the iso-cost line in equilibrium. This is diagrammatically shown for two locations—at distance d^0 and d^1 from CBD, respectively, $d^1 > d^0$.

As proved earlier, price-distance function $p(d)$ is downward-sloping, implying that the price that the consumers would be willing to pay for housing at distance d from CBD will be falling as distance d increases. Thus, $p(d^1) < p(d^0)$. As $\frac{\partial H}{\partial L} > 0$ (standard neoclassical assumption), from Equation (4.18), we get $r(d^1) < r(d^0)$. Thus, the absolute value of the slope of the iso-cost line at d^1, that is, $\frac{r(d^1)}{i}$, will be less than that for iso-cost line at d^0, that is, $\frac{r(d^0)}{i}$. Accordingly, the iso-cost lines will be as shown in Figure 4.11. The implications are $K(d^1) = K^1 < K(d^0) = K^0$, $L(d^1) = L^1 > L(d^0) = L^0$. These two inequalities yield $\frac{K^1}{L^1} < \frac{K^0}{L^0}$ implying that structural density at d^1, $S(d^1) = \frac{K^1}{L^1}$ will be lower than that at d^0, $S(d^0) = \frac{K^0}{L^0}$ (see Figure 4.11). Further, with capital K smaller and housing consumption q larger as distance d from CBD increases, the height of buildings is likely to be lower in suburbs than in central locations. Thus, while the central city area will have high-rise, high-density structures, sub-urban locations will have low-rise, low-density buildings and single-family homes. This conclusion seems to have been valid for several cities of developed countries in the past. However, it is not so in case of cities in developing countries like India where government regulations for FSI are not in conformity with the recommendations from theory. A general conclusion is that these cities have not exploited the power of density, land use and transport in securing efficient patterns of urban development.

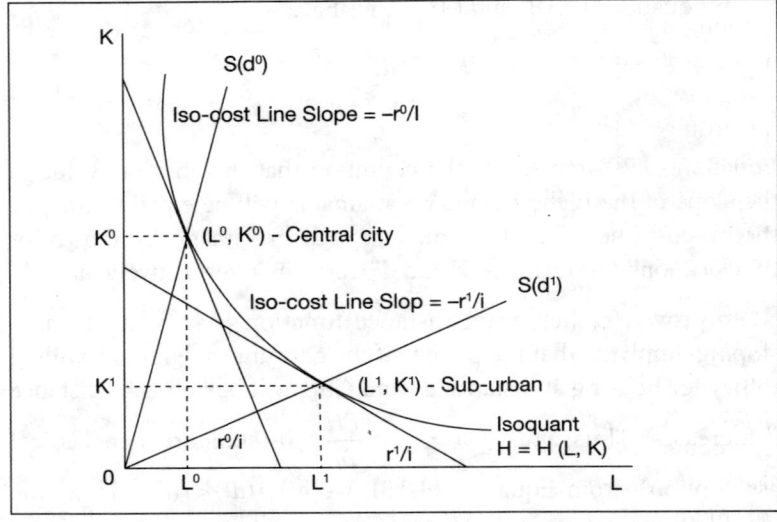

Figure 4.11 *Alonso–Muth–Mills Model: Housing Production: Central city versus Suburb*

Determinants of Land Use: Practice

Land uses in urban areas are shaped by not only market forces but also public policies. In particular, land use planning, alternatively called town and country planning, spatial planning or urban planning, plays a crucial role in land use decisions of firms, households and developers. Originating in the latter part of the 19th century following the Industrial Revolution, urban planning was a response to the problems of overcrowded and polluted cities of Western Europe. Its goal was to secure 'orderly' urban growth. Urban planning was regarded as a technical activity, linked to the planning and designing of human settlements. Later arguments in favour of urban planning were related to correcting for market failure due to externalities associated with pollution, congestion, noise and indiscriminate conversion of fertile agricultural land for urban uses, maintaining balance between various uses such as residential, commercial, institutional and recreational through zoning, providing infrastructure, housing and public amenities to city dwellers, resorting to land assembly through LA, land pooling and other mechanisms, etc. Further, land markets would not simply function without ground rules governing protection of property rights. Government legislation was advocated for defining, recording and enforcing land and property entitlements, conducting private transactions for the disposal of land, separating incompatible land uses and integrating infrastructure and land use planning. The role envisaged of government was not to replace the market but to remove its inadequacies and intervene when it fails.

The legal tools for urban planning consist of zoning, aimed at controlling the classification of land use, and planning permission, targeted at regulating land development for various uses. While local zoning ordinances were popular in the United States, planning permission system prescribed by national law took roots in the United Kingdom. Zoning regulations aim at controlling the type and intensity of land use. They prescribe norms for conforming and non-conforming land uses, densities, open spaces, infrastructure, housing, including light and ventilation, fire safety, etc. Zoning laws are supplemented by (a) subdivision regulations, prescribing street layouts, lot sizes, land allocation for public uses, taxes and charges for infrastructure financing, etc., and (b) building codes, setting standards of construction, use and maintenance.

In the United Kingdom, the Housing and Town Planning Act of 1909 empowered local authorities to restrict private development that does not conform with town planning principles. It enabled local authorities to develop TPS. A practical guide for the preparation TPS in accordance with the 1909 Act, published in 1911, states the objects of town planning as follows:

> ...land in the vicinity of town which is being or is likely to be developed for building purposes shall be developed in such a way as to secure proper sanitary conditions, amenity and convenience in connection with laying out of and use of the land and of any neighboring land. (Bentley and Taylor 1911, 1)

This guide also refers to the need for community control of town development with a view to providing 'health, convenience and beauty'.

The UK Town and Country Planning Act of 1947 legislated that 'all' land use in the future should be in accordance with plans prepared by local authorities. It prescribed that no material development could be undertaken without permission from local authority; ownership alone could not confer the right to develop land. The Act established the 'master planning' and 'planning permission' systems. While urban planning in the United Kingdom aimed at conformity with comprehensive master plan, the zoning system in the United States focused on mitigating negative externalities while meeting public service needs. The United States Department of Commerce issued the Standard State Zoning Enabling Act of 1926 to guide cities and towns, justifying the need for zoning to

> ...lessen congestion in the streets; to secure safety from fire, panic, and other dangers; to promote health and general welfare; to provide adequate light and air; to prevent the overcrowding of land; to avoid undue concentration of population; to facilitate the adequate provision of transportation, water, sewerage, schools, parks, and other public requirements. (United States Department of Commerce 1926, 6–7)

While some state laws require cities to prepare a 'general' or a comprehensive plan containing policies to guide long-term urban development and requiring zoning to be in accordance with the plan, comprehensive planning has not received much attention in the United States.

Regional and urban planning in India has adopted the master planning and planning permission systems in the United Kingdom with elements of zoning in the United States. Town planning and urban development laws in India articulate lofty objectives such as securing 'orderly urban development'. However, land use and DCRs based on these laws have become increasingly elaborate and stringent over the years. They have focused on detailed land use planning at multiple levels and, in essence, targeted at controlling development, rather than promoting it. As a result, Indian cities have not been able secure optimal land development, densities and land uses with a network of ordered central and sub-central districts as predicted by the urban economic model. This has led to acute shortage of floor space for economic growth–generating activities and affordable housing. Ironically, urban planners in India have chosen a narrow definition of development that does not consider the concepts of 'sustainable development' and 'inclusive growth'; for example, the Maharashtra Regional and Town Planning Act, 1966, in India defines development as:

> …carrying out of building, engineering, mining, or other operations in or over or under land, or the making of any material change, in any building or land or the making of any material structural change in heritage building or its precinct, and includes demolition of any existing building, structure or erection or part thereof and reclamation, redevelopment and layout and sub-division of any land.

A similar definition of development is adopted by town planning laws of other states in India. This is borrowed from Section 12(2) of the Town and Country Planning Act, 1947, in the United Kingdom which identifies development with 'the carrying out of building, engineering, mining or other operations in, on, over or under land, or making any material change in the use of any building or other land'.

The legal framework for land use planning in India is based on the Town and Country Planning Act, 1947, in the United Kingdom. While the planning system has undergone drastic changes in the United Kingdom with increased focus on decentralization and localism, it continues to remain centralized in India with a command and control approach. There is also no social benefit-cost analysis of how the system has fared with respect to key planning objectives. However, severe problems of air pollution in Delhi, environmental degradation in Bengaluru—once called a 'garden city'—devastating floods in Hyderabad in August 2000 and October 2020, in Chennai in November 2015, in Bengaluru in July 2016 and October 2020, and in Mumbai in July 2005 and August 2017 demonstrate how ill-prepared Indian metropolitan cities are to face exigencies and calamities. They reveal that not only land use planning but also infrastructure development and governance systems in urban areas have not kept pace with the challenges of urbanization. A key implication is that cities are not able to perform their legitimate role as drivers of economic growth and structural transformation. They are failing to function as efficient labour markets, exploiting agglomeration economies and mitigating congestion diseconomies with appropriate management of land use and infrastructure. A worrisome fact is that city regions, which are the creators of national wealth and tax bases of central, state and local governments, lack transportation and public health infrastructure to cope with land use densities and meet the backlog and current growth needs of infrastructure.

A major lacuna in master planning of India's city regions is the glaring disconnect between land use planning and land economics. Land use planning is not an end; it is an instrument to make cities discharge their fundamental functions: economic, social and environmental. With land use planning largely neglected by economists and land economics grossly ignored by planners, the integration between urban planning and economics has not occurred. Economists, emphasizing the virtues of the market, have hardly looked at the compulsions of land use and transportation planning in city regions. Planners, suspicious of the functioning of markets, have not recognized the contributions from land, transport and urban economics. Thus, the role of land as an economic good, and its links to externalities, has not been understood. Similarly, the importance of economic instruments such as land taxation, pricing of development rights and CC to correct for market failure, and various forms of rents to finance planned urban development has been neglected. An open question before policymakers in India today is as follows: Is the present command and control–based model of land use planning, which ignores theoretical development and practice in land, transport and urban economics, appropriate?

Lessons for Land Policy

The von Thünen and AMM models have limitations due to their simplistic assumptions. In particular, they do not explicitly incorporate the external economies of agglomeration and density in CBD, leading to higher wages and land rents as compared to peripheral locations. However, the models present a fundamental lesson: spatio-economic outcomes in an urban region, including location and land use, result from a trade-off between benefits and costs such as scale economies, wages, land rents, land values, housing prices, and commuting costs. They highlight the importance of accessibility considerations in land use decisions. The theories present some key propositions that can guide developing countries in the 'design' of interventions in urban land markets. These include

1. Land rent and housing price adjust to ensure locational equilibrium. Land goes to that use which bids the most for it—the principle of 'highest and best' land use.
2. Land uses are ordered away from CBD according to 'accessibility premium' to land and housing.
3. The household groups with steeper land rent or housing price function locate closer to CBD.
4. Land rent and housing price decrease, land and housing consumption increase, structural density and building height decrease, and population density decreases as the distance from CBD increases.
5. More populous cities tend to be spatially larger; higher income or lower commuting cost leads to geographically extended cities.
6. The poor and LIGs prefer to locate in central city areas in a bid to be close to workplaces, while saving commuting costs.
7. Transportation technology extends cities along highways. Commuters shift from low fixed cost technology like PT to high fixed cost technology like personalized automobile as they reside away from CBD.
8. Limiting city size by fixing rigid growth boundaries leads to higher urban land rents and housing prices and lower consumption of floor space.
9. Restricting building height or FSI results in a decrease in housing supply, increase in housing price, lower floor space consumption and sprawl.

Urban economics suggests that economic agents are confronted with a 'trade-off' between benefits of 'accessibility' and costs of 'affordability' in decision-making regarding location and land use. In the simplest model of residential location choice, households weigh the benefits of accessibility to workplace offering high wages against the costs of affordability in terms of land, housing, commuting and other expenditures. The high house rents and transport costs in cities such as Delhi, Mumbai and Bengaluru are conspicuous. Their other costs, such as shortages in basic civic services, overcrowding, traffic jams, air pollution, crime and hazards of communicable diseases, are also overwhelming. Yet, economic agents prefer to locate in such cities to gain from higher productivity and wages; access to a wider variety of amenities; and opportunities of learning, sharing and matching. Firms seek to benefit from scale and agglomeration, including specialization, diversity and competition. They strive to gain from knowledge spillovers, while reducing the costs of 4 Ts: transport, time, transaction and tariff. Developers choose locations to build, matching incomes and preferences of prospective buyers. Paradoxically, master planning in developing countries, by predetermining land uses, curtails the degrees of freedom with economic agents. It undermines the role of 'accessibility' and 'affordability' in location and land use and, therefore, the critical role of transport in land management.

Cities form and grow due to the collocation of many firms, households and developers. These agents will not cluster unless their benefits outweigh costs. However, actions of independent actors engaged in interdependent activities lead to externalities, centripetal and centrifugal forces, and cumulative and circular causation processes. These factors impact accessibility, affordability, density, land use, land rent, land value, housing price and other characteristics of locations and mobility in the labour market. They influence the supply of, demand for, and price of land and floor space in different locations. Demand for land depends on population, income distribution structure and economic activity. Supply of land depends on characteristics of land, including location, ownership and access to infrastructure, conditions of real estate market and government regulations, including zoning and FSI. If urban land supply is elastic and responsive to demand, land price would reflect the productive value of land. When urban land markets face structural bottlenecks and cannot readily adjust to demand, land price would be much higher than the productive value. Such bottlenecks include lack of investment in transportation infrastructure, restrictive zoning and stringent DCRs and speculative 'hold-outs' in land by owners to reap windfall gains. Land use planning in India, which is focused on regulatory controls, neglects the economic determinants of land use such as demand for, supply of and price of land. The planners also do not utilize the valuable market-based information on demand for and supply of land and housing, land value, housing price, office rent, transport cost, etc. to design evidence-based interventions in land markets. Thus, their prescriptions are often in conflict with the signals transmitted by the market.

While land use decisions by economic agents are determined by net benefits (benefits minus costs), urban planners in developing countries are obsessed with costs. According to them, the primary objectives of land use planning are to mitigate negative externalities such as incompatible land uses, vehicular congestion, air pollution, high land and housing prices, public health hazards, exclusion of the poor and indiscriminate conversion of rural land to urban use. However, the urban planners overlook the dynamics of agglomeration and networking externalities in city regions. Preoccupied with land use detailing, the planners have neglected developmental instruments, especially investment in PT, to address negative externalities. Further, they have ignored economic instruments such as highway toll, impact fee, special assessment, congestion pricing, carbon tax, motor vehicle tax, LVT, betterment levy, pricing of development rights, polluters pay charges and fiscal incentives. The neglect of a graduated VLT to push land held idle for speculation to productive uses is intriguing. Incidentally, skyrocketing land and housing prices in Indian cities signal that land and housing markets are severely constrained—due to stringent control on land use, density and FSI, chronic under-investment in transportation infrastructure to service land and rampant speculation.

Urban land markets in developing countries fail due to not only externalities, public goods, monopoly and speculation but also inappropriate land policy and unwarranted regulations. Governments in these countries are expected to invest in leading infrastructure; enable provision of serviced land for urban uses; address externalities of density, overcrowding and congestion; catalyse growth; promote affordable housing and workplaces; protect the environment; and maintain an efficient land information system to facilitate land market transactions. However, in practice, planning and development actions by public authorities have been far from achieving these goals. Urban areas in India present a picture of under-planning of economic growth and over-regulation of land markets. Many conspicuous problems of Indian cities such as exorbitantly high land and housing prices in relation to household incomes, failing public services, traffic congestion, sprawling development, exclusionary urbanization, etc. can be traced to land use–led master planning. This approach is focused on microcontrols over land use and FSI. By neglecting land, transport and urban economics, it also fails to present a coherent strategy to finance investment in transportation infrastructure to guide land development and use. Master planning ignores the fundamentals of urban public finance. Cities in developing countries are subjected to both market failure and government failure (Mohanty 2014, 2019).

Markets and public policies, in interaction with external economies and diseconomies, determine the net benefits of government interventions in city regions. However, public authorities in developing countries frame land use and density regulations and invest in urban projects without rigorous social benefit-cost analysis. They choose to control land development and use, while neglecting transport and their wider economic impacts. Land, transport and urban economics suggest that a top-down master planning model, focused on controls at regional, city, zonal, local and plot levels to attain a predetermined urban form, is ill-suited to guide the optimal allocation of scarce land resources in developing countries. They singularly point to the importance of PT in urban economic growth, inclusion and conservation. A PT-led and TOD strategy with phased investments in public transit and a hub and spoke model of development capable of benefiting from externalities are more appropriate for densely populated Indian city regions rather than land use–led master planning.

The economic importance of transport in land use planning derives from a number of reasons. First, transport positively impacts growth through multiple markets: land, housing, transport, labour, goods and services, etc. It promotes specialization, division of labour and scale economies. Second, it is critical to servicing land, expanding labour market, enhancing access to the economic mass, catalysing density and agglomeration economies, mitigating congestion diseconomies and increasing competition. Third, transport is instrumental in expanding employment and housing opportunities to the poor and LIGs, safeguarding the environment and promoting VCF of infrastructure. Ideally, transportation networks should play a 'leading' role in guiding land use, given their profound impacts on location, land value, housing price, mobility of the disadvantaged sections, environment conservation and economic growth. In fact, PT investment in anticipation of economic growth has been the single most important strategy to make urban land markets work in developed countries. However, master planning in developing countries has treated transportation as a 'residual', subservient to land use. Thus, cities have not been able to exploit the synergy between transportation, land use, density and development to promote inclusive growth. At this juncture of India's urban evolution, a critical policy intervention is to re-engineer cities by investing in PT, promoting TOD and transport–land use integration and implementing SLM with land as a resource. A walking time of 15 min to transit node and commuting time of 1 h to place of work may serve as a guide for designing SLM.

Investment and production in an increasingly globalizing and networked world are largely determined by market forces, supported by public policies as governments compete to attract investment. Location and land use decisions of economic agents in the spatial economy involve a trade-off between benefits and costs such as scale economies, wages, land rents, land values, housing prices and transport costs. A static model of planning that predetermines location, land use and density ignoring the dynamics of urban markets and public policies is bound to lead to socially suboptimal outcomes. International experience suggests that major projects often warrant changes in land use, density, FSI and other norms, prescribed by the planners at a time when they had no clue about the future economic activities or their land use requirements. In fact, cities like Bengaluru and Hyderabad could not have become information technology hubs had their master plans not been responsive to changing needs of the new economy. Developed countries like the United Kingdom, the United States and Australia follow flexi-zoning schemes to attract transformative projects.

Such schemes involve negotiations between the planning authority and the developer under law. If SDGs are to be achieved, economic agents across the board must have flexibility in making investment, production, location and land use decisions. Governments in developing countries must proactively facilitate such decision-making by investing in transportation infrastructure in anticipation of growth. They must also incentivize creative entrepreneurs and skilled workers to innovate and take risk. Land use zoning and development regulations are a means to attain development and welfare objectives, not ends in themselves. They must promote development, rather than controlling it.

An Appraisal of Land Use Planning

Exploring a New Paradigm for Developing Countries

Land Use Planning: Theory

Land use planning, alternatively called spatial planning, town and country planning, urban and regional planning or simply urban planning, has a long history. However, modernist urban planning originated in response to the social problems in cities following the Industrial Revolution. As Peter Hall observes, it *represents a reaction to the evils of the nineteenth century city* (Hall 1988, 7). Urban planning took roots in the aftermath of the 'chaos' in cities due to rapid industrialization, rural–urban migration and spatial concentration of population in urban areas. The problems of industrializing cities, which attracted a large number of migrants from rural areas within a short period of time, manifested in squalor, dirt, disease, disorder, ugliness, pollution, congestion, noise and overcrowded and unsanitary slums. These led to the emergence of urban planning as a profession, with planners stressing the need for more air and light, spacious housing and cleaner environments for urban residents, particularly the working class. To them, urban form was a key factor in maintaining a high quality of life, and modern technology made newer urban forms possible. The modernist desire of planners for a 'grand' city form called for clearance of ugly looking slums and rehabilitation of slumdwellers in orderly settlements. This pervaded not only theory but also practice of land use planning in developed countries. The modernist ideas soon spread to developing countries. Some key concepts, theories and approaches presented by modernist urban planning theories are presented below (see Mohanty 2019).

Howard: Garden City

Ebenezer Howard (1898/1902) proposed 'garden cities', laid out in a wheel-and-spoke pattern of settlements surrounding older, central cities, to address their problems of pollution, congestion and slums in the aftermath of the Industrial Revolution. His central idea was to combine physical design, social harmony and economic plan to promote decent living and working. The new satellite towns were to host small communities of single detached residential buildings with ample open space for every man, every woman and every child to live, to play and to develop. The central area of each garden city was to have civic buildings, a park and a shopping arcade. These cities were conceived to be beautiful, healthy, compact, efficient and self-contained—with community services, self-sufficient industries separated from residential areas and agriculture. To be built on cooperation with communal purchase of land at cheap agricultural prices, each garden city was proposed to house a population of 30,000 at the core and 2,000 at the periphery—at a density of 25–30 per acre. It was to contain 3,500 building lots of an average size of 20 feet × 130 feet, with the minimum space norm being 20 feet × 100 feet. Each garden city was to be collectively owned by the occupants. Economic growth would rely on each resident becoming an artisan entrepreneur, producing high quality goods for the community and generating export sales. This paradigm lacked an economic basis; business activities would hardly be present in Howard's utopia. Subsequent garden city projects eliminated the 'occupant ownership' and 'local industry' components. However, the scholastic theory of Howard's garden city was not implemented beyond two cities—Letchworth and Welwyn—in view of the impracticality of its economics and requirements such as 'cooperative commonwealth'.

Geddes: Social Evolution

Patrick Geddes (1915), widely recognized as the father of modern regional and urban planning, considered city as an evolution. He proposed to place societies in the wider socio-economic and environmental contexts of the region. He highlighted the role of integration of people, their livelihoods and the environment of the place and the region they inhabit in social and cultural progress. Geddes recognized the phenomena of 'conurbations' and ever-expanding communities. He advocated the acceptance of the inevitability of centrifugal forces and undertake spatial panning accordingly. Further, Geddes emphasized that planning must start with a detailed survey of the region—'diagnosis before treatment', 'survey before alteration' and 'analysis before synthesis'. He called for taking stock of physical, topographical, ecological, environmental, social and economic characteristics of the region; the challenges and opportunities they present; human response to the use of natural resource and other given factors; and the cultural landscapes created by relationships between 'place', 'work' and 'folk'.

Geddes, who spent considerable time in India guiding city planning, held the view that town planning is not merely place planning, nor even work planning. If it is to be successful, it must be folk planning. He suggested planning of cities in terms of planning of the whole region in which garden cities were to be rationally distributed. His conceptual approach led to the realization that urban planning must be undertaken in the broader concept of regional planning. Geddes was also the first scholar to place housing problem in the larger physical and social contexts of the city (Bauer 1934). His approach gave a methodological perspective, namely 'survey-analysis-plan' to urban planning. However, Geddes did not present a coherent theoretical framework for urban planning, addressing the role of power relations, political economy factors and social movements.

Burnham: City Beautiful

Daniel Hudson Burnham is credited for the launching of the 'City Beautiful' movement in the United States that flourished in the 1890s and 1900s. As director of works for the World Columbian Exposition in Chicago (1893), Burnham propagated the idea that design should not be separated from social issues like civic engagement and pride in city. The movement shifted attention from the concept of cities as symbols of industrialization and economic development. It emphasized that cities should aspire to generate aesthetic value and pride for their residents. Burnham advocated positioning the city around a central area connected by long boulevards so that the centre could be visible and accessible from all locations. Engaging architects, planners, businessmen, professionals and social reformers of the time, the City Beautiful movement emphasized the importance of beautification and design in building a functional and humane city. It promoted architectural grandeur of the city, focusing on consistency, proportion and detail. It also brought out the need for preparing a coherent city plan designed by 'conscious hand'—with teamwork by architects, surveyors and landscaping experts. The City Beautiful movement was prominently reflected in the plans of Chicago, Cleveland and Washington, DC. The movement did not proceed far due to its weak potential for attracting business enterprises. The 'City Beautiful' gave way to the 'City Efficient'.

Wright: Broadacre City

Frank Lloyd Wright, who envisaged that the United States become a nation of individuals, advocated a planned city called 'Broadacre', connected by superhighways. The 'Broadacre City' took forward the concept of decentralization from Howard's ideal community to individual family homes planned in a garden environment. Wright's view was that decentralization would permit each individual to live his own lifestyle on his own land. This view was influenced by three developments of the time: the automobile; radio, telephone and telegraph; and standardized machine-shop production. Wright regarded that the older, dense and crowded conglomerations like Chicago and New York were no longer modern. He hoped that the United States would reoccupy the rural landscape to benefit from rural virtues of individual freedom and self-reliance. He thought that fast transport and communication would create a 'community' sense. Wright believed that the Broadacre City would enable individuals to exercise three basic social rights: a direct medium of exchange, a place of ground to be held only by use and improvements and expression of ideas by which and for which one lives (Wright 1935).

Corbusier: Radiant City

Le Corbusier believed that cities were not dense enough and conceived of a vertical garden city to decongest city centres by increasing density with high tower blocks surrounded by parks and highways. In his own vision, large strips of land in the historical centre of Paris needed to be levelled and carefully filled with skyscrapers of enormous proportions in a symmetrical grid of streets. The Radiant City of Le Corbusier (*Cite Radieuse*) proposed a density of 1,200 inhabitants per acre to ensure that skyscrapers occupied only 5 per cent of the ground, while 95 per cent was left for gardens and connectivity infrastructure. High-income segments were to be accommodated in lower density luxury housing around courts, with 85 per cent of the site area being open. The design of the Radiant City of the future was meant to integrate effective means of transportation, adequate greenspace and sunlight, improved lifestyle and a better society (Corbusier 1933). However, the celebrated architect did not offer an economic logic for his proposal. His theory was nearly totalitarian and strict in terms of order, symmetry and standardization of design.

Modernist Planning: A Critique

Modernist urban planning theories, including Howard's 'Utopia', Burnham's 'City Beautiful', Wright's 'Broadacre City' and Le Corbusier's 'Radiant City' adopted a technocratic and deterministic view of planning. They believed that the form of an urban area determined its functions. They advocated physically planned cities with architectural grandeur, wide boulevards, extensive open spaces and decent housing to address the social evils of the industrial city. They also argued for large-scale clearance of slums in central cities and location of spacious housing for the working class in suburbs. Modernist urban planning theories did not consider the socio-economic fundamentals of cities: people at the centre of development; clustering of households, firms and institutions to reap external economies of agglomeration; localization of innovation and economic growth; employment generation in formal and informal sectors, etc. The theories ignore the basic premise that cities are products of processes, shaped by economic interactions and social relations. The proponents of the theories believed that cities require extensive central planning, including large-scale demolition of slums and reconstruction, to save them from disasters. They grossly neglected the human element in cities. The quest for a city's form overshadowed its functions, especially the economic and social functions. The view that the restructuring of urban form would solve the social problems in the industrial city proved to be wrong.

The fallacies of modernist planning are eloquently brought out by the eminent urbanist, Jane Jacobs in her seminal book of 1961: *The Death and Life of Great American Cities*. She criticizes the top-down, prescriptive paradigm that dominated the wisdom on city planning and rebuilding in the 20th century—led by Ebenezer Howard (1898/1902), Patrick Geddes (1915), Le Corbusier (1933), Henry Wright (1935), Lewis Mumford (1938), Clarence Stein (1939) and Catherine Bauer (1934). Jacobs attacked their theories on three grounds. First, local and on-the-spot knowledge is the most important resource for good planning. Second, local planning is the best way to use local knowledge and resources. Third, decentralized planning helps and maintains the spontaneous order that makes urban life work. This order results from the voluntary activities of many individuals and not the one created by government. Jacobs asks the fundamental question: 'who plans?' She explains that decentralized and market-driven decisions build the foundation of vibrant cities. She argues that large-scale, centralized and top-down systems of planning do not deliver. Jacobs held the view that cities evolve and subjecting them to too many technical controls seriously undermines their capacity to innovate and contribute to growth. Ironically, it is political action, rather than technocratic planning, that has been responsible for the most successful designs of cities around the world. Jacobs compared Le Corbusier's Radiant City with 'a wonderful mechanical toy' (Jacobs 1961, 23).

Jacobs attacked the anti-density perspective of modernist planning theories. These theories considered density as a problem and advocated decongestion of cities with self-contained, lower density fringes and suburbs. They did not recognize the crucial distinction between positive effects of density and negative consequences of overcrowding. They failed to consider the importance of density in the functioning of cities due to its links with external economies of agglomeration and the role of government in managing density. Modernist urban planning did not appreciate the significance of density in facilitating interaction, face-to-face contact, human capital accumulation, labour market efficiency and returns to sharing of local public goods. They also failed to recognize that the concept of density is not absolute; its impacts are shaped by the mix of economic activities and their access to PT networks. Jacobs observes:

> The development of modern city planning and housing reform has been emotionally based on a glum reluctance to accept city concentrations of people as desirable, and this negative emotion about city concentrations of people has helped deaden planning intellectually.
>
> No good for cities or for their design, planning, economics or people, can come from the emotional assumption that dense city populations are, per se, undesirable. In my view, they are an asset. (Jacobs 1961, 221)

Modernist planning articulated not only an anti-density perspective but also an exclusionary approach in the name of city modernization and provision of decent housing to the working class. The garden city approach of Howard advocated moving away from slum-infested cities and getting rid of their rat-infested neighbourhoods without addressing the root causes of slums. It culminated in large-scale, government-led slum clearance and rehousing subsidy schemes for LIGs in the United Kingdom. The approach was authoritarian. The City Beautiful movement pioneered by Burnham focused on architectural grandeur, exotic buildings, elegant public plazas, wide boulevards, large open spaces, recreational riversides and symmetric geometrical designs. The modernist planning theories considered slums and congested tenements inhabited by the poor in the industrial city 'ugly'. They were instrumental for large-scale demolition of slums and displacement of the poor in cities. They advocated government-supported low-income housing projects that, according to Jane Jacobs, became worse centres of delinquency, vandalism and general social hopelessness.

The Town and Country Planning Act 1947 in the United Kingdom provided legal frame to modernist planning theories. It started the 'master planning' regime. It advocated detailed land use planning at the city, zonal and local levels; compulsory acquisition of land to implement master plans; and a planning permission system to control land use and development. The model is adopted by most developing countries, including India. However, the experience with master planning reveals that a form-centric, land use–led and command and control–based approach does not work. It neglects the ways in which cities function and evolve. This is because location and land use decisions of firms and households are largely guided by market forces in interaction with public policies—not by the rigid master planning stipulations. Moreover, planning can also have high social costs, not simply benefits. These considerations have led to the abandonment of top-down planning in favour of decentralized and people-oriented paradigms in countries. However, the master planning model thrives in India.

Land Use Planning: Practice

The practice of modern land use planning started in early part of the 20th century in Europe and the United States. Prior to urban planning emerging as a profession, some key initiatives were taken by countries to modernize their cities, develop transportation networks, undertake public health interventions and regulate housing standards for the working class. These notably include the 'grid plan' 1811 of Manhattan, NYC; Public Health Act, 1848, in the United Kingdom; design of Central Park in NYC in the 1850s by architects Frederick Law Olmsted and Calvert Vaux leading to the parks movement; intense rebuilding of Paris by Georges-Eugene Hausmann in the 1850s and 1860s leading to urban renewal on a grand scale; opening of the world's first underground railway in London in 1863; New York State Tenement Housing Act, 1879; opening of first subway in North America in Boston in 1897; formation of Greater New York with merger of five boroughs in 1898; and Burnham's plan for Chicago in 1909.

The Housing and Town Planning Act of 1909 in the United Kingdom was the first major piece of town planning legislation. It was influenced by the 'garden city' movement championed by Howard, propagating principles of layouts and architectural design to create spacious, tree-lined avenues for housing the working population. The 1944 Greater London Plan of Sir Leslie Patrick Abercrombie was also influenced by the concepts of garden city. This plan proposed four concentric rings around London: the urban core, the sub-urban ring, the green belt and the outer ring. It called for construction of eight new towns beyond the green belt surrounding the metropolitan area to reduce population densities in inner London. Further, it proposed a circumferential highway to divert traffic from the inner core. The Greater London Plan was widely adopted in the United Kingdom and other European nations, including Germany, Netherlands and Scandinavian countries.

The approach to town planning in India during the first half of the 20th century was significantly influenced by the Housing and Town Planning Act of 1909 in the United Kingdom. The Act empowered local authorities to restrict private development that does not conform with stated town planning principles. It prevented the construction of back-to-back houses, required developers of homes to follow legal standards and limited the number of homes per acre. It enabled the preparation and implementation of TPS by local authorities—with the involvement of landowners on a land pooling basis. Further, the Act provided for the imposition of a 50 per cent betterment levy on increases in land values due to TPS. While providing for protection of rural amenities, preservation of buildings and objects of interest or beauty and acquisition of land for garden cities, the Town and Country Planning Act 1932 increased the betterment levy to 75 per cent. The Town and Country Planning Act 1947 advanced the general proposition that 'all' land use in the future should be in accordance with plans prepared by local authorities covering the entire country. Such plans would indicate land use for various purposes: residential, industrial, commercial and so on, along with norms for development control. This marked the beginning of 'master plan' or 'comprehensive plan', setting out detailed policies and proposals for the use and development of land within the planning area.

The Town and Country Planning Act 1947 separated land development right from ownership. It legislated that no 'material development' could occur without permission from the local authority; ownership alone could not confer the right to develop land. It assigned overarching powers to local authorities to undertake compulsory acquisition of land to implement the detailed land use plans. If a particular parcel could not be excluded from the benefits of development but the landowners were unwilling to contribute to the same, then the local authority could acquire that land. Further, the Act stipulated that all development value—difference between the value of land with permission to develop and existing use value—vested in the state. The Act provided for a tax of 100 per cent on the development value of land. It stipulated that all development value in the future would accrue to the state without compensation, except for those landowners who were able to show that their land had any development value in 1939. Master planning in India is rooted in the Act of 1947 and based on the twin system of comprehensive land use plan and planning permission for undertaking land development in conformity with the plan.

The spatial planning system in the United Kingdom consists of national planning policy guidelines, regional strategies till recently and local development frameworks. National restrictions include Town Centre First, Green Belt, Sites for Special Scientific Interest (SSSIs), and areas of outstanding natural beauty (ANOBs). Subject to national guidelines, land use planning takes place at the local level. The process has undergone drastic changes since 1947. With the passage of time, it was obvious in the United Kingdom that the numerous details prescribed by planners under the Town and Country Planning Act 1947 clogged the planning machinery. This called for a move to a much less detailed planning regime. The performance of the Act was dismal, but its prescription that no material development could occur without planning permission from the local authority has come to stay. This has, in essence, nationalized the development right on land.

The Planning Advisory Group Report 1965 in the United Kingdom advocated the concept of development plan (DP), comprising structure and local plans, to replace the detailed master plan. This was legalized in the Town and Country Planning Act 1968. The structural plans were envisaged to be strategic DPs presenting a broad framework of policies and strategies looking forward up to 20 years. Local plans were to be prepared in accordance with the structure plans. The Planning and Compulsory Purchase Act 2004 prescribed the replacement of structural plans by RSS and LDD. The Localism Act 2011 has eliminated regional strategies and mandated local and neighbourhood plans to reflect the aspirations of the people. It aims at making urban planning more democratic and participatory by recognizing neighbourhood planning as a right of the community. The Cities and Local Government Devolution Act 2016 empowers combined local authorities with directly elected mayors to use area planning and other tools to promote growth in partnership with the central government.

The Town and Country Planning Act 1990 in the United Kingdom introduced a novel feature in urban planning legislation to enable the local authority to capture a part of the development value created by planning. It permitted negotiation between a developer and the local authority to achieve socio-economic development objectives. Section 106 (1) of the Act stipulates that any person with an interest in land may, by agreement or otherwise, enter into a planning obligation, enforceable by the local planning authority:

(a) restricting the development or use of the land in any specified way;
(b) requiring specified operations or activities to be carried out in, on, under or over the land; (c) requiring the land to be used in any specified way; or (d) requiring a sum or sums to be paid to the authority on a specified date or dates or periodically.

Section 106 agreements, known as 'planning obligations', are legalized and regularized under planning acts and government circulars. Planning obligations require new developments to provide extra amenities as compared to what is required under law. The developers of housing projects are typically asked to construct a proportion of the total units for affordable housing to low and moderate-income households with a view to creating mixed and inclusive communities.

Unlike the United Kingdom, the United States adopted a decentralized approach to urban planning from the beginning. Local planning in the United States took strong roots with NYC's zoning ordinance of 1916, restricting land uses by district, separating commercial and industrial activities from residential uses, prescribing setbacks for buildings at different heights and limiting the maximum mass of a building that can be built on a plot of given size. The US Supreme Court in the case of *Village of Euclid, Ohio vs. Ambler Realty Company* upheld the constitutional validity of zoning in 1926 on grounds of public health, welfare and safety. Following this landmark judgement, zoning was extensively adopted by cities across the United States by 1930. The local zoning and subdivision decisions were not tied to comprehensive city plans, though same states later prescribed for the preparation of 'general plans'. The model of urban planning, combined with factors such as construction of interstate and intrastate highways, low-cost motor fuel, rise in income favouring automobile ownership and individual preference for consumption of larger quantities of land and housing in a garden city-type environment led to large lot zoning and low-density residential sprawl in the United States. Planning permission is not required by developers if the development fits into the zoning ordinance; the builders can then build 'as of right'. The federal government did not intervene in matters of housing and land use till the Great Depression in the 1930s. It passed some federal legislations relating to housing and urban renewal. During 1949–1974, a large federally funded urban renewal programme led to the creation of semi-independent urban renewal authorities in cities, most of which ceased to exist after funding was over.

A key observation on urban planning in the United States is that it fostered exclusionary zoning—manifesting in segregation in cities by income class, race, etc. The system led to a social movement demanding 'IZ' and 'inclusionary housing' (IH). The New Jersey's Supreme Court in the Mount Laurel Case, 1975, granted powers to municipalities, developers and lower-income people to approach the court directly to seek a judicial declaration of compliance with their affordable housing duties and rights. The decision mandated communities to use their zoning powers to provide realistic opportunities for the production of affordable housing to low- and moderate-income households. The Court included a constitutional obligation on all parties to create a 'fair share' of regional low- and moderate-income housing through IH or similar policies and zoning practices. It also provided immunity to towns from civil lawsuits attempting to demonstrate compliance through participation in the administrative process. Further, the Court's ruling permitted citizens with low income and developers the right to challenge legally under certain circumstances. Each municipality was mandated to develop an 'adequate housing plan' to bring the town in compliance with its 'fair share' of regional and prospective needs for housing by setting aside 15–20 per cent of its total housing units for affordable housing. The NYC's changes in zoning rules in 2016, called 'Zoning for Quality and Affordability (ZQA)', is a bold attempt in recent years to promote IZ and affordable housing through urban planning.

Evolution of Land Use Planning in India

The history of land use planning in India dates back to the Indus Valley Civilisation. However, modernist land use planning based on the concept of 'master plan' started in the country during the British Rule. The UK experience with industrialization, urbanization, slums and epidemics, along with the interests of the British rulers, formed the basis for urban planning legislation in India. The country witnessed two phases of town planning activities during the British era—town improvement programmes through appointed city improvement trusts (CITs) with focus on public health, sanitation, epidemic control and decongestion in the late 19th and early 20th centuries, followed by TPS along with public health improvement measures through local authorities. The interwar years did not witness much efforts towards town planning in India. The legal developments during the British period more or less followed the trajectory in the United Kingdom. After independence, Indian states have adopted the key features of comprehensive urban planning through master plans based on the UK Town and Country Planning Act 1947.

In 1864, the Military Cantonments Act XXII was promulgated in India, leading to planned Cantonments for troops and Civil Lines for the Whites to enable the segregation of Europeans from Indians. The Act also led to the establishment of Sanitary Commissions in Bombay, Madras and Bengal Presidencies. The public health concerns of the foreigners, especially those following outbreaks of cholera, plague and other diseases were met with response from administration through piped water supply systems and sanitary improvements. However, the conditions of the working class were grossly neglected. This led to congested slums, homelessness, footpath dwelling and 'dual' cities in India. The plague of 1896 resulted in setting up of CIT in all major towns. The Bombay CIT Act, 1898, provided for a board of trustees appointed by the government. The functions of the board were to undertake measures to improve sanitary and living conditions in the city. All vacant lands with the government and the Bombay municipal corporation were handed over to CIT, which widened roads, undertook sanitary improvement measures and opened up suburban developments.

The Bombay Act 1998 was instrumental for the enactment of legislations to set up of CIT in other cities—Mysore (1904), Calcutta (1911), Hyderabad (1912), Lucknow (1919), Kanpur (1919) and Allahabad (1920). CITs were entrusted with town improvement programmes, including slum clearance and housing for rehabilitation, of slum dwellers. The Bombay Improvement Act 1998 was largely structured on the pattern of Glasgow CIT Act 1866. The objectives of the Glasgow Act were to enable the destruction of appalling slums, development of housing for the working class and execution of improvement schemes. Reportedly, far more number of inhabitants were uprooted from slums in Glasgow than provided with legal space in the city. Following the experience in Glasgow and other cities in the United Kingdom, slum clearance emerged as a key theme of legislation relating to town improvement trusts in India in early parts of the 20th century; for instance, the Calcutta Improvement Act 1911 aimed at:

> ...the improvement and expansion of Calcutta by opening up congested areas, laying out or altering streets, providing open spaces for purposes of ventilation or recreation, demolishing or constructing buildings [clearing *bustees*, executing housing schemes and schemes for the rehousing of persons displaced by the execution of improvement schemes, acquiring land for the said purposes and all works relating thereto] and otherwise...

The Housing and Town Planning Act 1909 in the United Kingdom led to the first town planning legislation in India: the Bombay Town Planning Act 1915. This law introduced TPS by local authorities in areas potentially ready for development or redevelopment. It enabled land pooling with the involvement of landowners and levy of betterment charges to recover costs. The Act was followed by other legislations such as Madras Town Planning Act 1920 and Andhra Pradesh (Andhra Areas) Town Planning Act 1920. These laws aimed at regulating the development of towns to secure to their present and future inhabitants' 'sanitary conditions, amenity and convenience', and providing for TPS. Eminent scholars such as Patrick Geddes, H. W. Lancaster and Otto Königsberger came to India and spent many years in guiding the preparation of city plans between 1915 and 1947. However, the country did not witness any significant town planning legislation during that period. In fact, the Bombay Town Planning Act 2015 operated till the enactment of a new law by the Government of Maharashtra in 1954 that repealed it. The 1954 law introduced the concept of DP, while retaining TPS as an instrument to implement the same. The period 1912–1931 witnessed the designing and development of New Delhi as the new capital of the British empire. The plan was prepared by Edwin Lutyens and Herbert Baker, drawing from the garden city and City Beautiful movements. The plan for imperial Delhi, referred to as 'Lutyens' Delhi' combined monumental grandeur and geometrical symmetry with a network of straight and diagonal tree-lined avenues, extensive green spaces and a grand central axis. This contrasted sharply with old Delhi, characterized by narrow, winding streets and congested localities.

Some notable efforts for the preparation of master plans in India in the aftermath of independence include outline for the Master Plan of Bombay 1948, by N. V. Modak and Albert Mayer, Master Plan of Bhubaneswar 1948, by Otto Königsberger, Master Plan for Chandigarh 1951, by Le Corbusier and Master Plan for Delhi, 1962, by the Ford Foundation with involvement of Albert Mayer and other experts. A major urban planning and development law enacted after independence is the Delhi Development Act 1957. It prescribed for the constitution of Delhi Development Authority (DDA) by the central government as a body corporate. The law mandated the authority to prepare a master plan and zonal DPs for Delhi, dividing the planning area into zones for the purposes of land use and development. The Act defined development to mean 'the carrying out of building, engineering, mining or other operations in, on, over or under land or the making of any material change in any building or land and includes redevelopment…'. This was borrowed from Section 12 of the UK Town and Country Planning Act, 1947. The DDA Act influenced urban planning and development legislations in many states, leading to the establishment of urban development authorities (UDAs) as parastatals to prepare master plans and implement major urban projects in accordance with such plans. In some states, both master planning and plan implementation remained with UDAs, while in others, plan implementation tasks were assigned to urban local bodies (ULBs).

In 1960, the Town and Country Planning Organization (TCPO) circulated the Model Town and Country Planning Law providing guidelines for the preparation of town and country planning acts in states. This was revised in 1985 as Model Regional and Town Planning and Development Law (URDPFI Guidelines 2014, Volume IIA, p. 15). Some states adopted the TCPO guidelines to develop their regional and urban planning laws; others enacted laws based on their own requirements and perceptions. Two major acts enacted in the 1960s include the Maharashtra Regional and Town Planning Act 1966 and the Gujarat Town Planning and Urban Development Act (GTPUDA) 1976. The Maharashtra Act introduced regional planning and the Gujarat Act prescribed a two-stage planning approach: preparation of DP and its implementation through TPS with reservation of land for the socially and economically weaker sections (SEWS) to make city planning inclusive. Some major developments in regional and urban planning in last three decades include Constitution (74th) Amendment Act 1992 Urban DPs Formulation and Implementation (UDPFI) Guidelines, 1996 and Urban and Regional Development Plans Formulation and Implementation (URDPFI) Guidelines 2015 issued by the Ministry of Urban Development (MoUD), GoI. The guidelines were developed with support from TCPO and the Institute of Town Planners, India (ITPI). Key legislations for urban planning and initiatives for planned urban development in India over the course of history are presented in Table 5.1.

The current land use planning practice in India is based on the 'master planning' model. It aims at attaining socio-economic objectives

Table 5.1 Chronology of Key Urban Planning and Land Development Initiatives in India

Year	Initiative	Brief Details
1864	The Military Cantonments Act XXII	Establishment of Sanitary Commissions in Bombay, Madras and Bengal presidencies; creation of cantonments and civil lines segregating Britishers from Indians.
1894	LA Act	Acquisition of land for public purposes and companies subject to payment of compensation to landowners.
1898	Bombay CIT Act	CIT was set up to undertake schemes to improve sanitary and living conditions. All vacant lands with government and municipal corporation were handed over to the Trust.
1903	City of Mysore Improvement Act	Improvement and future expansion of Mysore city through an appointed board of trustees, undertaking schemes, including those based on land acquired under law with board's resolution.
1911	The Calcutta Improvement Act	Improvement and expansion of Calcutta by opening up congested areas, laying out or altering streets, providing open spaces, clearing bustees and housing the displaced by acquiring land.
1915	Bombay Town Planning Act	Preparation of TPS for areas potentially ready for urban development or redevelopment based on land pooling.
1920	Madras Town Planning Act	Regulate development of towns to secure to their present and future inhabitants' sanitary conditions, amenity and convenience; provide for TPS.
1920	Andhra Pradesh (Andhra Area) Town Planning Act	Regulate the development of towns to secure to their present and future inhabitants' sanitary conditions, amenity and convenience; provide for TPS.
1952	Punjab New Capital (Periphery) Control Act	Control and regulate the periphery of the new capital of the state of Punjab.

(Continued)

Table 5.1 (Continued)

Year	Initiative	Brief Details
1954	The Bombay Town Planning Act	Replaced the 1915 Act and introduced the concept of DP while retaining TPS as instrument to implement the plan.
1956	The Slum Areas (Improvement and Clearance) Act	Provide for improvement and clearance of slum areas in certain union territories and for protection of tenants in such areas from eviction.
1956	Orissa Town Planning and Improvement Trust Act	Development, improvement and expansion of towns in Odisha state to secure to their present and future inhabitants' sanitary conditions, amenity and convenience.
1957	The DDA Act	Establishment of DDA as a corporate body to provide for the development of Delhi according to plan and for matters ancillary thereto
1959	Assam Town and Country Planning Act	Development of towns and country sides in Assam on sound principles to secure proper sanitary conditions, to conserve and protect public health, safety and general welfare of residents.
1960	The Model Town and Country Planning Act—TCPO	Prepared by (TCPO) revising the earlier draft prepared by the ITPI, providing for constitution of State Town and Country Planning Board as coordinating and advisory body and setting up of local planning authorities for different urban and rural areas to undertake preparation of master plans and to enforce them.
1961	Karnataka Town and Country Planning Act	Regulating planned growth of land use and development and making and executing TPS; physical planning to precede economic planning to create healthy surroundings.

Year	Act	Description
1963	Maharashtra Ownership of Flats (Regulation of the Promotion of Construction, Sale, Management and, Transfer) Act	Regulation of the promotion of construction, sale, management and transfer of flats taken on ownership basis to tackle the problems of acute shortage of housing in several areas in the state of Maharashtra; duly addressing the issues of sundry abuses, malpractices and difficulties in possessing flats developed by promoters.
1966	Maharashtra Regional and Town Planning Act	Planning, development and use of land in regions with constitution of Regional Planning Boards, to make better provisions for the preparation of DPs with a view to ensuring that TPS are made in a proper manner and their execution is made effective, to provide for the creation of new towns by means of Development Authorities, to make provisions for the compulsory acquisition of land, etc.
1974	The Mumbai Metropolitan Region Development Authority Act (MMRDA)	Constitution of Development Authority for the Mumbai Metropolitan Region for planning and supervising proper, orderly and rapid development of areas within the region and executing plans, projects and schemes for the purpose.
1975	The Andhra Pradesh (Urban Areas Development) Act	Constitution of UDAs for urban areas (city and surrounding areas) to secure development according to plan—with power to acquire, hold, manage, plan, develop and mortgage or otherwise dispose of land and other property and carry out development works.
1976	The Gujarat Town Planning and Urban Development Act (GTPUDA)	Making and execution of DP and TPS in Gujarat with reservation of 10 per cent of land or such percentage as near thereto as possible to provide housing to SEWS.
1976	Urban Land (Ceiling and Regulation) Act	Imposition of a ceiling on vacant land in UAs, acquisition of such land in excess of ceiling limit, regulation of construction of buildings on such land, etc., to prevent the concentration of urban land in the hands of a few, speculation and profiteering therein and bringing about an equitable distribution of urban land to subserve the common good.

(Continued)

Table 5.1 (*Continued*)

Year	Initiative	Brief Details
1980	Integrated Development of Small and Medium Towns (IDSMT) Scheme	Launched by the GoI to promote dispersed urbanization with decentralized economic growth and employment generation, supported by durable infrastructure and remunerative projects in small and medium towns and integrated spatial and socio-economic planning.
1985	The National Capital Region (NCR) Planning Board Act	Constitution of planning board for the preparation of a plan for the development of the NCR for coordination and monitoring plan implementation and evolving harmonized policies for control of land uses and development of infrastructure in NCR to avoid any haphazard development.
1986	The Environment (Protection) Act	Protection and improvement of the environment and prevention of hazards to human beings, other living creatures, plants and property—environment includes water, air and land, human beings, other living creatures, plants, microorganisms and property.
1988	National Commission on Urbanization Report	Emphasized the link between urbanization and economic development and integration of spatial and economic development planning. Identified 329 cities as generators of economic momentum (GEM)—divided into national priority cities (NPCs) and state priority cities (SPCs), and special priority regions (SPRs) for planned development.
1988	National Housing Policy	Aimed at removing homelessness, improving conditions of the inadequately housed and providing basic minimum services to all. Identified the role of government as a provider for the poorest and vulnerable sections and facilitator for other income groups and private sector by removing constraints and increasing supply of land and services.

Year	Act/Policy	Description
1992	Constitution 73rd and 74th Amendment Acts	Included planning for economic and social development and urban planning under the legitimate functions of elected municipalities and mandated the establishment of district and metropolitan planning committees (MPCs) for the preparation of DPs—at district and metropolitan levels.
1996	UDPFI Guidelines	Issued by the Ministry of Urban Affairs and Employment for the preparation of spatial DPs and resource mobilization plans of urban centres, efficient plan implementation and innovative techniques for planned spatio-economic development of urban areas.
2005	Disaster Management Act	Aimed at effective management of disasters and connected matters with continuous and integrated processes of planning, organizing, coordinating and implementing; taking prevention, mitigation and other measures before, during and after disasters.
2005	Jawaharlal Nehru National Urban Renewal Mission (JNNURM)	First reform-led, demand-driven national mission to assist states and union territories for planned urban development with central support for infrastructure development and basic services to the urban poor—led to the repeal of the Urban Land Ceiling Act.
2006	National Urban Transport Policy (NUTP)	Launched in 2006 and revised in 2014—objective: to plan for the movement of people rather than vehicles by providing sustainable mobility and accessibility to all citizens to jobs, education, social services and recreation at affordable cost and within a reasonable time; calls for incorporation of UT as an important parameter at the urban planning stage rather than being a consequential requirement.
2013	Right to Fair Compensation and Transparency in Land Acquisition, Rehabilitation and Resettlement Act (replaced Land Acquisition Act 1894)	Ensure a humane and participative, informed and transparent process for LA for industrialization, development of infrastructure and urbanization with the least disturbance to the owners of the land and other affected families and provide just and fair compensation to the affected families whose land has been acquired or proposed to be acquired or are affected by such acquisition and make adequate provisions for such affected persons for their rehabilitation and resettlement (R&R).

(*Continued*)

Table 5.1 (Continued)

Year	Initiative	Brief Details
2014	URDPFI Guidelines	Guidelines issued by the MoUD, GoI, covering planning system framework, planning process, contents of plans, resource mobilization for plan implementation, regional planning approach, urban planning approach, sustainability guidelines, simplified planning techniques, infrastructure planning, simplified development promotion regulations, etc.
2015	Smart Cities Mission	Launched by the GoI to drive economic growth and improve the quality of life of people by enabling local development and harnessing technology as a means to create smart outcomes for citizens. Strategy includes pan-city initiative with at least one city-wide smart solution applied, area-based developments: retrofitting, redevelopment and greenfield.
2016	National Building Code	Initially published in 1970 and revised in 1983 and 2005, the National Building Code 2016 provides standards for administrative regulations, development control rules, general building and fire safety requirements, materials, structural design and construction (including safety); building and plumbing services; sustainability; and asset and facility management.
2018	NUPF	Recognizes cities as complex and changing agglomerations of people; calls for urban solutions to be local and contextual; urban design to be responsive to historic, geographic and economic contexts; planning process to be dynamic, adaptive, iterative, continuous and participatory; embracing mixed and changing land uses; infrastructure to anticipate and accommodate density and avoid sprawl.

through the development of spatially planned cities. The legal framework for the model derives from the Town and Country Planning Act 1947 in the United Kingdom. A typical master plan delineates land use and development patterns that should occur in the designated planning area, comprising the city and surrounding rural jurisdictions that are likely to be urbanized in the foreseeable future. It covers a horizon of about 20–25 years and presents a view of the built-up form of the planning area in its ideal end state. It prescribes for: (a) allocation of land to various uses, (b) regulation of land development and (c) installation of infrastructure to implement the land use plan. Key regulatory instruments for implementing the master plan include 'zoning' to classify land use at regional, zonal and local levels and 'planning permission' from the designated authority to carry out development in layouts and plots.

Town and country planning, urban development and municipal laws and regulations in India prescribe for the preparation and implementation of master plan, zonal plans and local area plans. They also prescribe development controls through layout approval and building permission. Further, they envisage the provision of infrastructure facilities at regional, zonal, local and layout levels to service land. Zoning and layout rules and building byelaws provide for norms to be followed by developers in public interest. These norms extend to land use, density, FSI, construction, public services, etc. Laws and regulations also cover procedures for conversion of agricultural land to urban use, institution of land use, change of land use from one category to another; approval for new developments in layouts; permission for construction of new buildings or additions and alterations to old buildings; advertisement permits; special requirements for environmentally sensitive zones such as coastal areas, wetlands and heritage precincts; enforcement of permission conditions; and penal action against unauthorized layouts and buildings, including demolition and prosecution of offenders. Plan implementation envisages: legal protection to the plan; enforcement of land use, layout, subdivision and building norms; infrastructure planning, capital budgeting and development; land assembly; and urban renewal. Other instruments include taxation and capacity building for plan preparation, implementing and monitoring.

Zoning: Classification of Land Use

Master plans allocate land for various uses in accordance with zoning regulations; for example, the Master Plan of Delhi 2021 (MPD 2021), prepared by DDA and notified in 2007, divides the Delhi development area into 10 land use zones under the Land Use Plan 2021: residential, commercial, industrial, recreational, transportation, utility, government, public and semi-public facilities, green belt/water body and mixed use. The Hyderabad Metropolitan DP 2031, prepared by Hyderabad Metropolitan Development Authority (HMDA) and notified in 2013, adopts a 12-fold land use classification: residential, peri-urban, commercial, manufacturing, public, semi-public facilities and utilities, multiple use, recreation and open space, water bodies, forest, special reservations, conservation (agriculture) and traffic and transportation. The URDPFI Guidelines, 2014, issued by the MoUD, GoI, suggests a 10-fold classification for allocation of land to various urban uses under the DP (Table 5.2).

Table 5.2 *URDPFI Guidelines: Urban Land Use Classification*

Level I			Level II		
N	A-N	Use Category	N	A-N	Land Use Zone
1	R	Residential	11	R-1	Primary residential zone
			12	R-2	Unplanned/informal residential zone
2	C	Commercial	21	C-1	Retail shopping zone
			22	C-2	General business and commercial district centres
			23	C-3	Wholesale, godowns, warehousing/regulated markets
			24	C-4	Service sector
			25	C-5	Regulated/informal/weekly markets
3	I	Industry	31	I-1	Service and light industry
			32	I-2	Extensive and heavy industry
			33	I-3	Special industrial zone—hazardous, noxious and chemical

Level I			Level II		
4	PS	Public and semi-public	41	PS-1	Government/semi-government/public offices
			42	PS-2	Government land (Use undetermined)
			43	PS-3	Police headquarters/station, police line
			44	PS-4	Educational and research
			45	PS-5	Medical and health
			46	PS-6	Social, cultural and religious (including cremation and burial grounds)
			47	PS-7	Utilities and services
5	M	Mixed use	51	M-1	Mixed industrial use zone
			52	M-2	Mixed residential zone
			53	M-3	Mixed commercial zone
6	P	Recreational	61	P-1	Playgrounds/stadiums/sports complexes
			62	P-2	Parks and gardens—public open spaces
			63	P-3	Multi-open space (maidan)
7	T	Transportation and communication	71	T-1	Roads/bus rapid transit (BRT) system
			72	T-2	Railways/mass rapid transit system (MRTS)
			73	T-3	Airport
			74	T-4	Seaports and dockyards
			75	T-5	Bus depots/truck terminals and freight complexes
			76	T-6	Transmission and communication
8	A	Primary activity	81	PA-1	Agriculture
			82	PA-2	Forest and horticulture
			83	PA-3	Poultry and dairy farming

(Continued)

Table 5.2 *(Continued)*

Level I					Level II
			84	PA-4	Rural settlements
			85	PA-5	Brick kiln and extractive areas
			86	PA-6	Others (fishing, pottery etc.)
9	E	Protective and undevelopable use zone	91	E-1	Water bodies
			92	E-2	Special recreation zone/protective areas such as sanctuaries/reserve forests and eco-sensitive zone
			93	E-3	Undevelopable use zone
10	S	Special area	101	S-1	Old built-up (core) area
			102	S-2	Heritage and conservation areas
			103	S-3	Scenic value areas
			104	S-4	Government restricted area (such as Defence)
			105	S-5	Other uses/spot zone*

Source: Ministry of Urban Development, Government of India (2015).

Notes:
N: Numeric code.
A-N: Alpha numeric code.
1. Overall, there could be 43 use zones at the DP level within 10 land use categories at the perspective plan level as given in the above table.
2. Areas of informal activities may be identified in the above land use categories at level II for 1–7 level I use zones only.
3. Mixed use zone shall be identified at the DP level, having dominant use and mixed use.
4. Use permissions for different activities can be provided at the project/action plan level or with the approval of the statutory authority as the case may be.
5. *The process of changing/relaxing/modifying land use of part or 'spot' of a 'zone' in a particular land use is termed as 'spot zoning'. This can be done for comparatively smaller area in a particular land use zone in such a way that it does not affect the overall DP.
6. Use zone regulations for the use permissibility could be decided by the town planner depending upon the requirement/feasibility.
7. Appropriate code in terms of both numerical and alphabetic letter are provided to facilitate the reference and to have a simplified procedure to follow.

Development Control Regulations

Development controls accompany zoning to ensure 'plan-led' urban development. These regulations are based on multiple laws and codes relating to urban and metropolitan area development, town and country planning, land management, municipal administration, environmental protection, etc., for example, developments in each of the 10 land use zones in Delhi development area are required to be carried out in accordance with regulations approved by the DDA under the DDA Act, 1957, including those under the Development Code. This Code aims at promoting quality built environment by organizing the most appropriate development of land in accordance with approved land development policies and land use proposals contained in MPD 2021. It aims at assisting authorities to regulate land use at two levels: (a) conversion of use zones into use premises or layouts and (b) permission of activities in use premises or buildings. More or less similar legal frameworks have been adopted by other cities.

Layout Rules and Building Byelaws

Layout rules specify norms for preparation of DPs and procedures for their approval. A layout plan indicates the subdivision of a large chunk of land with reference to regulatory norms and surrounding developments. Application for layout permission requires documents such as proof of land ownership, site plan, detailed plan showing subdivisions, including roads, plots for different user categories, open spaces, public facilities, reservation for LIGs, connectivity to external infrastructure such as water supply, sewerage, drainage, highways and public transit, payment of prescribed fees and security deposit, etc. Building byelaws are intended to secure standards for construction in accordance with the prescribed building code, while protecting the city from disorderly developments, traffic congestion, pollution and other environmental hazards. They prescribe norms such as width of approach road to plot, size of plot, coverage ratio, open spaces around building, facade, size of rooms, height of building, provisions for parking and fire safety, development-related charges, impact fees, guarantees for construction as per approval conditions, etc. The controls are meant to ensure lighting and ventilation, smooth traffic flow, public health, safety and convenience, etc.

Land Use Planning: An Appraisal

Over the years, countries around the world, including the United Kingdom, have moved away from an interventionist land use planning regime based on modernist urban planning theories to a decentralized approach. The reasons are many. First, the prescription that comprehensive planning, aided by expert inputs from technocrats—architects, planners, designers, engineers, etc.—would solve the social evils of the industrial city has been proved wrong. Second, while cities are products of actions of numerous firms, households and developers in connection with investment, production, location and land use decisions, the master planning model ignores the socio-economic dynamics of cities. The belief of planners in what anthropologists call 'environmental determinism' has led to treating cities as mechanical entities. Third, unrealistic planning standards have excluded the poor and LIGs from land markets as well as city plans. Peoples' movements against top-down, centralized and non-participatory planning around the world have led to the willingness of planners to take local preferences and democratic inputs into account. Fourth, the overriding concerns of economic growth and job creation have led to cities competing for investment nationally and internationally. This has prompted a movement to 'market-oriented' and 'people-centric' approaches to planning. However, master planning, with dictatorial connotations, thrives in developing countries like India. The legal-institutional framework for town and country planning in these countries, with multiple agencies undertaking land use, transport, socio-economic development and environmental planning, is fragmented.

India's Constitution (74th Amendment) Act, 1992, envisages that elected ULGs perform the functions of planning for economic and social development and urban planning, including town planning, regulation of land use and construction of buildings. It mandates the constitution of District Planning Committee (DPC) in every district to consolidate the plans of rural and urban local governments and to prepare draft district development plan (DDP). This plan shall consider (a) matters of common interest between rural and urban areas, including spatial planning, sharing of water and other physical and natural resources, integrated development of infrastructure and environmental conservation and (b) extent and type of resources available, whether financial or otherwise. The 74th Amendment further mandates the constitution of MPC in every metropolitan area to prepare draft Metropolitan Development Plan (MDP). This plan shall take into account (a) plans prepared by urban and rural local governments in the metropolitan area; (b) matters of common interest between urban and rural areas including coordinated spatial planning of the area, sharing of water and other physical and natural resources, integrated development of infrastructure and environmental conservation; (c) overall objectives and priorities set by the GoI and the state government concerned; and (d) extent and nature of investments likely to be made in the metropolitan area by central and state government agencies and other available resources. The logic behind the above provisions is appealing. However, due to poor implementation of the 74th Amendment Act and lack of actions at state level to empower ULGs, DPCs and MPCs, the objective of democratizing regional and urban planning is far from being achieved.

The 74th Amendment Act mandates that three-fourth of members of DPC and two-thirds of members of MPC shall be from out of the representatives of elected urban and rural local governments. This requirement is to ensure that DDP and MDP are formulated in a participatory manner. The Act also makes it mandatory for DPC and MPC to forward their respective plans to the state government. However, it does not clarify which authority is to approve them and how they are to be financed and executed. The implicit assumption is that the plans would be endorsed at the state level and included in state plans, integrating bottom-up and top-down approaches to regional and urban planning. Paradoxically, DPCs and MPCs are not yet operationalized in a meaningful way in most states. Where constituted, they also lack the authority to coordinate, prepare, finance and implement the DPs. As a result, master plans of metropolitan cities have not been able to address the broader regional concerns—multi-modal transport, conservation of environmental resources, integrated transportation-land use planning, sharing of resources for regional plan implementation, etc. (Ahluwalia, Kanbur and Mohanty 2014; Mohanty 2014, 2016, 2019).

An overview of the implementation of the 74th Amendment Act reveals that not much progress has been achieved to reform urban and regional planning in India. State, town and country planning and urban development laws continue to assign planning of urban areas to UDAs. These parastatals are expected to delegate local planning functions to ULGs. However, while DCR is entrusted to municipalities in most states, their involvement in plan formulation is marginal. As regards economic and social development, the ULGs are left out of the sectoral planning process led by State and District Planning Boards. Socio-economic and spatial planning are pursued separately. So also are transportation and land use planning. As regards regional planning, there is an institutional vacuum. The 74th Amendment Act does not clarify how district and metropolitan development plans, cutting across multiple jurisdictions, are to be financed. The most conspicuous lacune in master planning in India are objectives-instruments mismatch, narrow definition of development, mechanical process of plan preparation, lengthy procedure, anti-density perspective, neglect of conservation and transportation, exclusion of the poor, segregation of land uses, lack of financing strategy, poor plan implementation, institutional fragmentation, human resource bottlenecks and lack of community participation

Objectives-Instruments Mismatch

Town and country planning laws in India articulate multiple objectives to be attained through master plans; for example, laws in Andhra Pradesh state that while people should be free to build, there is a social need to ensure a healthy, orderly, disease-free and fire-proof habitat that is not polluted, allows circulation of people and goods, protects the environment and promotes privacy. However, master plans pay scant attention to the instruments needed to achieve such objectives. Obsessed with land use detailing and controls at multiple levels, they neglected strategic aspects of urban development such as conservation of environment, protection of heritage resources, investment in infrastructure, especially rail-based transit, public health and disaster management, transportation-land use integration to promote labour market mobility, making affordable housing and workplaces available to the poor and LIGs and sustained financing of urban and regional development.

Narrow Definition of Development

Following British town and country planning laws, urban planning legislations in India have defined 'development' as carrying out building, engineering, mining or other operations in, over or under land or making of any material change in any building or land. Such narrow definition, confined to physical aspects of land and the city, fails to capture concepts such as 'sustainable development' and 'inclusive growth'. Master plans in the past largely focused on designing cities to achieve a grand urban form, neglecting their social, economic and environmental functions, including preparation and implementation of plans for economic development and social justice, as envisaged under the 12th Schedule of the Constitution of India.

Anti-density Perspective

Master planning of cities in developing countries is rooted in the anti-density perspective of modernist urban planning. It has led to very low FSI in central areas, sprawl, increased infrastructure costs and unwarranted annexation of agricultural lands to urban jurisdictions. It has resulted in scarcity of floor space for productive economic activities, affordable housing and informal workplaces that engage the bulk of the urban poor. The master planning model undermines the role of clustering of firms in catalysing agglomeration economies. These externalities call for actions by government to support density at strategic locations and mitigate congestion diseconomies with investment in PT and other infrastructure facilities. Since they accord primacy to land use and neglect transport, master plans have not been able to exploit the power of density and accessibility integration to catalyse economic growth.

Technocratic Plan Formulation

Master planning is mechanical. It projects the population of planning area as the first step in plan formulation. The projected increase in population between the base and plan horizon years is divided by an estimated household size. This gives the increase in number of households. That figure is multiplied by the space norm for an average middle-class household fixed by the planners. The exercise yields the land required for residential use. Projections of land for non-residential uses—office, retail, industry, community, recreation, etc.—are tagged to projections of economic activities and space norms adopted for them. This methodology treats critical urban uses like conservation and transportation as 'residual' in the planning process. It ignores the role of dynamic interactions between location and land use factors in shaping spatio-economic outcomes.

Lengthy Process of Planning

A conspicuous drawback in comprehensive master planning is its inordinately long process; for example, the first Master Plan of Hyderabad started in 1965 but came into force in 1975. Its revision started in 1995, but notification of the revised plan occurred in 2008. The second Master Plan of Mumbai began in 1977, but it was completed in 1994. Preparatory actions for the second Master Plan of Delhi began before 1980, but the plan came into operation in 1990. Experience shows that zonal and local area plans do not get ready for years, defeating the very purpose of comprehensive planning. While the capacity for such detailed planning is absent in Indian cities, the process naively assumes that future economic activities would fit into a rigid spatial frame.

Neglect of Conservation

The master planning process treats conservation, including protection of natural and heritage resources, as a residual. Accordingly, ecologically sensitive areas such as water bodies, wetlands, forests and natural and man-made heritage precincts are neglected. Master plans reserve land for open space, often exceeding 10 per cent of the total planning area. Planning laws prescribe for acquisition of such lands by public authorities within a period of 10 years from the notification of plan. However, endemic constraints of financing make such acquisition nearly impossible. In the meantime, vested interests get zoning changes effected, and the very purpose of conservation is defeated. Thus, most cities in India lack statutory open spaces as envisaged by their master plans.

Neglect of Transportation

Transport makes or mars a city. However, the land use–led master plans have grossly neglected transportation networks and their financing. They fail to recognize the 'leading' role of transport in guiding location, land use and local economic development. As a result, cities have been unable to exploit the WEBs of major transportation projects through the expansion of labour markets, increased competition and agglomeration economies. It has also led to a lack of spatial and functional integration between the city, suburbs, rural growth centres and satellite towns.

Exclusion of the Urban Poor

Master planning adopts unrealistic norms, covering minimum lot size, road width, open space, setbacks and a host of other requirements. This has led to 'exclusionary' urbanization. The poor are weeded out of formal land markets as well as master plans. The mushrooming of slums in large cities is related to the high standards of master plans which the poor cannot satisfy. Informal sector activities also find no place in the formal plans. Master plans have invariably failed to allocate land and floor space to the urban poor for living, working and vending. They also do not cater to the mobility concerns of the lower-income groups who need residential location with access to PT.

Segregation of Land Uses

The master plans in developing countries in the past promoted segregated land uses as in the West. However, mixed uses are appropriate for Indian living, with the majority in cities owning no automobile and large numbers engaged in self-employment pursued from home. Such informal workplaces do not find a place in the master plans. Thus, master planning has resulted in employment-housing-transport mismatch, longer and wasteful commuting, unsustainable energy consumption, environmental degradation and adverse impacts on climate change.

Lack of Financing Strategy

The master plans lack a coherent strategy to finance development due to their failure to incorporate economics. There has been little attempt by cities in developing countries to harness the synergy between spatial planning, transport, density and zoning. These factors lead to unearned benefits to a lucky group of owners of land at vantage locations. However, master plans have neglected benefit taxes and value capture tools to finance infrastructure. In particular, they have not exploited land-based sources such as LVT, VLT, planning gains tax (PGT), development gains tax (DGT), impact fee, developer exaction, special assessment district, betterment levy, purchasable and transferable development rights, planning obligations and tax increment financing (TIF). Further, cities have neglected taxes on various forms of unearned increments: land rent, monopoly rent, scarcity rent, agglomeration rents, planning and infrastructure-induced rents, etc.

Poor Plan Implementation

Master plans prescribe zoning and FSI regulations to implement their 'grand' vision of the city. Such regulations tend to be elaborate and restrictive. Focused on land use controls at regional, city, zone, local and plot levels, they lead to rent-seeking. Master plans in the past also relied heavily on compulsory acquisition of land to achieve the plan objectives. The failure of such interventions is conspicuous. The preparation of master plans takes a long time. In the meantime, haphazard growth takes place in anticipation of future land uses. Unauthorized developments take place, especially in the urban fringe and areas reserved for public purpose. Ironically, planning practice in Indian cities reveals that though the master plans claimed to be rigid, discretionary changes in land use and FSI occurred on a fairly large scale. Such changes reduced the space earmarked for public amenities and conservation.

Institutional Fragmentation

Cities in developing countries, including India, are subjected to multiple plans prepared by multiple authorities—regional plan, DDP, MDP, city DP, master plan, city utility and infrastructure plan, city sanitation plan, city mobility plan, slum-free city plan, city investment plan, heritage conservation plan, disaster management plan, etc. The institutional structure for plan preparation, financing and implementation is fragmented; for example, planning and development of Delhi involves DDA, Delhi Metro Rail Corporation (DMRC), Delhi Urban Art Commission, New Delhi Municipal Committee, three municipal corporations, Delhi Jal Board, Delhi Urban Shelter Improvement Board, Government of National Capital Territory of Delhi (GNCTD), NCR Planning Board and Ministries of Urban Development, Home and Railways, GoI. The multiplicity of authorities leads to plans working at cross purposes, leading to under-investment in infrastructure and over-regulation of land development and use.

Human Resource Constraint

The capacity for urban planning in developing countries is severely constrained by the lack of planners: physical, transportation, environment, social, economic, etc. Only about 2,100 master plans have been notified in India so far. For many of them, the zonal and local area plans are not completed. With more than 7,900 cities and towns in India, including 53 metropolitan cities requiring MDP and about 670 districts requiring DDP mandated by the 74th Amendment Act, the country needs a huge increase in the number of town and country planners from the current level of about 5,000. An expert group set up by the Ministry of Human Resource Development, GoI, projected the requirement of urban planners in the country by 2031 at 300,000 (MHRD 2011). However, there are about 20 recognized institutions in India, producing nearly 600 qualified planners annually.

Lack of Community Participation

Prepared by professionals, the master plans are neither people-centric, nor people-driven. The planning process does not ensure adequate participation by the majority in cities, comprising the poor and LIGs. In most states, UDAs are entrusted with the preparation of master plans. These authorities are parastatals—not accountable to the people—unlike elected ULGs. Ironically, spatial planning function around the world is performed by local governments in view of their proximity to the people and access to local knowledge. JNNURM mooted the concept of 'community participation law' as a mandatory reform to enable the close participation of people in local affairs in India. While several states have enacted such a law, implementation in the field has been poor.

A New Paradigm for Urban Planning

The top-down, static and land use-centric master planning model is ill-suited to deal with dynamic urban problems, including land market failure. The model, rooted in modernist planning theories, is authoritarian. It adopts a narrow interpretation of land, focusing on land use and ignoring the importance of density and accessibility to transportation infrastructure. Further, it fails to take into account the determinants of location and land use in the spatial economy. It does not utilize the valuable information transmitted by the market on demand for and supply of land and housing, land rent, land value, housing rent, housing price, transport cost, etc. The master planning approach ignores a fundamental premise of urban economics, namely cities are products of processes shaped by 'economic interactions' and 'social relations'. It fails to recognize what Jane Jacobs calls the 'organised complexity' of cities. The latter arises due to *dealing simultaneously with a sizable number of factors which are interrelated into an organic whole* (Jacobs 1961, 432). Jacobs refers 'systems', 'processes' and 'self-organization' in the evolution of cities. These factors suggest that spatial, socio-economic and environmental outcomes in a city region depend on complex interactions between numerous firms, households and developers in the pursuit of economic activity. Subjecting these agents to many mechanical controls adversely impact enterprise. Ironically, it is political action rather than technocratic planning that has been responsible for the most successful designs of cities globally.

Developing countries practising master planning have focused on regulatory interventions in land markets, neglecting developmental tools and ignoring economic instruments. They have not evaluated land use zoning and DCRs. However, Cheshire and Hilber (2008) find that planning restrictions have typically imposed a 'tax' on office development in England that varied from around 250 per cent of development cost in Birmingham to 400–800 per cent in London. This tax amounted to about 300 per cent in Central Paris, 200 per cent in Amsterdam but 0–50 per cent in New York. Cheshire et al. (2014) also find that the restrictive town planning system in the United Kingdom has severely curtailed the supply of land and housing, turning them to something like 'gold' or 'artwork'. It increases housing prices with regressive impacts on low- and middle-income dwelling units, housing market volatility and office rents. It also lowers retail productivity and employment in small independent retailers. Further, it fails to assess the true social cost of brown field versus green field development. Glaeser (2011), Koster et al. (2011) and Brueckner and Sridhar (2012) find that building height restrictions typically reduce the positive effects of agglomeration economies.

The conspicuous failure of cities in developing countries to meet the infrastructure needs of growth; provide housing, basic services and employment to the people; allocate land and floor space to the poor and LIGs; prevent environmental degradation; and manage disasters indicate that master planning has culminated in high social costs. These costs are compounded by the long neglect of PT and transport–land use integration. They manifest in exorbitant land values, housing prices, living costs and office rents. The master plans have resulted in acute scarcity of serviced land and floor space for productive economic activities at central city locations and shortage in affordable housing for not only the poor and low-income segments but also the middle-income groups (MIGs). While the formal land markets have weeded the urban poor out, the formal master plans have deprived them of the 'right to the city'. The urban poor are also handicapped due to the lack of PT, which results in their inability to access affordable housing and employment opportunities. Ignoring the economics of land, transport and cities, the master plans have invariably failed to present a coherent strategy to finance urban plans. Assigning a subsidiary role to transport, they have failed to exploit value creation, capture and recycling instruments to finance infrastructure. Master planning has led to chronic under-investment in infrastructure, spotty development, sprawl, longer commuting, energy wastage, increased service costs, social exclusion, public health hazards, vulnerability to disasters and adverse impacts on agriculture, rural livelihoods and climate change.

The failure of public authorities in developing countries to make urban land markets work is mainly due to three broad factors: under-provision of public goods, over-regulation of land markets and neglect of economic instruments. Cities have neglected infrastructure and affordable housing due to abysmal finances. They have not exploited 'beneficiaries pay', 'polluters pay', 'congesters pay', 'exacerbaters pay' and 'growth pays' instruments. Due to their neglect of land-based taxes, especially VLT, cities have not been able to curb speculation in land markets, which has resulted in the withdrawal of large chunks of land from contiguous development. Under-investment in transport has hindered the functioning of cities as unified labour markets. The failure to create synergy between transport, mobility, accessibility, density and land use has resulted in the inability of firms to exploit agglomeration and networking economies. This has led to environmental degradation. Lack of investment in connectivity infrastructure, rampant speculation in land market and stringent restrictions on land use and FSI have led to scarcity of 'accessible' and 'affordable' locations to firms and households. They have constricted the choice of creative entrepreneurs and skilled workers in pursuing chosen economic activities.

A major problem with present master planning in India is that while it is inherently inequitable, it does not incorporate instruments to correct for planning-related inequities. The master plan proposals are not based on social benefit-cost analysis. On the one hand, they exclude the poor from land and floor space allocation processes, and on the other hand, zoning and FSI regimes lead to windfall benefits to some lucky landowners. However, the latter are not required to pay for 'planning gain'; they are not subjected to 'differential taxation'. Similarly, speculators who keep their land idle benefit from infrastructure development as free riders. However, they do not contribute towards 'development gain'. Landowners whose lands fall under conservation or no-development zone in the master plan are not compensated for 'planning loss'. They are provided with neither monetary compensation nor TDR. Similarly, rural habitations that provide garbage dumping yards to cities are not compensated for the pollution hazards caused to them. Rural lands annexed to urban areas lead to agricultural production and rural livelihood losses, apart from lost amenities and ecological functions. However, master plans do not take such 'invisible' effects into account. They do not recognize the principle that the gainers from government actions must compensate the losers. Ironically, under 'conservation easement' programmes in the United States, landowners can voluntarily give up development rights temporarily or permanently in exchange of compensation from government. European Union countries provide subsidy for farmland conservation and sustainable agricultural practice. Such policies are absent in developing countries.

Modernist urban planning, which underlies the master plan approach, is weak in theory. It also has a poor record in practice. The paradigm is not appropriate to address SLM and sustainable development issues in developing countries. Relying on a command and control approach, it neglects the role of people in city building. Planning theory, in the course of its evolution, has moved to newer paradigms such as 'rational planning', 'incremental planning' and 'planning as a political process' (Allmendinger 2009; Faludi 1973; Taylor 1998). However, master planning in developing countries has not kept pace with theoretical developments in literature. Taylor's criticism of 'imprecise', 'vague', 'ambiguous' and 'opaque nature' of complex and normative concepts is applicable to master planning.

Jacob's criticism of modernist planning as mechanical, based on an 'anti-density' perspective, and incapable of addressing the 'organized complexity' of cities is also applicable. Master planning ignores the importance of co-location and density in the 'collaborative brilliance' of cities (Glaeser 2011). While cities are economic entities, master plans fail to use tools of economics such as social benefit-cost analysis and optimization subject to constraints.

City regions lead to important benefits and costs due to actions of multiple actors, including central, state and local governments. Firms, households and developers take decisions regarding location and land use. However, independent actions by economic agents regarding interdependent activities lead to externalities and market failure, calling for government intervention. Extreme urban land markets, characterized by rampant speculation and withdrawal of large chunks of land from contiguous development, lead to socially suboptimal outcomes. Governments also fail to correct for market failure by resorting to unduly restrictive land use norms and FSI controls while neglecting core infrastructure, especially transportation. Inability to regulate haphazard developments has led to more stringent and elaborate controls, dampening initiative to develop and build. Master planning has also led to rent-seeking and corruption. City regions of developing countries suffer from double jeopardy: market failure and government failure.

Seven decades of land use–led master planning in India has failed to achieve the core objectives of spatial planning: environmental conservation, social inclusion and infrastructure provision to support economic growth. A multi-tier planning model with rigid land use controls at regional, city, zonal, local and plot levels is simply unwarranted. Such controls, reminiscent of pre-liberalization era, have dampened development. Accordingly, a two-tier planning structure led by transport is suggested. The first tier aims at a regional strategic plan, focused on conservation of national, state and regional heritage and environmental resources and development of core regional infrastructure networks, especially public transit, HSR and a grid of arterial and radial roads. The second tier envisages a series of land pooling schemes (LPS) at local area level led by TOD and SLM, incentivized by government and driven primarily by private developers. It is anticipated that the proposed model will integrate transportation, land use, density, development, IZ, carrying capacity-based planning and VCF strategies, with flexibility in plan implementation. Land and urban policies in developing countries must exploit the organic links between transportation and land use, spatial and economic, and rural and urban planning. They must harness the benefits of transportation-accessibility-affordability-density-land use integration to promote sustainable land management and development.

Urban planning in India must be reformed to enable cities to discharge their fundamental economic, social and environmental functions. The country must liberalize master planning, which has been left untouched by economic liberalization reforms from the 1990s, to promote development rather than control it. A key direction for reform is to incorporate the basic tenets of land economics and related disciplines of transport economics, urban economics and NEG to enable urban land markets to work. This warrants, among other things, recognizing land as a composite, spatial, economic and environmental good and as an input, output and a resource; role of cities as unified labour markets; symbiotic relationship between transportation and land use; pivotal importance of transport in 'leading' land and local economic development; major PT projects creating 'accessibility premium' to locations and 'WEBs' to the economy; land rent as a 'surplus'; and LVT, benefit taxation and VCF as ideal instruments for debt financing of infrastructure. The country must shift from a top-down, prescriptive, technocratic, rigid, land use–based and comprehensive urban planning approach to a decentralized, responsive, people-driven, flexible, transport-led and strategic planning paradigm. Public transit investment, density, TOD, transport–land use integration, social inclusion and DP financing need to be designed together as part of a holistic approach to land policy and urbanization strategy.

Sustainable Land Management

Connecting Transport, Land Use and Development

Challenges of Spatial Transformation

Every developed country has passed through two fundamental processes of development: structural and spatial transformation. Developing countries are also passing through the same. Table 6.1 provides comparative data on urbanization in the world in 2018. Globally, the level of urbanization is expected to increase from 55 per cent in 2018 to 68 per cent in 2050. About 90 per cent of the increase of 2.5 billion in cities and towns would be in Asia and Africa. Three countries, that is, India, China and Nigeria, would account for 35 per cent

Table 6.1 Population of Urban and Rural Areas at Mid-year and Percentage Urban 2018

Region or Country	Urban (in Million)	Rural (in Million)	Total (in Million)	Percentage Urban (%)
World	4,219.8	3,413.0	7,632.8	55.3
More developed regions	993.8	269.4	1,263.2	78.7
Less developed regions	3,226.0	3,143.6	6,369.6	50.6
India	460.8	893.3	1,354.1	34.0
China	837.0	578.0	1,415.0	59.2
Nigeria	98.6	97.3	195.9	50.3

Source: United Nations (2019).

Table 6.2 Percentage of Population of Urban Areas at Mid-year (1950–2050; in %)

Region or Country	1950	2015	2035	2050
World	29.6	53.9	62.5	68.4
More developed regions	54.8	78.1	82.7	86.6
Less developed regions	17.7	49.0	59.0	65.6
India	17.0	32.8	43.2	52.8
China	11.8	55.5	73.9	80.0
Nigeria	9.4	47.8	62.2	69.9

Source: United Nations (2019).

Table 6.3 India: Demographic Trends and Projections During 1950–2050

	1950	2015	2035	2050
Total population (in million)	376.32	1,309.05	1,564.57	1,658.98
Urban population (in million)	64.13	429.07	675.46	876.61
Percentage	17.0	32.8	43.2	52.8
Rural population (in million)	312.19	879.98	889.11	782.36
Percentage	83.0	67.2	56.8	47.2

Source: United Nations (2019).

of the global urban population growth during 2018–2050. India is expected to add 416 million; China—255 million; and Nigeria—189 million. Table 6.2 presents trends in world's urbanization and projections to 2050. Table 6.3 portrays salient demographic data for India covering the period 1950–2050.

Urban population in India, which increased by 365 million over the 65-year period, 1950–2015, is likely to rise by 448 million over the 35-year period, 2015–2050. Rural population is expected to decrease only marginally from 880 million in 2015 to 782 million in 2050. Thus, the country would face dual challenges of rural and urban development over many decades. While the projected increase in population of cities is overwhelming, some researchers contend that the level of urbanization in India as reported by official documents is an underestimate. They argue that the figure does not capture the 'hidden' urbanization in the peripheries of large cities. Using the concept of 'agglomeration index', a globally applicable alternative measure of urban concentration, a World Bank study has estimated the share of India's population living in areas with 'urban-like' features in 2010 at 55.3 per cent (World Bank 2015).

A key feature of India's urbanization is its top heavy structure. The number of metropolitan agglomerations, containing 1 million or more, increased from 1 in 1901 to 9 in 1971, 35 in 2001 and 53 in 2011. Their share in urban population rose from 6 per cent in 1901 to 38 per cent in 2001 and 43 per cent in 2011. In 1950, only two Indian cities figured in the list of 30 largest UAs in the world—Kolkata with 5 million at 9th place and Mumbai with 3 million at 15th place as against New York-Newark with 12 million at 1st place. By 2015, the number of such agglomerations in India swelled to 4—Delhi with 26 million (2nd), Mumbai with 19 million (6th), Kolkata with 14 million (13th) and Bengaluru with 10 million (29th)—compared to Tokyo with 37 million (1st place). Delhi is projected to be the world's largest UA in 2035 with 43 million people. Five other Indian cities, Mumbai, Kolkata, Bengaluru, Chennai and Hyderabad, would then be among the 30 largest UAs globally (United Nations 2018).

Large city regions propel growth. In 2016, the 300 largest metropolitan economies in the world, containing 24 per cent of global population, contributed nearly 50 per cent of global GDP. These economies, which include nine from India, also concentrated and accelerated growth between 2014 and 2016. They explained 67 per cent of real GDP growth and 36 per cent of employment growth in the world. McKinsey (2014) projects that by 2025, India would have 69 metropolitan cities. About 77 per cent of India's economic growth from 2012 to 2025 would emanate from 49 clusters of districts with metropolitan cities as nucleus. While metropolitan regions are India's growth engines, central cities in such regions are witnessing a premature industrial suburbanization. Exorbitant land and housing prices, traffic congestion, air pollution and shortages in infrastructure are prompting manufacturing firms to move away from central cities to suburbs even before they could exploit agglomeration economies.

A key challenge of urbanization in India is to transform land use and development in metropolitan regions.

Urbanization calls for effective management of scarce land resources in order to cater to housing, workplace, infrastructure and other needs. Making serviced land and floor space available to meet the demands of economic growth while conserving the environment is central to India's sustainable development. McKinsey (2010) projects that India will need 700–900 million m^2 of commercial and residential space each year till 2030. Connecting these spaces requires 2.5 billion m^2 of new roads and 7,400 km of new metros and subways, representing 20 times the infrastructure capacity that was added in India since 1999. While the challenges are daunting, urban growth also has crucial implications for sustainable rural development. Cities consume a huge amount of rural resources. They annex agricultural lands to accommodate increased urban population. Large villages get converted into towns in situ. Further, rural lands cater to the needs of urban areas for raw materials, energy, food, water, waste disposal, labour force and landscape amenities, apart from preserving natural habitats and biodiversity that support life. SLM is critical for rural development. It is also the key to attaining the objectives of economically efficient, socially equitable, environmentally sustainable and financially viable cities.

Urbanization presents a unique opportunity to developing countries to accelerate economic growth and reduce poverty. India must harness SLM as a resource for planned urbanization. In particular, policymakers must address the dilemma of 'building upward' or 'building outward' to accommodate urban population growth. The options have ramifications for infrastructure, land use, sprawl, public health and environmental externalities and carrying capacity of the ecosystem. This chapter focuses on land management for sustainable development: procuring, assembling, financing, developing, renewing, connecting, servicing, using, reusing and regulating land. It is based on the premise that land management issues cannot be meaningfully studied in isolation of the interactions between market forces, externalities and public policies. Land is a heterogeneous good with multiple dimensions: horizontal, vertical, access to infrastructure and close links to externalities. Land markets fail and are subjected to zoning and FSI regulations. Government policies for PT, economic growth and environmental conservation significantly impact spatio-economic outcomes. Transport is the key to managing density, land use and congestion externalities.

Land and transport have symbiotic relationships. Transport makes or mars a city. It creates access, and access creates value. No meaningful discussion on land management is possible without referring to the role of transport in 'location' and 'land use' by impacting accessibility, affordability, density, externalities and economic development. As the FSI levels in Indian cities are very low, a strong case exists for re-engineering cities with phased investments in mass transit, HSR and grids of arterial and radial roads and calibrated increases in FSI in strategic locations. These projects promote agglomeration economies, mitigate congestion diseconomies and catalyse growth. They lead to 'accessibility premiums' to locations and 'WEBs' to the economy. The benefit principle of public finance suggests that a value creation, capture and recycling strategy is eminently suitable for financing PT investment. Transport also assists the poor in accessing employment and housing opportunities. Further, it leads to key environmental benefits. Planned increases in city densities obviate the necessity to extend urban boundaries by encroaching upon fertile agricultural lands.

The remaining parts in this chapter deal with the changing land use patterns in India, socio-economic and environmental impacts of land use changes and key elements of SLM strategy to address such changes. We refer to the centrality of PT in SLM. Transportation-density-land use integration is perhaps the single most important instrument available with planners in developing countries to pursue sustainable regional and urban development. This chapter makes a strong case for transport-led, transit-oriented and hub and spoke-patterned spatial development to exploit the synergy between accessibility, affordability, density, land use and local economic development. This strategy calls for investment in PT in anticipation of growth, TOD and LPS with landowners as partners. It also advocates strategic densification, urban renewal and new township development programmes with carrying capacity–based planning and IZ. Further, it makes a strong case for financing land and infrastructure development based on value creating intergovernmental partnerships that lead to enhanced tax bases for local, state and central governments and make debt financing of planned urban development feasible. Benefit taxes and earmarked intergovernmental transfers could be escrowed to leverage long tenor debt to finance transit.

Changing Land Use Patterns in India

India accounts for 17 per cent of population and 2.4 per cent of area of the world. The country has adopted a nine-fold classification of land use in five groups (see Box 6.1). Table 6.4 presents salient data on changes in land uses in India between the years 1950–1951 and 2014–2015.

Box 6.1: India: Classification of Land Use

1. Forests: Includes all lands classed as forest under any legal enactment dealing with forests or administered as forests, whether state-owned or private and whether wooded or maintained as potential forest land. The area of crops raised in the forest and grazing lands or areas open for grazing within the forests should remain included under the forest area.
2. Not available for cultivation
   a. Area under non-agricultural uses: Includes all lands occupied by buildings, roads and railways or under water, for example, rivers and canals and other lands put to uses other than agriculture.
   b. Barren and unculturable land: Includes lands such as mountains and deserts. Land which cannot be brought under cultivation except at an exorbitant cost should be classed as unculturable whether such land is in isolated blocks or within cultivated holdings.
3. Other unculturable land, excluding fallow land:
   a. Permanent pastures and other grazing lands: Include all grazing lands whether they are permanent pastures and meadows or not; village common grazing land is included under this.
   b. Land under miscellaneous tree crops, etc.: Includes all cultivable land which is not included in 'net area sown' but is put to some agricultural uses. Lands under casuarina trees, thatching grasses, bamboo bushes and other groves for fuel, etc. which are not included under 'orchards' should be classed under this category.
   c. Culturable waste land: Includes lands available for cultivation, whether not taken up for cultivation or taken up for cultivation once

> but not cultivated during the current year and the last 5 years or more in succession for one reason or other. Such lands may be either fallow or covered with shrubs and jungles, which are not put to any use. They may be assessed or unassessed and may lie in isolated blocks or within cultivated holdings. Land once cultivated but not cultivated for 5 years in succession should also be included in this category at the end of the 5 years.
> 4. Fallow lands:
>   a. Fallow lands other than current fallows: Includes all lands, which were taken up for cultivation but are temporarily out of cultivation for a period of not less than 1 year and not more than 5 years.
>   b. Current fallows: Represents cropped area kept fallow during the current year; for example, if any seeding area is not cropped against the same year, it may be treated as current fallow.
> 5. Net area sown: Represents the total area sown with crops and orchards. Area sown more than once in the same year is counted only once.
>
> *Source:* Ministry of Statistics and Programme Implementation. *Nine-fold classification of land use.*

While the geographical area of India stood at 328.73 million hectares (ha) in 1950–1951, 1980–1981 and 2014–2015, the land uses reported for these years were 284.32, 304.16 and 307.82 million ha, respectively. The 'gross cropped area' increased from 131.89 million ha in 1950–1951 to 198.36 million ha in 2014–2015. Over the same period, the 'net area sown' rose from 118.75 million ha to 146.13 million ha. The 'area under non-agricultural use' went up from 9.36 million ha to 23.32 million ha. The area 'not available for cultivation' reported in Table 6.4 includes area 'under non-agricultural uses' and 'barren and un-culturable land'. The share of 'non-agricultural uses', comprising lands occupied by buildings, roads and railways or under water and other non-agricultural uses including urban, increased by nearly 5 percentage points between 1950–1951 and 2014–2015. However, the share of 'barren and uncultivable' lands declined by 8 percentage points over the period. Presumably, a part of the increase in land devoted to urban use is explained by such decline. Two notable changes in land use patterns in India over the years are (a) concentration of agricultural landholdings at the top end and marginalization

Table 6.4 *India: Changing Pattern of Land Use (1950–1951 to 2014–2015)*

Sl. No.	Land Use Category	Percentage of Total Land Area Reported for Land Utilization Statistics (%)		
		1950–1951	1980–1981	2014–2015*
1.	Forest	14.24	22.18	23.32
2.	Not available for cultivation			
	Area under non-agricultural use	3.29	6.44	8.73
	A. Barren and unculturable land	13.42	6.56	5.52
3.	Other unculturable land excluding fallow land			
	A. Permanent pasture and other grassland	2.35	3.94	3.33
	B. Land under miscellaneous tree crops and groves not included in net area sown	6.97	1.18	1.01
	C. Culturable wasteland	8.07	5.51	4.05
4.	Fallow lands			
	A. Fallow lands other than current fallows	6.14	3.20	3.60
	B. Current fallows	3.76	4.88	4.90
5.	Net area sown	41.77	46.12	45.42

Source: Ministry of Agriculture and Farmers' Welfare (2019).

Note: *Provisional estimate.

at the bottom in rural areas and (b) lack of access to land for shelter by large sections living in urban areas, leading to slums and squatter settlements.

Rural and Urban Land Uses

Land ownership and use patterns in India present a highly skewed picture. Further, landlessness has increased over the years. Landless households are defined by NSSO to include all households with less than 0.002 ha. They are officially recognized as the 'poorest of the poor'. Socio Economic and Caste Census 2011 (SECC 2011) indicates that 56.41 per cent of rural households did not own any land (https://www.secc.gov.in/statewiseLandOwnershipReport [accessed 10 July 2020]). NSSO (2006) reports that 48.5 per cent of urban households in India in 2003 were landless. Census 2011 reveals that 35 per cent of urban population in India lived in one room or less. The corresponding figure for slums was 49 per cent.

Table 6.5 presents the distribution of land holdings and operated area in India in 2010–2011 and 2015–2016 based on the Agricultural Census. Small and marginal holdings (0.00–2.00 ha) accounted for 86.08 per cent of the total number of holdings in India in 2015–2016 as against 85.01 per cent in 2010–2011. Their share in total operated area was 46.94 per cent in 2015–2016 compared to 44.58 per cent in 2010–2011. Large holdings (10.00 ha and above) were merely 0.57 per cent of total holdings in 2015–2016 compared to 0.70 per cent in 2010–2011. However, they had a share of 9.07 per cent in operated area in 2015–2016 as against 10.59 per cent in 2010–2011. The average size of holding in ha decreased from 2.28 in 1970–1971 to 1.84 in 1980–1981, 1.55 in 1990–1991, 1.33 in 2000–2001, 1.15 in 2010–2011 and 1.08 in 2015–2016. The increasing fragmentation of land holdings is adversely affecting agricultural productivity in India, making agriculture uneconomic.

As in rural areas, cities and towns in India are faced with highly uneven distribution of land ownership and use. About 60 per cent of the population in Mumbai lives on only 7 per cent of the city's land. In Pune, 36 per cent of population occupies just 1.55 per cent of land

Table 6.5 India: Distribution of Landholding and Operated Area (2010–2011 and 2015–2016)

Size Group (ha)	Agricultural Census 2010–2011		Agricultural Census 2015–2016	
	% of Holdings	% of Area Operated	% of Holdings	% of Area Operated
Marginal (<1.00 ha)	67.10	22.50	68.45	24.03
Small (1.00–2.00 ha)	17.91	22.08	17.62	22.91
Semi-medium (2.00–4.00 ha)	10.04	23.63	9.55	23.84
Medium (4.00–10.00 ha)	4.25	21.20	3.80	20.16
Large (≥10.00 ha)	0.70	10.59	0.57	9.07
Total	100.00	100.00	100.00	100.00

Source: Ministry of Agriculture and Farmers' Welfare (2019b).

area. According to Census 2011, more than 30 per cent of households in nine metropolitan cities reside in slums. In India, slums are largely a metropolitan phenomenon. In terms of the percentage of population of metropolitan cities living in slums in 2011, Visakhapatnam tops the list with 44.1 per cent, followed by Jabalpur Cantonment—43.1 per cent; and Greater Mumbai—41.3 per cent (54% in 2001). Among the largest municipal corporations, apart from Greater Mumbai, Kolkata and Chennai have more than 25 per cent of households residing in slums. The number of slumdwellers in India is estimated at 65.5 million in 2011. This figure is an underestimate as it does not take into account squatters not notified as slums. The lack of tenure security and access to lifeline amenities, precarious shelter, high exposure to water- and air-borne diseases, vulnerability to eviction by municipal officials and to disasters like floods and cyclones are common problems facing slumdwellers in India.

Slums in India's large cities present islands of subhuman living and multidimensional poverty, not captured by the standard income-based criteria. They have health indicators often more appalling than their rural counterparts. Slums are vivid expressions of failure of urban land markets, exacerbated by failure of governments to correct for deficiencies in the market. The slumdwellers are subjected to a double jeopardy: market failure and government failure. Urban land markets, characterized by extreme speculation, lead to exorbitant prices of urban land and floor space which the poor and LIG cannot afford. The formal master plans of cities also neglected the space needs of the urban poor. They allocated land and floor space to urban uses based on the space norms of the average middle-class household. The master plans also did not recognize the informal sector, which engages the bulk of the urban poor. The problems are compounded by the long neglect of PT, depriving the poor of access to livelihood opportunities in the new knowledge economy (Mohanty 2014, 2016, 2019).

The Census of India data reveal that the area occupied by ULBs constituted 3.19 per cent of India's total area in 2011 as against 2.44 per cent in 2001 and 2.04 per cent in 1991 (Ramachandran 2017). The figure is not large, considering that cities account for 3–6 per cent of a country's land area in developed countries. However,

India is only 34 per cent urban and has to go a long way in urbanization. Cities must carefully weigh the option of building vertically and utilizing the underused urban land rather than extending boundaries. However, state governments in India in the past indiscriminatingly extended the limits of cities, especially metropolitan cities, by annexing agricultural lands. This is a concern as large chunks of strategically located land in urban areas remain underused by speculators due to rent-seeking. Further, considerable extents of 'high value' lands are locked in 'low density' slums, without being integrated with the city. Additionally, public authorities in central, state and local governments hold large extents of idle land without worthwhile plans for utilization.

Impacts of Land Use Changes

Ecologists differentiate between 'land cover' and 'land use'. Land cover depicts the natural and anthropogenic features observed on earth's surface such as terrestrial ecosystems, natural resources and habitats. It includes vegetation—natural and man-made, water bodies, wetlands, grasslands, built-up or developed area, etc. Land use represents operations or activities on land, carried out by human beings to obtain products or benefits through utilization of land resources, for example, agriculture, recreation, industry, commerce, single-family homes, multi-family apartment complexes, parks, water reservoirs, sewerage treatment plants, transportation networks, etc. While land cover describes the surface cover on ground, land use describes the purpose served by land. Land use changes, leading to changes in land cover, lead to a mix of private and social benefits and costs. Benefits include economic growth and employment; costs include environmental damage and climate change effects.

Land use changes have major impacts on socio-economic and environmental outcomes. The conversion of farmland and forests to urban and industrial uses reduces the land available for food, fodder and timber production. Pressure on agricultural lands manifests in soil erosion, salinization, desertification and other forms of land degradation, leading to loss in agricultural production. Deforestation diminishes land quality and agricultural productivity. Rural land use for non-agricultural activities reduces the amount of open space and other environmental amenities available for local residents. While leading to productivity benefits and cost savings, urbanization reduces the 'critical mass' of farmland necessary for economic survival of agrarian economies. It impacts lives and livelihoods and the way society is organized. Haphazard urban growth in Asia and Africa has encroached upon many rural communities to such an extent that their identity is lost. Poorly planned density leads to overcrowding, pressure on infrastructure, traffic congestion, pollution and deterioration in public services. The urban poor are the worst-affected population due to lack of access to shelter and basic amenities, exposure to public health hazards and vulnerability to disasters. Suburbanization has intensified income segregation and economic disparities around the world.

Apart from socio-economic impacts, land use changes impact the quality and productivity of environmental resources, including air, water, soil, plants and animals. Agricultural run-off is a leading source of water pollution in both inland and coastal areas. Draining of wetlands for crop production and diversion of irrigation water for aquaculture have negatively impacted wildlife species. Irrigated agriculture has changed the water cycle, causing groundwater levels to dwindle to abysmal levels. Deforestation due to industrialization and urbanization leads to adverse impacts on wildlife and human habitats. It increases soil degradation and landslides, destroys biodiversity and adds to GHG effects. Haphazard development pollutes the environment, creates congestion, increases urban flooding and has adverse implications for climate change. Habitat destruction, fragmentation and alteration associated with urbanization are a leading cause of biodiversity decline and species extinction. Urban development in coastal areas constitute a major threat to health, productivity and biodiversity of the marine environment. It is also responsible for contamination of rivers, lakes and other water bodies and destruction of wetlands. Metropolitan areas are the hubs of fossil fuel activity and unsustainable consumption of energy and environment resources. Globally, cities account for 75 per cent of natural resource consumption, 80 per cent of energy use and 75 per cent of carbon emissions (Mohanty 2019; UNEP 2015; UN-Habitat 2016). SLM is critical for addressing the adverse consequences of urbanization.

Sustainable Land Management

The United Nations identifies SLM as a key tool to attain SDGs 2030. The concept was introduced in the Earth Summit held in 1992 in Rio as the use of land resources, including soil, water, animals and plants for production of goods, to meet the demands of human beings over time, while simultaneously ensuring the long-term productive potential of these resources and maintenance of their environmental functions. SLM was advocated to address key concerns in 'development-environment debate' such as degradation of land, water and vegetation; depletion of non-renewable resources; emission of GHGs that contribute to climate change; and adverse effects of haphazard urbanization on agricultural productivity. The literature on SLM is mostly focused on agriculture, food security, ecology and environment. It emphasizes rural land management and environmental regulation. However, with rapid urbanization in developing countries, SLM is receiving increasing attention from urban researchers and policymakers. It is considered indispensable for achieving UN SDG 11 that calls for making 'cities and human settlements inclusive, safe, resilient, and sustainable'.

SLM instruments for rural areas focus on food, fodder, fibre, fuel and freshwater needs. They include measures to prevent land degradation and deforestation, conserve natural and cultural resources and protect biodiversity. They provide support services to landowners and farmers such as soil conservation, nutrients to improve soil quality, water conservation and recycling and livelihood protection and promotion. Environmental regulations relate to water quality and quantity, non-renewable energy use, waste management, air pollution, traffic congestion, carbon emission, and mitigation of public health hazards associated with water- and air-borne diseases and environmental damages due to natural and man-made disasters. SLM instruments for urban areas focus on land use and floor space to address the demands of economic growth while paying utmost attention to carrying capacity of the ecosystem. They aim at balancing vertical development in cities with horizontal expansion to minimize the adverse impacts of urbanization on agriculture and the environment. The SLM approach sharply contrasts with master planning that treats conservation and transportation as residuals in plan-making. It emphasizes PT–led urban development rather than being driven by personalized automobiles. It considers environment as an intergenerational resource and its conservation as a non-negotiable principle of urban planning.

A major lacuna with urban planning through master plans in developing countries is that it accords primacy to land use on the premise that land use determines transport needs. The opposite view is perhaps more appropriate for developing countries like India in view of the crucial role of transport in promoting higher densities, agglomeration economies, labour market mobility and economic growth, while avoiding sprawl and mitigating congestion diseconomies. SLM considerations also make a compelling case for TOD. First, the population density, composition and income distribution structure of cities, the majority belonging to LIG and MIG, favour PT-led development. Second, the concerns of agricultural productivity, food security and livelihoods in rural areas, accounting for two-thirds of total population and imperatives of conservation of land, water, energy, forests and biodiversity, favour dense development in cities rather than sprawling urbanization. Key components in SLM include investment in transport infrastructure in anticipation of economic growth, TOD, transport–land use integration, TOD-based LPS with landowners as partners in urban development, IZ to promote affordable housing and workplaces for the poor and VCF of transportation infrastructure.

SLM calls for timely investment in core infrastructure to meet the demands of economic growth and urbanization: public health care and disaster resilience, including water supply, sewerage, stormwater drainage, solid waste management, preventive and promotive health care and non-polluting, energy-efficient, multi-modal PT. Key PT options include BRT, light rail transit (LRT), MRT, HSR and a grid of arterial and radial roads. They need to be supplemented by non-motorized transport (NMT) and transport-led LPS with landowners as partners; transport–land use integration, strategic densification of transit nodes with potential for agglomeration in existing cities and new townships on growth corridors; IZ to address the concerns of affordable housing to the poor and LIG; motor vehicles taxation and

CC to promote use of PT; and financing of public transit with benefit taxation and value creation, capture and recycling instruments (Mohanty 2014, 2016, 2019).

Primacy of Public Health

Even metropolitan cities in India, the generators of national economic momentum, lack adequate public health and environmental infrastructure. These cities are ill-prepared to handle disasters like floods, cyclones and pandemics like Covid-19. Ironically, they have not learnt lessons from the experiences of their counterparts in the developed world. Cholera outbreaks in London in the early 19th century led to massive investments in sewerage and sanitation in the city. Tuberculosis surge in NYC in the early 20th century led to a phenomenal response from government through tenement regulation, affordable housing and urban renewal interventions and public transit investments. SARS outrage in the early 21st century in some Asian countries witnessed considerable investments in medical and health infrastructure in their cities. Dense cities around the world continue to hold their advantages in terms of education, skills, access to cutting-edge technology, innovation, economic growth, employment, housing, social interaction, culture and recreation. There is no reason why India's metropolitan cities, with land values among the highest in the world, cannot finance robust public health and PT systems in anticipation of growth and be disaster-resilient.

Leading Role of Transport

Transport creates access, and access creates value through direct, indirect and induced effects. 'Accessibility' reduces money, time and inconvenience costs of travel to reach valued destinations: workplaces, homes, schools, shopping malls, cultural and recreational centres, railway stations, airports, etc. Transport also enhances 'affordability' of locations. Further, it facilitates face-to-face interaction, information exchange, collaboration, innovation and knowledge-led growth. Transport impacts city functions and form by inducing land use and development. It leads to 'accessibility premium' to locations and 'WEBs' to the economy. Such benefits arise due to agglomeration economies in central locations, more efficient functioning of cities as large labour markets, enhanced competition and increased outputs under monopolistically competitive markets (Venables 2007).

Transport has been a major factor in the transformation of world's great cities (Kennedy 2011). The importance of visionary transportation planning is singularly demonstrated by the 1811 'grid plan' of Manhattan, NYC. The plan provided a blank state for guided urban development with accessible streets and adaptable blocks. The built-up area of Manhattan grew seven-fold along the 'grid' in the 19th century (Angel 2012). 'No invisible hand guided Manhattan towards rectangular blocks of private property embedded in a public grid of avenues and streets. A real hand did that of John Tandel Jr., the engineer hired by a state commission to survey the island'. (Fuller and Romer 2014, 3). The government acquired land for roads as per plan and protected the same for decades. It took up development of the grid and connectivity infrastructure in a phased manner. It required landowners to finance the cost of construction of road adjacent to their properties based on the benefit principle of public finance. This led to increase in their property values far more than they paid through betterment levies.

The growth of NYC was strongly shaped by transport resources: the Erie Canal, protected harbour, shipping hub, connectivity to vast network of national railways, national highways and international airports, and a comprehensive, well-used public transit system. The opening of the Erie Canal in 1825, connecting the Hudson River to Buffalo, linked New York to the Great Lakes hinterlands. Integrated transportation-land use planning and proactive investment in PT, together with economic forces, enabled New York to grow into an economic colossus. London triumphed because of its port, railway networks and telegraph cables. The Saint Gotthard tunnel in the Alps facilitated the rise of Zurich and Milan as major financial centres. Frankfurt benefited from its hub airport. London started its metro in 1863 (population 3.2 million), Paris in 1900 (population 4.2 million) and New York in 1904 (population 3.5 million). The developed countries invested in metro rail even when their income distribution structure did not generate the ridership numbers to ensure financial viability. They regarded transport as a catalyst of land use for productive economic activities, while catering to the mobility needs of urbanization.

Re-engineering Cities with Transit

Apart from SLM and economic growth considerations, the importance of MRT and HSR in India can be gauged from the fact that the road system in cities will not suffice to accommodate the projected per hour per direction traffic (PHPDT). India is only 34 per cent urban; its urban population is projected to double between 2014 and 2050 (United Nations 2019). Metropolitan city regions are already dense and subjected to serious congestion. They need to be re-engineered with transit. Transportation planners recommend transit options for urban areas based on PHPDT as follows: BRT—10,000–15,000; light rail–15,000–35,000; medium rail—30,000–60,000; and heavy rail—55,000 and above. High-speed trains, running at about 250 km/h, are suitable for megacity regions. External economies and spillover effects make a strong economic case for investment in MRT and HSR, along with a grid of arterial and radial roads, transport–land use integration, TOD and VCF to promote sustainable development.

HSR originated in Japan in 1964, with Japanese national railways launching the Tokaido Shinkansen, connecting Tokyo Central and Shin Osaka and running with a speed of 210 km/h. By 2017, China reportedly established a HSR network of about 23,914 km, Japan—3,041 km; Spain—2,871 km; France—2,142 km; and Germany—1,475 km (Mohanty 2019). Huge investments in HSR and public transit networks have enabled China to drive growth through cities. In their studies of HSR in China, Salzberg et al. (2013) found the presence of WEBs of a significant scale. These benefits of larger and better-connected markets accrue to individuals and businesses even when they do not travel. Transport economics suggest that when the wider economic impacts of transportation projects on land development and use, mobility, economic growth, environmental conservation, social inclusion and resource generation are combined, HSR can be justified based on social benefit-cost analysis. It will save time and money, reduce pollution, promote energy security, support technology clusters, expand tourism, revitalize derelict areas and enhance the competitiveness of regions. It will enable cities to harness the external economies of density, diversity and networking and benefit from decongestion. It will also spur economic development in the second-tier tiers cities and rural growth centres along the rail routes. Further, HSR will lead to unified labour markets, offering opportunities to urban and rural workers to choose from a wider set of employers and vice versa.

Grid of Arterial Road Networks

Shlomo Angel presents four simple ways that cities in developing countries could expand their areas to meet population growth in the future. The first step is to project population and the land area needed. The second is to secure new municipal boundaries that include the feasible areas for urban expansion. The third step is to acquire the right of way for a grid of arterial roads in the expansion area, connecting the city's existing arterial roads network. Arterial roads are those which carry trunk infrastructure lines like water and sewer mains, storm water drains, telecommunication networks, etc. and also cater to PT services. Lastly, cities should acquire the land for public open spaces in the expansion area in advance before development occurs. Angel suggests that the arterial roads be designed with about 30 m width to support designated bus lane, bike path and median apart from regular traffic. Such roads may be located about 1 km apart to ensure that no individual lives at more than 10–15 min of walking distance from public and private transportation services that will make use of the arterial roads (Angel 2012).

Angel's approach enables cities to add infrastructure inexpensively on a 'just-in-time' basis as their urban footprint expands. It does not rely on top-down master plan schemes that make predetermined prescriptions about land use, density and FSI. The model is non-intrusive as land development between the arterial roads is market-driven, thereby producing structural and spatial diversities and contributing to the urban vitality. Apart from arterial roads, land needed for radial roads and future MRT and HSR networks may also be reserved to promote TOD in a phased manner. Strong incentives may be put in place to encourage development near transit corridors and nodes. Land for such projects may be procured, wherever possible, through TPS as in Gujarat. The 76 km-long Sardar Patel Ring Road developed by the Ahmedabad Urban Development Authority (AUDA) with land secured free of cost through TPS presents an excellent initiative for wider replication.

Transit-oriented Development

TOD is rooted in the planning movements of 'new urbanism' and 'smart growth' from the 1980s. The movements advocated the restructuring of urban planning to concentrate housing, jobs, shopping and other activities around transit stations. TOD aims at (a) enabling more people to live close to transit services and use the same, (b) providing a rich mix of uses within walking distance of a transit station, (c) providing pedestrian facilities and multi-modal connectivity to move people, not vehicles, (d) making transit station a gateway to the community and (d) revising city planning regulations to encourage high FSI and ground coverage along major transit corridors and around transit nodes. The most widely used tool to promote TOD and PT-using communities is zoning. It aims at channelizing development to transit nodes and corridors by increasing density, FSI and land use incentives. Policies to intensify development in and around transit stations with workplaces, retail outlets and high-density low- and middle-class housing are necessary to make TOD succeed. Under Greater Copenhagen's 'finger plan', developments are required to be concentrated along railway corridors and radial expressways. Large office buildings are required to be located within 600 m of train stations.

Curitiba in Brazil has successfully implemented TOD, integrating transportation, land use and urban design. From the 1970s, the city has executed a linear growth strategy along a series of structural axes. Each axis includes a 'trinary' road system comprising three parallel roadways, located a block apart. The structural axes constitute the first level in a hierarchy of an integrated road system. The central lane of the central road is exclusively dedicated to high-capacity express busway. The two lateral roads cater to through traffic while providing access to adjacent development. In the land parcels situated within one block from a structural axis, FSI was increased to 6, permitting buildings that could reach a volume of construction six times the plot area, at gross population densities up to 600 inhabitants per hectare. FSI permitted along other routes served by PT was fixed at 4. Curitiba's master plan provided for decreasing FSI as distance from PT network increased. Owners of properties which could not be developed because of zoning restrictions were allowed to sell a standard FSI by way of TDR to developers who could use the same for high-density construction along the structural axes.

Considerations of economic efficiency, social equity, environmental sustainability and financial viability make a strong case for cities in developing countries to adopt PT–led and transit-oriented urban development as a core principle of spatial planning. India's NUTP, 2014, argues the case for TOD as follows:

> High density urban growth offers the opportunity for trip lengths to be short. It promotes a high level of accessibility for Non-motorized Transport (NMT). It fosters successful, financially viable PT, and enables cities to have low levels of energy use per person in UT. The Government of India would encourage Transit Oriented Development (TOD) with increased FAR along transit corridors with high density of population...

NUTP, 2014, recognizes the organic link between transportation and land use planning in promoting TOD. It advocates that both should be undertaken together to serve the entire population and yet minimize the travel needs. It calls for integrated plans to channel future growth around a pre-planned regional transport network rather than developing the same after uncontrolled sprawl occurs. Indian cities such as Indore, Ahmedabad, Pimpri-Chinchwad, Bengaluru and Mumbai have embarked on TOD. The Delhi MRTS Line 3 was extended to Dwarka subcity, planned by the DDA, over 5,500 ha in 29 sectors to house one million residents. DDA entered into an agreement with DMRC for extending Line 3 by 6.5 km to connect Dwarka to South Delhi. Under this agreement, DDA, apart from giving free land, provided ₹750 crore to DMRC towards the cost of construction and rolling stock and also met the cost of rehabilitation of project-affected families. The MRTS Line 3 has significantly reduced the commuting time from Dwarka to Central Secretariat in New Delhi.

TOD requires up-front investment in transit networks in phases and development of transit nodes and corridors with high-density, non-residential space and low- and middle-income housing. It also calls for flexible zoning to promote density and mixed land uses in transit nodes and facilitate transit ridership to make the networks financially viable. TOD also warrants supporting policies such as development of feeder transport for last mile connectivity, motor vehicle and fuel taxation to discourage the use of personalized vehicles and subsidy to promote public transit use. TOD presents a unique opportunity to developing countries like India to make urbanization inclusive by connecting the poor and LIG to housing and employment opportunities. Further, it has a significant potential to reduce congestion and pollution, promote conservation and make value increment financing of transit investments feasible. TOD can act as a key instrument of SLM when developmental, regulatory and fiscal instruments are combined as part of holistic strategy to planned urban development.

Transport–Land Use Integration

Transport–land use integration is perhaps the single most important tool available to policymakers and planners in developing countries to promote sustainable cities. Transport and land use have symbiotic relationships. Institution and change of land use and density lead to changes in demand for transportation. Major transportation investments such as highways, BRT, LRT, MRT and HSR also call for changes in land use and development intensity to make them viable. A well-planned public transit system with higher commercial and residential densities on transit nodes and corridors and mixed land uses facilitates multi-modal travel: walking, bicycle, PT and automobile. Locations with good accessibility also have higher chance of being developed with higher density than remote locations. However, the master planning model neglects PT by according primacy to land use based on a myopic view.

The American planning literature refers to 'land use–transport feedback cycle' in recognition that trip and location decisions co-determine each other. This cycle is presented as follows:

1. Distribution of land uses determines the location of human activities such as living, working, shopping, education and leisure.
2. Geographic distribution of human activities calls for trips in the transport system to overcome the physical distance between activity locations.
3. Distribution of infrastructure in the transport system creates opportunities for spatial interactions measured by accessibility.
4. Differential accessibility co-determines location decisions and results in changes in land use.

The two-way relationship between transport and land use suggests that the land use impacts envisaged by the master plans cannot be achieved without integrating transportation and land use. However, it is difficult to isolate the pure effects of transport on land use as the impacts on land development are reaped in the medium or long run and through multiple markets: land, labour, transport, goods and services, etc. The following factors were found to contribute to developments around new public transit nodes in North American and European cities: benefits of accessibility to economic agents, overall growth scenario and demand for development in the region, relative ease of land assembly around transit nodes, presence of complementary land use policies such as rezoning and density bonus and extent to which a transit node is integrated with surrounding developments and the urban fabric (Mohanty 2019; Salon and Shewmake 2011).

In order for a transit project to generate the largest beneficial impact from land use, the transit authority and the local government must work in coordination. The transport system needs to be implemented according to a predetermined schedule to maximize gains. The local government must be in a position to use zoning and FSI regulations to support transit ridership. It must also have the legal tools to capture unearned increments to landowners due to execution of transit project and regulatory interventions. Integrated transportation-land use planning can also be more effective if they combine economic instruments such as LVT, benefit taxation, CC and VCF with developmental and regulatory tools. instruments. Together, they promote density, accessibility, affordability, mobility and sustainable land use, while preventing sprawl. As the benefits of transport–land use integration capitalize into land values, VCF is a fair and efficient method to mobilize unearned increments to land. If a transportation project passes the social benefit cost test, the rise in land values in the project impact area is expected to exceed its cost. Therefore, the project cost can be covered by reclaiming a part of the uplift in land values, leaving the rest to landowners as net windfall. VCF offers a significant opportunity to cities to leverage resources to finance UT.

Strategic Densification of Cities

Many urban economic activities do not require land per se, but floor space built upon it. Demand for urban land uses, barring conservation and transportation, is essentially a 'derived' demand for built space. Density and FSI are key parameters in urban planning to make floor space available for various uses. While density is an area-wide instrument, FSI is a plot-level control. Density captures the intensity of development, proxied by population or employment per unit of land. It is a key instrument to attain SDGs as a denser city, *ceteris paribus*, obviates the necessity of indiscriminatingly expanding the city boundaries, encroaching agricultural land, reducing conservation areas and increasing energy consumption. Density also enables the cost-effective provision of local public goods by facilitating exploitation of scale economies. Effective management of density and FSI calls for proactive investment in PT networks.

Density enables the substitution of capital for costly land in constructing floor space. *Ceteris paribus*, the higher the FSI, the larger will be the buildable space over a plot. However, this could lead to greater pressure on infrastructure. Higher FSI in nodes with growth potential catalyses agglomeration and networking economies and enables cities to function as efficient labour markets. Planning regulations around the world, thus, prescribe very high FSI in city centre, moderately high FSI in subcentres and very low FSI in areas far away from CBD. Urban economics also suggest that density, land rent, land value and housing price decline as distance from CBD increases. However, while land values and housing prices in central areas of Indian cities are exorbitant, restrictive density and FSI regulations prevent more floor space being built up. FSI in Indian cities is very low, for example, 1.2–3.5 in Delhi and 1.5 in Chennai. In Mumbai, FSI is 1.33 for the island city; it is 1.00 in suburbs subject to 0.33 additional FSI as incentive on payment and fulfilling certain conditions. Internationally, FSI is seen to increase during the course of development. However, in Mumbai, FSI has decreased from 4.5 in 1964 to 1–1.33, discouraging redevelopment of dilapidated buildings.

Downtowns in cities globally have very high FSI: Denver—17; Los Angeles—13; Chicago—12; San Francisco—9; Vancouver—9; Tokyo—20; Singapore—12–25; Hong Kong—12; Shanghai—8; and Bangkok—8. FSI of 15 in financial district of Manhattan and 10 along main avenues in NYC has been successfully superimposed on the 'grid plan' from 18th century. In Singapore, FSI of 12–25 in CBD is accompanied by a radioconcentric transit system with an extensive network of feeder bus routes. In Seoul, FSI of 10 in CBD and 8 in subcentres is supported by the third longest MRT network in the world. Sao Paulo follows a policy of FSI of 1 as a right to the landowner, but additional FSI up to 5 is permitted through a system of incentive zoning and purchasable development rights that take into account the accessibility to PT (Mohanty 2014, 2019).

Indian cities have not only low but also uniform FSI over large stretches. Globally, high FSI and public transit accessibility go together. However, master planning in India in the past did not integrate accessibility, density and land use. Accordingly, cities have not developed centres of agglomeration linked to subcentres based on a hub and spoke pattern of spatial organization. Ironically, low FSI across the city affects low- and middle-income households more adversely than other groups, apart from reducing productivity of the non-residential sector. For a given floor space consumption and population, a low FSI increases the demand for more land, warranting new infrastructure. In the absence of finance to develop infrastructure, the supply of new urban land and floor space falls short of the natural demand generated by increased urban income, population and economic activity. Further, restriction on building heights leads to deadweight welfare losses by increasing commuting costs. There is a need to liberalize FSI in Indian cities. Hyderabad presents a pioneering example in this regard.

Liberalization of Floor Space Index: Hyderabad

Hyderabad has substantially increased FSI and saleable built-up area for all types of properties by changing the basis on which built-up area is controlled, linking FSI to a formula and payment of impact fee. The formula is based on a combination of (a) width of abutting road, (b) building setbacks and (c) special controls in designated areas for fire safety, air traffic clearance or other local reasons. The liberalization of FSI is most remarkable for large plots on wide streets; properties along roads with 30 m width or more have no applicable building height restriction provided they adhere to the prescribed setbacks. Properties along roads with width ranging from 24 m to 30 m can have building height ranging from 30 m to 50 m depending on setbacks, which increase with height. The planning regulations in Hyderabad also provide for 'skyscraper zones' with minimum height of building permissible at 36 m (12 floors), minimum plot size at 4,000 m^2 and minimum width of approach road at 24 m. They stipulate city-level infrastructure impact fee levy for all buildings with height above 15 m to raise resources for area and city-wide infrastructure. The scales of impact fees differ between buildings depending on use such as residential, commercial, institutional and office and height of building. Additional building height is permitted subject to larger setbacks around the building.

While FSI regulations under master plans in India impose flat area-wide restrictions on FSI, Hyderabad has broken a new ground by allowing for a more dynamic determination of FSI based on carrying capacity of abutting road and plot size. Though the initiative is criticized by some planners as favouring new areas at the cost of inner-city locations, its contribution lies in linking FSI objectively to accessibility parameters and impact fee. The formula-based approach to FSI has also freed it from the discretions of planners. It recognizes that keeping FSI rigid in the face of large investments in infrastructure and economic growth is inefficient. The liberalization of FSI in Hyderabad has kept land and housing prices in the metropolitan area within reasonable limits unlike many other metropolitan cities in India.

New Towns on Growth Corridors

Even with strategic densification of city centres and subcentres, the existing cities in India would not be able to accommodate the huge numbers to be added due to urbanization. Instead of indiscriminately extending urban boundaries, it is desirable to develop ring towns, satellite towns and rural growth centres on TOD principles based on social benefit-cost analysis. They may be connected to metropolitan cities with MRT, HSR, dedicated BRT and other networks with a commuting time of about 1 h. India's ambitious programme of national highways may finance bypasses and ring roads to decongest metropolitan cities and facilitate the emergence of economic growth hubs. Such projects can be eminent candidates for public-private-partnerships (PPPs) in view of their potential to generate agglomeration externalities. The TOD model may also be extended to 'twin cities' such as Bengaluru and Mysore, Ahmedabad and Gandhinagar, Delhi and major cities in the NCR, etc. by linking them with HSR/MRT and enabling the connected cities benefit from mutually reinforcing agglomeration economies. South Korea has successfully implemented regional planning to decongest Seoul through the creation of five new towns—Bundang, Ilsan, Pyeongchon-dong, Jeong-dong and Sanbon-dong. These are strategically located within 20–25 km radius from CBD of Seoul and connected to it by expressways and rail transit. Started in the mid-1990s, the towns were developed within 5 years, catering to about 3 million new residents.

India is in the midst of a highway revolution. Planned expansion of highway networks such as the Golden Quadrilateral, North-South and East-West and other corridors present opportunities to develop new towns at vantage transportation hubs linked to major cities. The Delhi-Mumbai Industrial Corridor (DMIC) aims at the establishment of global manufacturing and commercial hubs with self-contained, state-of-the-art townships equipped with world-class infrastructure facilities. Twenty-four investment nodes spanned over 6 states are identified—11 investment regions (IRs), each spreading over about 200 km², and 13 industrial areas (IAs), each covering about 100 km². Both employment location and residential township require to be planned together, with adequate space for LIG who are bound to migrate to the cities spurred by industrialization. Special Economic Zones (SEZs) may be developed as integrated townships to avoid slums around them in the future. While the existing metropolitan cities in developing countries like India exhibit agglomeration economies, new cities would be able to generate agglomeration momentum only when the incentives to attract economic growth activities are strong. In this regard, countries provide a range of zoning and fiscal dispensations to invite private entrepreneurs and investment to cities.

Land for Affordable Housing

A study by the Ministry of Housing and Urban Affairs (MoHUA), GoI estimates the urban housing shortage in the country in 2012 at 18.78 million. More than 95 per cent of this pertains to economically weaker sections (EWS) and LIG. The figure comprises homeless and people living in congested, obsolescent and non-serviceable *kutcha* houses. Census 2011 also revealed that 3 per cent of the households have no homes; nearly 80 per cent of housing shortage owes to congestion; and another 12 per cent is due to obsolescence. Paradoxically, 10.1 per cent of the houses in India remained vacant in 2011, compared to 9 per cent in 2001. Such vacant houses presumably belong to HIG, including non-resident Indians. Outdated rent control laws discourage homeowners from renting their houses out due to difficulty in getting the tenants evicted when needed and the fear of being dragged into litigation. Perverse incentive to build houses for others, apart from own use, is a major cause of rental housing shortage in cities. The rural migrants who come to cities in search of work need 'rental', not 'ownership' housing. The lack of availability of litigation-free, serviced land for housing LIGs at appropriate locations is a major factor behind the affordable housing problem in Indian cities.

Location in a central place with PT connectivity provides the poor access to employment opportunities. However, these sections, accounting for a quarter of India's urban population, are forced to take shelter in slums, leading to sprawl. Slums arise due to failure of both land market and planning system. Some directions to make land and floor space available to the urban poor in developing countries are (a) providing tenure security and basic services to slumdwellers as well as 'no eviction guarantee', (b) promoting IZ in urban expansion areas as in TPS, reserving up to 10 per cent of the total land for weaker sections, (c) re-engineering cities with public transit and TOD to locate low- and middle-income housing in high-density complexes around transit nodes and (d) prescribing IH for service personnel in all individual houses and apartments beyond a particular size. Ahmedabad metropolitan DP has demarcated 1 km area around the 76-km long Sardar Patel ring road as R-AH zone, permitting FSI of 4 for the construction of residential units of 36–80 m² of built-up area. Such inclusive initiative needs to be replicated throughout India.

Land Assembly and Development

Making serviced land, floor space and public facilities available in tune with the demands of economic growth and urbanization is a central issue in developing countries. It calls for land assembly by private developers and public authorities—procuring, consolidating, developing and subdividing land; servicing it with internal and external infrastructure; renewing dilapidated areas; and generating floor space. Urban planners in India in the past have favoured large-scale compulsory acquisition of land to implement master plan proposals. However, the procedural requirements under the new LA Law, 2013, make it difficult to acquire land for implementing master plans. They suggest exploring alternative models of land assembly such as LPS and TPS.

Delhi presents a prominent example of compulsory acquisition of land for planned urban development. The responsibility of land development in Delhi is entrusted to DDA under the DDA Act,

1957. The Land and Building Department of the GNCTD acquires land for DDA, which then undertakes land development for various purposes. DDA also allocates land to private developers for construction of houses. However, over the years, DDA has failed to fulfil the bourgeoning demand for land and housing in Delhi. Only an average of 777 ha of land was acquired annually instead of 1,372 ha targeted over the period 1962–1981. During 1981–2001, against a planned acquisition of 24,000 ha, only 9,507 ha were acquired by 2001—39.6 per cent of the target. Around 14,479 ha of land was proposed to be developed during the plan period 1961–1981. However, by 1984, the land actually developed for residential purpose was only 7,316 ha. In the various subcities envisaged under MPD-2001, of the total 17,493 ha proposed to be developed, only 8,388 ha (48%) of serviced land were made available by 2001 (Centre for Civil Society 2009, 147).

The model of large-scale public acquisition of land to achieve the planners' vision of a modernist city has not worked in Delhi or any other city in India. This is largely due the strong resistance by farmers following gross under-payment of compensation and deprivation of the huge benefits of urban development on their land. Many LA proceedings have been stuck in courts for years. Nevertheless, the model of compulsory acquisition of land for planned urban development is going to be difficult in view of the elaborate requirements prescribed under the new LA Act, 2013, as may be seen from the following:

Notification for social impact assessment (SIA) study—notification for commencement of consultation and of SIA study and publishing the same as per prescribed procedures.
Conduct of SIA—completion of SIA study within 6 months from the date of commencement and making it available to the public.
Appraisal by expert committee—evaluation of SIA report by an independent multidisciplinary expert group, which would make recommendations within 2 months from the date of its constitution.
Preliminary notification for LA and R&R: —public notification about the details of the land as per prescribed procedure.
Food security—no irrigated multi-cropped land to be acquired; such land may be acquired only in exceptional circumstances, as a demonstrable last resort.

Hearing of objections—objection to the competent authority in writing within 60 days from the notification.

Preparation of R&R scheme—census in the affected area and preparation of draft R&R scheme, including particulars of R&R entitlements of each landowner and landless persons whose livelihoods are primarily dependent on the lands.

Publication of declaration—declaration of the land under the act along with the summary of the R&R scheme; it should be published as per prescribed procedures.

LA award—LA award in the prescribed form after an enquiry into and disposal of objections, if any, raised.

R&R award—R&R award to each affected family.

Compensation—compensation for land acquired; it should be a multiple of the market value by a factor of at least one to two times. Solatium will be paid at 100 per cent of the compensation, including market value and value of assets.

Land Pooling Scheme

South Korea has used 'land readjustment' and Taiwan 'land consolidation' successfully to undertake land assembly for planned urban development through land pooling, while capturing a part of the resultant land value increase to finance development cost. Under these techniques, once an area is selected for development, the municipality declares it as a special area under law as the unit for physical planning. A site plan is prepared, and about one-third of the area is set aside for streets, parks, schools and other public uses. The cost of civic infrastructure and services like water supply, sewerage, drainage, roads, electricity, etc. is then estimated. The next step is to project the likely market value of improved sites and estimate the ratio of capital costs needed by infrastructure to such market value. This gives the percentage of area meant for residential and commercial development that has to be sold to meet the infrastructure costs. The extent of the area so determined is called the 'cost equivalent area'. In most cases, this turns out to be nearly 10 per cent of the total area. About 43 per cent of the area under a LPS is required to support a self-financed planned project. Experience of South Korea and Taiwan reveals that even if landowners lost up to 50 per cent of the area they held, the value of improved sites exceeded that of the original holdings by many times. In South Korea, the 'cost equivalent area' sites are auctioned through a competitive bidding process.

In Gujarat, TPS is based on the concept of land pooling adopted by land readjustment and land consolidation schemes. TPS has been the predominant mechanism in the state to undertake integrated urban development over more than half a century. Urban planning in Gujarat is a two-step process outlined under the GTPUDA, 1976, and its rules. The first step is to prepare a DP for a designated area. The second step is to prepare TPS. DP presents a broad vision for the city's development; it is a dynamic document that is detailed gradually. The new areas to be opened up for development are clearly marked and divided into smaller areas of about 100–200 ha, typically involving 100–250 landowners. Each such area is called TPS. The scheme provides for laying out or relaying out land, either vacant or already built upon, allocating land areas for roads, water supply, drainage, sewerage, street lighting, open spaces, gardens, green belts, recreation grounds, schools, markets, etc., and undertaking development. It also caters to preservation of objects of historical or national interest and of natural beauty.

TPS involves the following steps: topographical survey of the TPS area, establishment of ownership details of each land parcel, reconciling survey and landownership records to prepare a base map, defining the boundary of the area, marking original plots on the base map, tabulating ownership details and plot size, laying out roads, carving out plots for amenities, tabulating deduction and final plot size, delineating final plot, working out infrastructure costs and betterment charges, conducting landowners' meeting, modifying draft TPS and obtaining approval by state government. Each landowner gets back proportionately reduced developed land, contributing for reservations and land sale component to meet infrastructure costs. Every TPS is legally required to reserve land to the extent of nearly 10 per cent of total area for SEWs. The allotment of land from the scheme area is made as per the following general standards: 15 per cent for roads; 5 per cent for parks, playgrounds, gardens and open spaces; 5 per cent for social infrastructure such as schools, dispensary, fire brigade and public utilities; and 15 per cent for sale by the appropriate authority to meet the cost of infrastructure in the scheme area.

TPS offers the following advantages: (a) the planning process has all the freedom that a new town offers without being burdened with LA, associated costs and court litigation; (b) the reduction in land area, costs and returns of the scheme are spread across all landowners; (c) inclusive development occurs with sizable land being made available for the weaker sections through the planning system itself; and (d) the local authority is enabled to levy betterment charges on landowners in proportion to land value increment due to planning and infrastructure improvements. TPS is an effective alternative to compulsory acquisition of land, as it is more beneficial to landowners and also more equitable. It promotes planned urban expansion without strains on the public exchequer. A shining example of land pooling by farmers as shareholders is provided by Magarpatta city in Pune, Maharashtra.

Farmers as Shareholders

Magarpatta city presents an innovative example of landowners-farmers as shareholders in development, creating a world-class, self-contained township based on 'walk to work, walk to school' principle. This township, spread over 430 acres, is located in the outskirts of Pune. The land has been part of Pune Municipal Corporation since 1960, and it falls under agricultural zone. A community of 120 farmers organized themselves and set up the Magarpatta Township Development and Construction Company. This company prepared the Magarpatta city plan and approached the Government of Maharashtra with an integrated township proposal under the Maharashtra Regional and Town Planning Act, 1966. After receiving approval for the project and change of land use, the township was started in 1994 and developed over 10 years. Today, with environment-friendly development, high-quality urban services, excellent modern facilities for education and health and state-of-the-art workplaces, Magarpatta city is home to over 35,000 residents and a working population of 65,000.

The farmers in Magarpatta agreed to use money from land only for asset creation, thereby providing a safety net for the next generation. They used a part of the value of their land to buy flats and shops in the township, thereby securing lease rentals. Funding for new business ventures came from banks. Over 250 entrepreneurs in non-agricultural ventures have, thus, emerged from the farming community. These first-generation entrepreneurs account for a gross annual turnover of ₹150–200 crore. The business strategy of the company ensured that a farmer with 1 acre of land at the time of its formation today earns a dividend of about ₹15–16 lakh per year. Social integration of the farming community with residents of Magarpatta township was carefully planned. Allocation of flats to the farmers was done in such a way that they were located in different parts of the township. Today, it is difficult to differentiate the farmer community from other residents.

Magarpatta city provides an excellent case of township development by the private sector facilitated by government—without arduous LA and at no cost to public authorities, while generating sizable tax increments to central, state and local governments. The innovative features of the model are (a) landowners, as shareholders in township development, are entitled to profit-sharing; (b) they are also entitled to receive a percentage of land sale proceeds in proportion to their land holdings, thereby benefiting from escalating land prices; (c) no landowner is displaced from his ancestral land; instead, land is used to empower him; and (d) landowners have the opportunity to turn into entrepreneurs, thereby creating employment for themselves and others. One limitation of the Magarpatta township development model is that it did not provide for reservation for the weaker sections as in TPS in Gujarat.

Road Widening Scheme: Hyderabad

Countries around the world resort to incentive zoning through instruments such as premium FSI, density bonus and 'up-zoning' aimed at a more favourable land use to rejuvenate derelict areas. Hyderabad has been implementing a similar scheme to widen master plan roads since the 1980s with a remarkable success. By March 2014, the city widened 307 roads with 260 km of length, securing land estimated at ₹1,200 crore from landowners free of cost under the novel 'road widening scheme'. The state government empowered the city municipal corporation with relaxation of zoning regulation and grant of concessional FSI to secure land for widening master plan roads. The corporation was assigned the authority to relax FSI up to an extent of 1.0, grant concession in setbacks and ground coverage and permit conversion of land remaining after the extent surrendered free of cost to commercial use. The landowner is also entitled to TDR to be used in the remaining land or anywhere within the city; allowed to construct an extra floor with an equivalent built area for the extent surrendered subject to public safety requirements; or permitted to avail concessions in front, side and rear setbacks, relaxation of height and permission for construction of a cellar floor keeping in view its feasibility on ground. The road widening scheme has been popular with landowners in Hyderabad as they perceive that the benefits are much more than the foregone cost of land surrendered for road widening.

Addressing Public Land Management

Central, state and local governments in India own large extents of high value lands, lying unused or underused. Such lands thwart contiguous area development, while a huge surplus value remains locked and unavailable for economic growth and affordable housing. Thirteen major Port Trusts in India hold about 100,000 ha of land; the Airport Authority of India—20,400 ha; Ministry of Defence—283,000 ha; Indian Railways—43,000 ha; and Wakf Board—240,000 ha. The Mumbai Port Trust holds one-sixth of the island city's land, while only 16 per cent of the land is required for port-related activities. Data on lands held by state and local governments are not available. However, they also keep sizable extents of land unused and underused. Government departments and undertakings, operating in silos, are often reluctant to develop the lands with them to avoid parting with the surplus generated to the consolidated fund of government for general purpose expenditures.

The management of land with public authorities in India suffers from multiple problems. Land-owning authorities do not maintain land inventories and lease records properly. While encroachments on public lands have been rampant, the enforcement machinery with authorities is not equipped to protect such lands, which are often embroiled in social sensitivities and political controversies. Lack of transparency regarding lease of public land, conditions of lease, fixation of and collection of lease rent, enforcement of lease conditions and revision of lease have often led to suspicious, below-market rate deals on rent-seeking consideration. Such deals lead to prolonged court disputes and non-payment of lease rents over long periods. They hinder realization of the economic value of land. Sometimes, collusive encroachments and litigations occur on prime government lands. Public land governance in developing countries like India does not recognize land as a valuable asset. Government officials also lack skills and incentives to manage public lands or develop them on the 'highest and best use' principle by resorting to PPPs. Many expert committees in the past have suggested entrusting the management of public land in India, including monetization of surplus land, with government departments by professionally managed, specialized and centralized public land development agencies that work as real estate management companies. The suggestions have not been implemented.

Lessons for Urbanization Strategy

SLM is a fundamental tool to promote sustainable development. It calls for urban development approach much broader than envisaged under the master planning paradigm. SLM recognizes that spatio-economic outcomes in a city region depend on dynamic interplay between market forces, externalities and public policies. In particular, land, transport, labour and goods markets; agglomeration, networking and knowledge externalities; and spatial planning, infrastructure development and economic growth policies of governments interact. Such interactions lead to 'organized complexities' of cities, making them dynamic. Thus, a top-down and static master planning model is ill-suited to address the concerns of land market failure. Further, a Geddes-type survey-analysis-plan methodology to project economic activities and their land use requirements, 20–25 years ahead is fraught with methodological problems. The economics of urban land and cities in developing countries are too dynamic and complex to be captured by projections based on extrapolation of trends. A command and control approach does not leave much scope to manage transport, land use, density, externalities and local economic development with SLM tools. Transport-led urban planning is more appropriate for developing countries to promote SLM and sustainable development than land use–led master planning.

Unlike master planning, SLM considers land in all its dimensions, including horizontal, vertical, access to infrastructure and links to externalities. It aims at harnessing the synergy between accessibility, affordability, land use, development, density, land value, housing price and other characteristics of locations, connectivity infrastructure and economic growth drivers. SLM envisages integrating sustainability considerations into land use, transport and economic development planning, land and development regulations, land assembly and infrastructure development, transport-density-land use integration and public land management. It focuses on making serviced land and floor space available for economic growth and urbanization, while promoting social inclusion and mitigating adverse impacts on eco-carrying capacity, agricultural productivity, energy security and climate change. SLM calls for PT–led and transit-oriented development, transport–land use integration and mixed-use zoning. TOD warrants proactive investments in BRT, MRT, HSR and grids of arterial and radial roads in anticipation of growth. It also calls for channelizing high-density low- and middle-income housing and employment-generating non-residential developments to transit nodes and corridors.

PT is a unique instrument for SLM in that it promotes density and agglomeration economies, while mitigating congestion diseconomies and avoiding sprawl. It expands labour markets, generates WEBs, promotes competition, catalyses growth and facilitates conservation. It also enables the poor and LIG to access affordable housing and employment opportunities in the new knowledge economy. Further, it makes VCF of infrastructure feasible. Historically, transport has been the single most important factor in the take-off of nations and rise of great cities. Empirical studies also document WEBs of major PT investments, which are not captured by conventional social cost-benefit analysis. The London Cross Rail provides a recent example. The mega programme is expected to lead to huge benefits to the UK economy by improving transport links, promoting house building, creating business opportunities and jobs and supporting wider regeneration. There are strong reasons to suggest that MRT and HSR will lead to such results in India—through direct, indirect and induced impacts. However, investments in transit and TOD must be combined with other instruments to promote financial viability. Government action is also necessary to discourage developments that promote use of personalized automobiles. Complementary instruments to facilitate TOD include 'up-zoning' and 'density bonus', vehicles and motor fuel taxes, CC and a graduated tax on vacant land, with tax rate increasing depending on the period during which land is held idle. Enhanced connectivity between cities, sub-urban nodes, rural growth centres and new towns with agglomeration potential will expand labour markets, address congestion in central areas and facilitate inclusive growth.

The master planning approach, which aims to attain socio-economic objectives through a predetermined urban form is mechanical. Being rigid, it is not suitable for internalizing the externalities arising from dynamic interactions in the spatial economy. Neglecting plan financing, master plans also fail to address land market failure due to under-provision of public goods and merit goods. Ironically, land use–led master plans have seriously curtailed the degrees of freedom with firms, households and developers in deciding economic activity location and land use. Comprehensive planning to attain development objectives by enforcing land use controls at regional, city, zonal, local and plot levels may thus be an exercise in futility. Accordingly, a two-tier planning structure is considered adequate to make market forces and public policies complement and supplement. The first tier envisages a strategic or structural plan at the regional level, focused on conservation and trunk infrastructure development in a phased manner. The second tier envisages TPS or area development schemes at local level, focused on combining accessibility, density, land use, development, social inclusion, environmental protection and VCF through urban design. TPS may be executed through the private sector or PPP, incentivized by the government as in the case of Magarpatta city, Pune. Flexibility is necessary in urban planning and design to accommodate the drivers of growth, while addressing the concerns of health, environment, climate change and disaster resilience. The government could even consider OODC and CEPAC type schemes, being implemented in Brazil, to promote densification and LPS.

Transportation-land use integration lies at the core of TOD. However, transportation planning and land use planning in India have been pursued as separate exercises, without exploiting the synergy between the two. Thus, transport, land use, density and development are not integrated while managing externalities. The standard argument by planners for continuing with low FSI in cities is that they lack infrastructure to support density. However, it is not understood why public transit investment, TOD and flexi-zoning instruments cannot be combined under a value creation, capture and recycling strategy to finance public transit. Such a strategy could be linked to debt financing from the market with escrowed revenues from benefit taxes and charges, including LVT, VLT, property tax, motor vehicles and fuel taxes, impact fee, betterment levy, special assessment district, pricing of development rights and dedicated funds from higher levels of government to repay debt. The case for such transfers follows from the logic that income tax and GST are general benefit taxes connected with living, working and shopping in the city (Bahl, Linn and Wetzel 2013). As metropolitan projects like MRT and HSR are likely to lead to significant uplifts in such tax bases, a strong economic case exists for central and state governments to allocate dedicated funds for such projects.

The fact that large metropolitan cities in India are implementing MRT and considering HSR options offers a unique opportunity to pursue TOD along with zoning, density and other subventions to support LPS. The effectiveness of MRT systems in Toronto and Seoul is attributable to an urban strategy that channelled growth into transit nodes and corridors. This was facilitated by zoning changes that permitted higher densities and mixed land uses in designated zones. By increasing land use intensity around transit stations, Singapore has facilitated land development based on the 'highest and best use' principle. Urban policy in Singapore includes subsidization of transit ridership and electronic road pricing (ERP) that directed developments to transit nodes and corridors. In Hong Kong, land policies have promoted compact, high-density townships and property development around transit stations. They have generated substantial revenues to finance mass transit while increasing ridership. In Shanghai, rail is considered as a 'magnet' that attracts new development; it has shaped urban expansion and restructuring through land use changes. The experiences of South Korea and Japan suggest that the larger the city, the more important it is to invest in public transit and to integrate transportation and land use (Mohanty 2019; Suzuki, Cervero and Iuchi 2013; Suzuki et al. 2015).

Apart from neglect of investment in public transit and transport–land use integration, land management in India has been plagued by other factors. The latter include blanket restrictions on conversion of agricultural land to urban uses; outdated rent control laws that discourage rental housing; high stamp duties that adversely affect property transactions; poor land records that make property rights obscure; difficulties in acquisition of land for infrastructure, making land assembly difficult; discretionary changes in land use on rent-seeking considerations; and deficient land, transport and urban governance. As India has to go a long way in urbanization, a national land policy is necessary to address the emerging issues of land markets, especially in metropolitan regions. However, except for a sporadic attempt at the national level through the Urban Land Policy Committee, 1965, the issues of land management have not engaged the attention of policy-makers. The 1965 policy deliberations also reflected the command and control approach to urban planning typical of the pre-liberalization era. India needs to develop land policy and liberalize urban planning, according a central role to SLM.

The current state of suboptimal urban affairs in India is an outcome of seven decades of land use–led planning. It is traced to the lack of empowerment of the 'third tier' and neglect of urban planning, financing and governance. The country needs to develop a national urbanization strategy, backed by land and transport policies with a key role for empowered urban and metropolitan governments. Aimed at re-engineering cities with transit, the strategy needs to focus on implementing SLM through transport-led and transit-oriented development, integrated transport–land use planning, environmental conservation, social inclusion and VCF of infrastructure. India must move from a land use–led to a transport-led and transit-oriented regional and urban planning regime. This strategy must balance densification, infill development, expansion and new township development alternatives. However, Indian cities are ill-equipped to finance public transit, HSR and grids of arterial and radial networks due to their precarious finances. They also lack transportation planners and engineers. The limited transportation planning exercises they undertake are conducted by physical planners, but physical planning in cities suffers from acute shortage of town and country planners. Thus, while reforming land management, India must address the issues of resource mobilization for investment in public transit and institutional and human resource capacities to implement SLM. Transportation-land use-density-development-financing integration will be the key to reconciling the objectives of economic efficiency, social equity, environmental sustainability and financial viability in urban development.

Financing Land Development

Designing a Toolbox of Land-based Instruments

Urban Land as a Resource

Land has been recognized as an ideal resource to finance public infrastructure for long. Some economists and political scientists proclaimed that private ownership of land was a historical mistake. Others contended that as land values arose from 'circumstances', 'progress of society', 'community enterprise' and 'public investment', private appropriation of such values was scandalous. Some scholars favoured nationalization of land, arguing that the public right to appropriate land values depended on the public right to land. Most thinkers, however, advocated a special tax on land—a levy different from that on other factors in tax base. Their views relied on special attributes of land such as permanent nature, inelastic supply, immobility and link to locational externalities and role of spatial planning and infrastructure in land values. In the context of cities, an oft-cited argument is that land values increase due to urban prosperity, contributed by society as a whole. Initially, the debate on urban land taxation focused on impropriety of private property rights, inequities in distribution of landholdings, land as a prime source of unearned income and unearned income as a legitimate object of taxation. Subsequent arguments have highlighted the role of land taxes in implementing city DPs and preventing speculative withdrawal of land from the market.

Economists regard land-based taxes and charges as ideal instruments to finance local public goods, correct externalities and reduce inequalities. These instruments subscribe to efficiency, equity and benefit principles of public finance. Land taxes act against speculative landholding, encourage investment in productive land uses and prevent sprawl. They are progressive; those who own land only are required to pay taxes according to the extent held. Moreover, spatial planning and public investments in infrastructure lead to windfall gains to landowners. It is, thus, fair to make them pay towards the cost of projects and welfare of the society. Land-related instruments implemented internationally can be divided into three groups:

Land-based taxes: Levied under the sovereign powers of the state by urban local governments (ULGs). They include property tax, VLT, real estate transfer tax (RETT), LVT, site value tax (SVT), land value increment tax (LVIT), PGT, DGT, land use conversion tax, etc.

Development of financing tools: These are upfront payments for development of land by private developers with permission from the local authority. Based on 'growth pays', 'polluters pay' and 'exacerbaters pay' principles, these include developer exactions, development charges, impact fees, planning obligations, development contributions, land pooling/TPS, etc.

LVC instruments: These are post-development levies to recoup land value increments arising from community initiative and enterprise in the form of spatial planning, infrastructure development, economic growth, etc. They include LVT, LVIT, VLT, property tax, RETT, sale of developer land, project land and development rights, land monetization, joint development mechanism (JDM), special assessment district, betterment levy, TIF, etc.

Developed countries have extensively used land-based tools to finance public expenditures during their urban transition. Local property tax, levied on the capital value of land and buildings dominated the US public finance till 1933, by which time urbanization surpassed 50 per cent. By the Great Depression of the 1930s, local governments in the United States accounted for over half of the total tax revenues collected by all levels of government (Wallis 2000). However, land-based mechanisms are yet to be exploited by ULGs in India. This is intriguing as landowners benefit far more than they contribute. This chapter delves into theories of land-based revenue instruments and international practices on their implementation (Andelson 2000; Bahl and Linn 1992; Dye and England 2010; George 1879; Mishra 2019b; Mohanty and Mishra 2014; Mohanty 2014, 2016, 2019; Peterson

2009; Prest 1981; Vyas, Vyas and Mishra 2020). The objective is to enable policymakers in developing countries like India to design a toolbox of land-based instruments that are theoretically sound and practically attractive.

Land-Based Financing: Theory

In 'The Wealth of Nations (1776)' Adam Smith argued that after all the proper subjects of taxation are exhausted; if the exigencies of the state still continue to require new taxes, only then can the taxes be imposed on improper ones. He regarded land as a proper subject for taxation, land rent being an unearned income. His reference to landowners runs as follows:

> They are the only one of the three orders whose revenue costs them neither labor nor care, but comes to them, as it were, of its own accord, and independent of any plan or project of their own. That indolence, which is the natural effect of the ease and security of their situation, renders them too often, not only ignorant, but incapable of that application of mind which is necessary in order to foresee and understand the consequences of any public regulation. (Smith 1776, Book 1, Chapter 11, 277)

Smith distinguished between different taxes on landowners: taxes on historic land rents, taxes on current land rents, taxes on produce of land, taxes on buildings and taxes on land transfer. Taxes on buildings were divided into taxes on structures and on ground rents.

Adam Smith was in favour of taxing rents to land vis-à-vis rents to housing to meet the needs of good government:

> Ground rents are still a more proper subject of taxation than the rent of houses. A tax upon ground-rents would not raise the rent of houses. It will fall altogether upon the owner of the ground-rent, who acts always as a monopolist, and exacts the greatest rent which can be got for the use of his ground.

> Both ground-rents and the ordinary rent of land are a species of revenue which the owner, in many cases, enjoys without any care or attention of his own… Ground-rents and the ordinary rent of land, are therefore, perhaps, the species of revenue which can best bear to have a peculiar tax imposed upon them.

> Nothing can be more reasonable than that a fund which owes its existence to the good government of the state should be taxed peculiarly, or should contribute something more than the greater part of other funds, towards the support of that government. (Smith 1976, Book V, Chapter II, Part II, Article 1: Taxes upon the rent of land, 843–44)

Smith's arguments for taxation of land rents ran on the following lines:

1. Efficiency argument: taxes on land rents are neutral in terms of effects on resource allocation.
2. Equity argument: it is fair to tax away surpluses that are more due to extraneous factors than to individual efforts.
3. Benefit principle: people should pay for government actions and services, which benefit them.

In 'On the Principles of Political Economy and Taxation (1817/1951)', David Ricardo considered land as distinct from all other factors of production in view of its fixed supply and unique feature that the whole of the return on land was a surplus. He defined rent as the portion of the produce of earth paid to the landlord for using the original and indestructible powers of the soil. According to Ricardo, rent accrues to landowners, not due to contribution to productive economic activity but because of ownership of land. It stems from differential fertility of land; marginal land does not receive rent. Ricardo did not pay attention to taxation of land rents, while discussing the intensive and extensive margin of cultivation in rural land. He simply argued that a tax on land rents could not be shifted.

The first fully developed arguments for special taxation of urban land emanated from John Stuart Mill (Mill 1848/1909, 817; Prest 1981). Considering land rents as 'created by circumstance', he made the following observations regarding landlords:

> They grow richer, as it were in their sleep, without working, risking or economizing. What claim have they on the general principle of social justice, to this accession of riches? (Mill 1909, 818)

Mill was of the view that private property rights in land were a historical mistake, and the unique features of land made it an appropriate object for special taxation. However, he identified two major impediments to taxing land rents at a high rate:

1. It is difficult to distinguish between the elements of current land values due to private efforts and 'circumstances' or factors connected to the progress of society.
2. The present landowners may not be the beneficiaries of accumulated rent from history. They might have recently purchased land at market value based on expectations regarding future rent.

Mill favoured taxation of unexpected windfalls. This required tracking the present value of land so that all future increments, not attributable to individual effort, could be taxed at a high rate.

In 'Progress and Poverty' (1879), Henry George argued that land values were attributable entirely to 'general forces': natural or social and not to landowners' efforts. He distinguished between returns to labour and capital, which are earned and returns to land, which are unearned. George articulated the view that landlords had no moral right to land values, existing land rents or land value increments resulting from future economic expansion. He argued that as public investments capitalize into land values, the economic rent to land was the most appropriate form of public finance. George also proclaimed that a 100 per cent tax on land rents was the only tax needed to meet public expenditures and such a tax was non-distortionary. This started the 'single tax' movement in the United States. The Henry George theorem (HGT) states that under certain conditions, the aggregate spending on public goods generates adequate land rents to finance such goods (Arnott 2004; Arnott and Stiglitz 1979; George 1879; Stiglitz 1977).

Karl Marx distinguished between differential rent, absolute rent, building lot rent and ground rent (Marx 1909, Chapters XXXVII–XLVII). He regarded land rents as 'surplus value' and argued that landowners had no right to properties or rents derived therefrom. In 'Principles of Economics (1890)', Marshall argued that Ricardo's concept of intensive and extensive margin of cultivation was equally applicable to urban land as it was to agricultural land (Marshall 1890, Book V, Chapter XI). Marshall considered land as distinct from all other factors of production in view of its inelastic supply and the whole return to land being a surplus. He stated that a tax on site value (or public value) was in essence a tax on monopoly profits. Marshall also recognized that additional local public spending due to taxation of public value of land might benefit landowners more than they pay through tax. Pigou distinguished between tax on site value, reflecting general progress of society and tax on windfalls, representing unexpected increments in land. He favoured both the taxes (Pigou 1927).

The case for taxing urban land has figured not only in theory but also in national debates around the world for more than a century (Mohanty 2014, 2016). The Committee on Urban Land Policy, appointed by the then Ministry of Health, GoI observed in their report of 1965:

> While discussing the various measures for tackling the problems in the developed and undeveloped urban land we had stated that unearned increases in urban land and property values being in the nature of 'social surpluses' must be mopped up for the benefit of the society as a whole. After all development in and around a town takes place as a result of Government and municipal development activities and there is no reason why the huge profits should be allowed to be digested by speculators and profiteers. (Ministry of Health 1965)

The United States National Commission on Urban Problems in their report in 1969 stated as follows:

> The owners of the land can go to Hawaii and rest languidly on the beaches or make prolonged safaris into the inmost regions of Africa. They may study Shakespearean literature at Stratford-upon-Avon or Zen Buddhism in Japan or ponder urban problems in Washington. They can go up in space capsules or down a hole in the ground. They will become richer and richer without trial or sweat. For as Dr. Johnson once remarked in another connection here are "riches beyond the dreams of avarice". (1969, 396)

The Vancouver Action Plan of the United Nations Conference on Human Settlements 1976 contained the following:

> The unearned increment resulting from the rise in land values resulting from change in use of land, from public investment decision, or due to

the general growth of the community must be subject to appropriate recapture by public bodies (the community). (United Nations 1976, Recommendation D.3)

Land-Based Financing: Practice

Globally, more than 30 countries have adopted land-based instruments to finance urban public expenditures. They include the United Kingdom, the United States, Canada, Mexico, Jamaica, Argentina, Australia, New Zealand, Denmark, France, Finland, South Africa, Kenya, Tanzania, Zambia, South Korea, Taiwan and Japan. Table 7.1 presents a summary of such instruments (Andelson 2000; Anderson 2009; Dye and England 2010; Hagman and Misczynski 1978; Mohanty 2014, 2016, 2019; UoH-HSMI 2017).

Land-Based Taxes

Land-based taxes aim at raising resources while curbing speculation in land markets and acting against the concentration of land ownership. Key land-based tax instruments adopted globally include the following (see Mohanty 2014, 2016, 2019 for greater details and sources of information/data):

Land Value Tax

Following Henry George's single tax movement, Hyattsville, Maryland became the first city in the United States to enact LVT in 1898. Pennsylvania authorized Pittsburgh and Scranton in 2013 to adopt the 'split-rate' property tax—tax rate on value of land higher than on value of buildings thereon. Pittsburgh implemented LVT from 1913 to 2001. It taxed land at a rate twice that on structures till 1970s. Subsequently, the tax on land was raised to about 5.77 times than that on improvements. The city has, however, rescinded its two-part property tax after nine decades of implementation. This is reportedly due to infrequent and inaccurate assessments and clumsy rate-setting procedures. Other states in the United States also levied LVT. Virginia and Connecticut authorized their municipalities to levy 'split-rate'

Table 7.1 A Toolbox of Land-based Instruments

Sl. No.	Instrument	Description	Region Where It Is Practised
A. Land-based taxes			
1.	LVT	Based on capital value of land or related parameters.	Taiwan, Australia, New Zealand, Denmark, South Africa and the USA.
2.	property tax	Levied on both land and buildings on capital value, rental value or area-based method. The global trend is moving to a capital value base to exploit the ongoing increases in property values.	All over the world. Most Indian cities follow area-based property tax linked to location, plinth area and use of building.
3.	RETT	Paid by buyer/seller (buyer in India) on transfer of property or property rights to another party.	All over the world. In India, the buyer pays the tax. In some states in the USA, both buyer and seller share the tax.
4.	VLT	Tax on capital value of land held idle beyond a specified period—at a rate exceeding that applied to built-up property.	Brazil, Taiwan, South Korea, Andhra Pradesh and Telangana
5.	LVIT	Tax on increase in land value between base and assessment years; levied at local level and differs from capital gains tax (CGT)	Taiwan, Germany, Denmark, South Korea and Latin America
6.	Land Gains Tax (LGT)	Tax on gains in the value of land held beyond a period—paid by seller in addition to CGT on income.	The USA (Vermont State) and Canada (Toronto)
7.	Real Property Gains Tax (RPGT)	Tax on gains from disposal of real property or of interest, options or other rights in or over land and disposal of shares in real property companies.	Malaysia

8.	PGT/DGT	Tax on gains in land/property value due to planning or development permission, including rezoning and change in land use.	The United Kingdom and Ireland
B. Development financing tools			
1.	Developer extractions	Contributions from land developer towards on- and off-site infrastructure necessitated by new development based on negotiations permitted under land use regulations.	The USA, Canada, China (Shanghai), Thailand (Bangkok)
2.	Development charges	Charges collected by local authority under law towards internal (on-site) and external (off-site) infrastructure costs while granting permission for development.	Several countries, including India (notably Haryana Urban Development Authority (HUDA)
3.	Development impact fees (DIF)	Charges on new development to pay for impact or cost of new or expansion of old infrastructure, especially off-site, but are required to serve new development.	The USA, India (Hyderabad city)
4.	Planning obligations	Provision of infrastructure or affordable housing based on negotiation under law between developer and local authority—as conditions of planning permission.	The United Kingdom
5.	Development contributions	Contributions from developers towards infrastructure facilities as conditions of permission for rezoning/development.	Australia
6.	Land pooling/readjustment/TPS	In-kind instrument based on land pooling or sharing with land-owners/farmers as partners in urban expansion, sharing costs and benefits.	South Korea, Taiwan, Japan, Latin America and India (Gujarat)

(Continued)

Table 7.1 (Continued)

Sl. No.	Instrument	Description	Region Where It Is Practised
C. Land value capture (LVC) methods			
1.	Sale of developer land	Developers provide internal and external infrastructure in layouts and recover costs through sale of land or housing.	Developed countries and India
2.	Lease/sale of extra project land/excess condemnation	Lease or sale of land in vicinity of major infrastructure projects like highways and MRT after development; often accompanied by favourable changes in land use zoning and development rights.	Hong Kong, France and Australia
3.	Lease/sale of development rights	Lease or sale of FDI/additional zoning/land use/development rights than normally permitted.	Brazil and India (Karnataka state—Bengaluru Metro)
4.	TDRs	Transfer of development rights from one zone in a city to another subject to fulfilling the requirements set by the master plan.	The USA, Brazil and India (Mumbai, Hyderabad and Bengaluru)
5.	Monetization of land assets	Sale or lease of publicly owned unused or underused land with rezoning and higher FSI that lead to enhanced land values.	India (Mumbai), Egypt (Cairo), Turkey (Istanbul) and South Africa (Cape Town)

6.	JDM	Partnership between public authority and private developer to build real estate on land owned or controlled by the public authority.	Japan
7.	Special assessment district	Local governments set boundaries within which differential taxes are imposed on land and property whose values are expected to increase due to spatial planning and new infrastructure facilities.	The USA, Canada and Europe
8.	Betterment taxes and charges	Levies on increments in land value due to infrastructure development and spatial planning in demarcated areas or city-wide.	Colombia (Bogota), Argentina and India (Hyderabad)
9.	Tax/value increment financing	Public authorities earmark whole or part of the revenue increments arising from land and infrastructure development in a designated area to service the debt incurred for financing.	The USA and Australia

Source: Mohanty (2014, 2016, 2019); UoH-HSMI (2017).

property tax. Hawaii imposed such tax from 1963 to 1977. Every state in the United States, today, has some form of property tax based on capital value and, hence, in part, a tax on land value.

Australia presents a leading case of reliance on LVT to meet public spending needs. The states of South Australia, Tasmania and New South Wales (NSW) resorted to 'SVT' years before the Australian federation was formed in 1901. The federal government enacted the Land Tax Assessment Act in 1910, introducing a levy on land value alone. This was repealed in 1952 to accord additional tax base to states and local bodies. Currently, every state in Australia levies a tax on land value—Queensland under the Land Tax Act, 1915, South Australia under the Land Tax Act of 1936, NSW under the Land Tax Management Act, 1956, and Victoria under the Land Tax Act of 1958. LVT is universal in Queensland and NSW. Sydney is the world's largest city deriving the bulk of revenues from LVT. In New Zealand, LVT was introduced under the Valuation of Land Act, 1896. This law permitted local governments to choose from three alternative property tax systems: (a) capital improved value: total value of land, buildings and other improvements; (b) unimproved value or land value only; and (c) annual rental value. However, since 1985, there has been a noticeable shift towards capital improved value as the base of property tax in New Zealand.

In Europe, Denmark presents a pioneering example of LVT—introduced in 1926 with tax rate on land much higher than on buildings. In Asia, Taiwan presents an outstanding practice of LVT. The country adopted four principles under the Statute of Equalization of Urban Land Rights in 1954: (a) fair assessment of land value; (b) taxation according to declared value; (c) optional public purchase of land at declared value; and (d) public enjoyment of land value increments in the future. In Taiwan, LVT is based on official declared value (ODV), assessed by local authority every 3 years. It is highly progressive, with tax rates ranging from 1 per cent to 5.5 per cent, depending on percentage difference between ODV and a starting accumulative value assigned by the government. In South Africa, municipalities were authorized to choose among three bases of property tax: site rating (unimproved land value), flat rating (capital improved value) and composite rating (value of land and improvements rated differently). By

1920, several South African provinces had adopted LVT; for example, SVT was introduced in the Transvaal in 1916. However, the three-rate system has been abolished in South Africa by the local government: Municipal Property Rates Act of 2004 on administrative grounds.

Property Tax

Property tax is levied on land and buildings: residential and non-residential. The collection from property tax in India is estimated at 0.15 per cent of GDP, which is very low in terms of international comparison (Table 7.2). Some economists argue against non-residential property tax on the ground that it gets 'exported' when jurisdictions are fragmented and creates distortions. Those paying the tax may not be the ones receiving civic benefits. However, this does not pose a major problem in developing countries like India where city jurisdictions are fairly large. Empirical evidence also suggests that agglomeration economies in large cities create sizable benefits to industry and business. Thus, if non-residential property tax is escrowed to finance core infrastructure projects, these entities may gain by much more than they pay through tax.

Table 7.2 Levels of and Trends in Property Tax Revenues for Groups of Countries (as Percentage of GDP)

	1970s	1980s	1990s	2000s
OECD countries	1.24	1.31	1.44	2.12
	(16)	(18)	(16)	(18)
Developing countries	0.42	0.36	0.42	0.60
	(20)	(27)	(23)	(29)
Transitional countries	0.34	0.59	0.54	0.68
	(1)	(4)	(20)	(18)
All	0.77	0.73	0.75	1.04
	(37)	(49)	(59)	(65)

Source: Bahl and Martinez-Vazquez (2008, 40–41)—based International Monetary Fund data.
Note: Figures in parenthesis show the number of countries.

Real Estate Transfer Tax

RETT is an ad valorem tax on value of property or interest therein transferred. In Australia, Japan, Sweden, the United Kingdom and India, it is known as stamp duty. In the United States, the tax is levied by states and cities. In Pennsylvania, the state and cities each adopt a tax rate of 1 per cent. Ontario province, Canada levies land transfer tax (LTT) at 0.5–2 per cent of property value. From 2008, Toronto has introduced an additional municipal land transfer tax (MLTT) applied to purchase price of land with rate similar to that in Ontario. In Indonesia, land and building transfer tax has become a local tax since 2011; Jakarta can levy its own tax up to a maximum of 5 per cent. In India, the tax is imposed by states; only a few southern states share it with local governments. In general, RETT is paid by the buyer. In New York State, the tax is paid by the seller. If the seller does not pay or is exempted, it falls on the buyer.

Vacant Land Tax

Cities like Rio de Janeiro, Bogota, Buenos Aires, Mexico City, Cape Town, Durban, Johannesburg and Manila levy VLT—at a rate higher than that on built-up property. The Constitution of Brazil, under Article 182, empowers municipalities to demand owners of unbuilt, underused, or unused urban land to provide for adequate use thereof as per the master plan, subject to imposition of a graduated VLT—at rates that are progressive in time. In the Philippines, cities can levy 'idle land tax' with a maximum surcharge up to 5 per cent. In Quezon City, the tax rate on idle land abutting a national highway is 3 per cent over and above property tax. For other locations, the surcharge is 1 per cent. In Taiwan, VLT is levied at a much higher rate than LVT. Vacant land is defined as private urban land designated for building use in TPS but not developed within the time period stipulated by local authority. For the purpose of taxation, an improved site on which the value of buildings constructed is less than 10 per cent of the land value is considered as vacant.

Land Value Increment Tax

Imperial Germany started LVIT in 1911, first at local level and then at central level. Taiwan levies LVIT in addition to LVT and VLT. It is a steeply progressive tax based on realized gains from land transaction. It is levied at rates ranging from 40 per cent to 60 per cent, depending on the percentage increase in land value from base year. LVIT constituted 23.03 per cent and LVT, 8.21 per cent of all local taxes collected in Taiwan in 1982. The figures rose to 31.79 per cent and 20.58 per cent, respectively, in 2004. Vermont in the United States introduced LGT in 1973 to discourage speculation in land. Sellers of land are liable to pay LGT in addition to capital gains income tax. LGT is imposed on the gain from sale or exchange of land, if held by the seller for less than 6 years. It is highly progressive; the tax rate varies from 5 per cent for gains of less than 100 per cent on land held between 5 and 6 years to 80 per cent for gains over 200 per cent on land held less than 4 months. Property held longer than 6 years is exempted from LGT. Ontario initiated LGT in 1974 with a tax rate of 20 per cent on realized gains from all real estate.

Planning/Development Gains Tax

PGT/DGT differs from LVIT and CGT in that is based on land value increase due to TPS, planning permissions and infrastructure investments. It differentiates land from other assets liable to LVIT or CGT on the ground that a landowner can fortuitously make huge windfall gains simply due to the decision by public authorities. Several countries around the world adopted PGT, DGT or their variants at some stage or other. They include the United Kingdom, Denmark, Poland, Ireland, etc. Table 7.3 presents the efforts by the United Kingdom for taxation of planning/development gains over the course of a century.

A special land development gain tax called *frigørelsesafgift* is levied in Denmark when agricultural land is brought into urban zone. The rate is about 50 per cent of the increase in land value due to rezoning.

Table 7.3 The United Kingdom: Evolution of Taxation of Planning/ Development Gain (1909–2010)

Measure to Extract Planning/ Development Gains	Description of Levy	Years
Betterment charges (Housing and Town Planning Act of 1909)	50% levy on increases in land values due to TPS.	1909–1932
Betterment charges (Housing and Town Planning Act of 1932)	Not exceeding 75% levy on increases in land values due to TPS.	1932–1947
Development charge (Housing and Town Planning Act of 1947)	100% of tax on increase in land value arising due to planning permission or a levy equal to development value of land.	1947–1953
CGT (Finance Act, 1965, and CGT Regulations, 1967)	CGT at 30% on gains from disposal of capital assets, including land.	1967
Betterment levy (Land Commission Act, 1967)	40% of net development value realized through land transaction or development.	1967–1971
DGT (Finance Act, 1974)	Tax on disposal or notional disposal of land or building with development value.	1974
Development Land Tax (Development Land Tax Act, 1976)	Tax of 80% on development value of land with intention to raise it to 100%; rate reduced to 60% in 1979.	1976–1985
Planning obligation (Town and Country Planning Act, 1990: Section 106)	Contributions from developers negotiated by local authority towards cost of specific public facilities as condition of planning permission.	1990–
Community Infrastructure Levy (Planning Act, 2008, and Community Infrastructure Levy Regulations, 2010)	Hypothecated levy by local authority to fund new infrastructure—in addition to developer contribution—under planning obligations.	2010–

Source: Town and Country Planning and other Acts in the United Kingdom, Mohanty (2014, 2016).

In Poland, a tax at 30 per cent is levied on land value increment if the land is sold within 5 years of change in zoning. Ireland introduced windfall tax in 2009, with a rate of 80 per cent, on profits and gains on the disposal of 'development land' with rezoning. It is applicable to conversion from non-development to development, agricultural to residential, single use to mixed use, etc., and planning permission to undertake development that materially contravenes the area DP. Development land is defined as land (including buildings) disposed of for a price higher than its 'current use value'. Windfall connotes the increase in market value of land due to planning decision.

While PGT/DGT has a huge potential to raise resources for planned development in metropolitan regions, they are grossly neglected in developing countries like India due to their faulty master planning model.

Land Development Charges

These are upfront charges levied by local authority while according permission to developers to undertake land development. These take several forms as follows:

Developer Exactions

Developer exactions require a land developer to contribute to infrastructure necessitated by new development. They aim at protecting public health, safety and welfare of urban residents and mitigating against the negative impacts of urban growth. They assist in protecting the community from increased infrastructure costs through cost sharing with new residents. Exactions allow local governments to pass on a part of the cost of public facilities to the developer when development begins rather than waiting until taxes or charges are levied and collected from new residents. Since the 1920s, private developers in the United States have been required to provide for public use such facilities as streets, sidewalks, water lines, sewers and parks that were within or adjacent to new development. The Standard Planning Enabling Act of 1928 issued by the US Department of Commerce stipulated that as a condition of subdivision approval, developers be required to construct a range of civic facilities. After World War II, the developers' responsibility was expanded to off-site infrastructure that benefited the community as a whole. In the 1950s and the 1960s, the authority of local government to collect 'voluntary' contributions or 'developer exactions' on a case-by-case basis as a negotiating tool was established.

Globally, developer exactions take several forms: dedication—donation of land and/or infrastructure facilities like water supply and roads for public use; tap fees—for connecting new development to existing infrastructure networks such as highways, water and sewer lines; fee in lieu—monetary levy in lieu of installation of facilities like parks and utilities; and linkage fee—towards mitigation of secondary effects of development such as affordable housing, employment, schools, and health care facilities. In Bangkok, commercial centres desiring connectivity to metro stations were required to pay connection charges and contribute towards the cost of connecting bridges. In Shanghai, developers met the costs of construction, maintenance and security arrangements for a pedestrian link between metro station and shopping centre.

Development Charges: Internal and External

State legislations in India provide for levy of development charges on new developments while according approval. These charges include internal (on-site) and external (off-site) costs. HUDA presents a good example of EDC levied on colonizers. Under the Haryana Development and Regulation of Urban Areas Act (HDRUAA), 1975, external development works are defined to include water supply, sewers, drains, necessary provisions for disposal of sewage, sullage and storm water, roads, electrical works, solid waste management and disposal, slaughterhouses, colleges, hospitals, stadium/sports complexes, fire stations, grid substations, etc. and any other work that the Director of Town and Country Planning may specify for execution outside the colony/area for the benefit of the colony/area. The Act mandates the developer to pay 'proportionate development charges' in external development works to be carried out by the government or local authority. The proportion and modality for such payment are determined by the Director of Town and Country Planning. Development authorities for other urban areas in India also collect development charges. In general, they underestimate the costs of external development works, leading to substandard urbanization.

Development Impact Fees

Most states in the United States authorize local governments to levy impact fees as 'one-time' charges to make the developer pay a 'fair share' of the cost of public facilities and services necessitated by new development. These charges are levied as a condition of permission to undertake development. They aim at offsetting the impact of additional development and residents on existing municipal infrastructure. The principal use of impact fees, which distinguishes them from developer exactions, is the financing of 'off-site' capital works to support new development. Impact fees differ from land taxes in that they aim at eliminating the potential negative impacts of additional development on the community. They also differ from user charges in that they are not based on 'pay according to use'. They are levied on 'polluters pay' and 'exacerbaters pay' principles; those who create cost impacts on the society must pay for mitigating the same.

Impact fee legislations in the United States cover a vast range of new public facilities intrinsic and extrinsic to the development upon which the fee is levied. These include roadways, streets, sidewalks, bridges and traffic control devices; water source, treatment and distribution facilities; wastewater collection and treatment facilities; reclaimed water treatment and distribution facilities; storm water drainage; solid waste collection equipment and disposal; hazardous toxic waste disposal; underground utilities; electricity generation and distribution; street lighting; roadside tree plantation and median landscaping; regional and local parks; recreational facilities; city hall, civic centres and public libraries; day care centres; schools; public art, museum and cultural facilities; preservation of heritage precincts; protection of environmental resources including endangered species; law enforcement facilities and equipment; fire protection facilities and equipment; harbour, port and airport improvements; mass transit facilities and equipment; emergency medical services; low- and moderate-income housing; training of civic personnel, etc. Laws prescribe the preparation of capital improvement plan (CIP) for earmarking impact fees for new area to finance the same. The United States Supreme Court has ruled that impact fee is within the legal powers of local government to finance all types of public facilities subject to 'reasonably related', 'rational nexus' and 'proportionality' tests. An impact fee must demonstrate a reasonable relationship between the fee and demand for infrastructure created by new development. Second, an essential nexus between the conditions of development permission and legitimate state interests must be established. Third, there should be a proportionality between a development's projected impact and the fee. Proportionality refers to the portion of the cost that reasonably relates to the needs of and benefits to new development (Mohanty 2016; USDHUD 1993).

Impact fees have demonstrated a significant potential to raise local revenues in the United States. Local governments there prefer impact fees to finance new development due to mounting opposition from old residents to pay higher property taxes for projects that do not benefit them directly. Impact fees are also less administratively cumbersome, more predictable, more equitable and less prone to political and bureaucratic discretions than 'negotiated' exactions. They are considered the most 'rational' step in the evolution of local government financing of infrastructure in the United States. However, these instruments are yet to be adopted by cities in developing countries like India, excepting Hyderabad.

Planning Obligations

Section 106 of the Town and Country Planning Act, 1990, in the United Kingdom empowers local authorities to negotiate with developers, while according development permission to make commitments known as 'planning obligations'. Any person interested in land in the area of a local authority may, by agreement or otherwise, enter into 'a planning obligation' enforceable by the authority. Such obligations may cover executing capital works, making financial or in-kind contribution or providing affordable housing. They are formalized by legal agreements known as Section 106 agreements. A planning obligation may be unconditional or conditional. It may impose any restriction or requirement, including payment of specified sums indefinitely or for such period as may be specified. If there is a breach of condition in a planning obligation, the enforcing authority may (a) enter the land and carry out the operations and (b) recover from the person or persons against whom the obligation is enforceable any expenses reasonably incurred by them in doing so. A planning obligation is a local land charge enforceable under law by the local authority.

Development Contributions

Australia has been using 'development contributions' extensively to fund urban projects, including major headwork infrastructure such as arterial roads, sewerage treatment plants, community facilities and affordable housing. Development contributions are similar to upfront user charges in respect of future infrastructure services when a close connection is established between the type of development, its infrastructure requirement and the contribution mandated. When such a nexus is not established, they are akin to taxes. Australian states permit negotiations between local authorities and developers for (a) contribution in-kind—land gifted to government by the developer for public facilities; (b) work in-kind—public infrastructure works and facilities constructed by the developer and handed over to public authorities; and (c) monetary charges—financial contributions for acquisition of land for public use or provision of infrastructure and affordable housing. Where development contributions are insufficient to meet the infrastructure costs, the gap is financed from other sources, including fiscal transfers and borrowing. In New Zealand, local authorities collect development contributions from developers under the Local Government Act, 2002, towards infrastructure costs; financial contributions under the Resource Management Act, 1991, towards recovery of environmental costs, for example, those associated with mitigating, avoiding or remedying negative impacts on environment; and targeted rates under the Local Government (Rating) Act, 2002, for collecting funds from identified groups benefiting directly from or impacted upon by projects.

Town Planning Schemes

For a long time, Gujarat state in India has been practising TPS to undertake planned expansion of urban areas. TPS is based on land readjustment/pooling practised in South Korea and Japan. Urban planning in Gujarat is a two-step process under the GTPUDA, 1976. The first step is to prepare a DP for a designated urban area. The second step is to prepare TPS. DP is a broad-brush development vision for the city—a dynamic document that is detailed gradually. It clearly marks the new areas to be opened up for development and divide them into smaller areas of about 100–200 hectares, typically involving 100–250 landowners. Each such area is called TPS. TPS has been the predominant mechanism for undertaking integrated urban development in Gujarat on a self-financing basis. It offers an effective alternative to compulsory acquisition of land, being more beneficial to landowners and also equitable. TPS has a significant scope for application in all large cities in India.

TPS provides for laying or relaying out land, either vacant or already built upon, allocating land for roads, water supply, drainage, sewerage, street lighting, open spaces, gardens, green belts, recreation grounds, schools, markets, etc., and undertaking development. It also caters to the preservation of objects of historical or national interest or natural beauty. Every TPS is legally required to reserve land to the extent of nearly 10 per cent of total area for SEWS. The allotment of land from the scheme area other than for SEWs is made as per the following standards: 15 per cent for roads, 5 per cent for parks, playgrounds, gardens and open spaces, 5 per cent for social infrastructure such as schools, dispensary, fire brigade and public utilities, and 15 per cent for sale by the appropriate authority to meet the cost of infrastructure in the scheme area. The remaining land, often exceeding 50 per cent of the total land pooled, is handed over to landowners with substantial increase in value—after development.

Land Value Capture Tools

LVC tools aim at capturing and recycling public-funded windfalls accruing to landowners. Unlike impact fees, the rationale for LVC has nothing to do with the charges for beneficial infrastructure. It relates to the paradigm that unearned increments in land values owe to community action and not to landowner's effort. LVC instruments enable public authorities to trade anticipated future revenues for a present infrastructure programme. They include fiscal and non-fiscal, recurrent and one-time instruments. Recurrent instruments include leasing of space benefiting from infrastructure, special assessments and TIF backed by LVT, LVIT, property tax, business tax, local benefit taxes, etc. One-time instruments include developer exactions, impact fees, betterment levy, sale of land and development rights, JDM and land pooling. Some key LVC instruments, in addition to the land-based taxes discussed earlier, include the following:

Sale of Developer Land

Developed countries promoted considerable investments in urban housing and infrastructure by requiring real estate developers to provide internal and external infrastructure works, while recovering costs through the sale of plots and housing units. These investments follow DPs prepared by public authorities and planning permissions accorded. Developing countries are also requiring developers to provide basic infrastructure facilities as per permit conditions and/or pay development charges. Such charges cover internal and external infrastructure, extending to water source development and transmission lines, sewerage lines and treatment plants, freeways, regional parks and even maintenance of public facilities for a stipulated number of years. Denmark and South Korea have successfully developed new towns linked to central cities with MRT and limited access expressways by mobilizing resources through sale of land and housing. Ørestad in Denmark and Bundang, Ilsan, Pyeongchon-dong, Jeong-dong and Sanbon-dong in South Korea present good examples of such new towns.

Lease/Sale of Project-related Land

This involves lease or sale of land in the vicinity of public infrastructure like highways and mass transit after development—often with rezoning and enhanced development rights. The instruments work where the government owns land or can buy land at pre-development prices, and zoning laws are not rigid. Often a public authority acquires land adjacent to an infrastructure facility before development. After installation of infrastructure, it sells land or enters into long-term lease with developers for use of sub-surface, ground or air rights, recouping outlays. In case the lease period is very long, substantial payment is received upfront. Hong Kong metro provides a premier example of land lease to capture value created by public investment. Urban land in Hong Kong is state-owned and is leased to property developers for long periods, generally 50–99 years. Station areas are developed with high density based on TOD principle. Lease revenues include initial upfront amount secured through public auction, payment for modification or renewal of lease and land rents.

When Baron Haussmann rebuilt Paris during the Second Empire, he used government authority to acquire land for grand avenues along with extra parcels on both sides. The excess land was used as collateral for debt to finance new roadways, water and sewer lines and natural gas grids. Land-value gains on the extra property acquired were used to repay debt. In Australia, public land within a certain distance from alignment for major urban highways is transferred to a public-private development corporation. This corporation borrows against the land as collateral and finances highway construction. The loan is repaid through the sale of adjoining land after its value has gone up due to enhanced accessibility. Where land is owned privately, the public authority acquires more land than required, and this excess land is sold after its price has increased due to the development of infrastructure development. This method is known as 'excess condemnation'.

Lease/Sale of Development Rights

Brazil has mobilized sizable resources for planned urban operations through the sale of development rights. The scheme of *Outorga*

Onerosa do Direito de Construir (OODC) is based on a basic FSI cap on the landowner's right to build beyond which a fee is charged. Between 2002 and 2004, Sao Paulo reduced FSI in most parts of the city to 1 as a right to the landowner. It permitted additional FSI up to 5 through a scheme of purchasable development tights and TDR, linked to PT access. Sao Paulo has also implemented *Certificados de Potencial Adicional de Construção* or Certificate of Potential Additional Construction (CEPAC) from 1995 to auction construction rights. This is based on the concept that new development potential due to rezoning, permission for additional construction and public investment in infrastructure should not be in a laissez faire way but be auctioned among those desirous of taking advantage of future benefits. The city issues CEPAC bonds corresponding to additional construction rights for purchase by competing developers. Such bonds are publicly sold in electronic auctions regulated by *Comissão de Valores Mobiliários*, the Brazilian Securities and Exchange Commission.

Monetization of Land Assets

Public authorities in developing countries like India own large extents of unused and underused land in many cities. While these cities suffer from acute shortages in infrastructure, it makes good sense to sell or lease some such land, with rezoning and increased FSI to generate funds for servicing the land and the city with infrastructure. Effective monetization of idle land leads to 'unlocking' of land values for growth and productive use of unproductive assets. Sale or lease of public land has the additional advantage of channelizing private investments to areas where they are most productive. Effective land management calls for making an inventory of public lands and periodic comparison of values of land in public use and in the open market. It facilitates putting public land to 'highest and best' uses, duly exploiting the benefits of spatial planning and land management, including zoning and FSI. Peterson (2009) provides examples from cities around the world demonstrating the significant potential of conversion of land assets to infrastructure assets in cities, including Mumbai.

Joint Development Mechanism

JDM is a partnership between a public authority and a private developer to build real estate project on land owned or controlled by the authority. The benefits to public authority under JDM falls into three categories: (a) donation of public land and grant of development right to private developers in return for private investment in public infrastructure, (b) sale of publicly owned land and development rights to private developers with the proceeds used to finance public infrastructure and (c) allocation of increased land value created by public infrastructure through taxes to capture the gains accruing to private landowners, or by voluntary gain-sharing agreements negotiated prior to public investment. Tokyo has long used JDM along with privatization of transport services as a value capture strategy. It has a long history of privately built, owned and operated railways. There are twelve railway corporations in Tokyo, out of which 11 are privately owned. These entities, which declare rail as their 'core' activity, earn more profits from associated real estate business such as departmental stores and construction enterprises. The government provides direct subsidies and low interest loans to corporations to meet upfront capital costs. It promotes transit ridership through congestion pricing, direct control on car ownership, vehicle and fuel taxes and tax breaks for PT users.

Special Assessment District

Special assessment districts are widely used in the United States. Local authorities demarcate boundaries within which differential taxes are assessed on properties expected to increase in value due to proximity to new infrastructure. The origin of special assessment can be traced to the 1691 levy by NYC to fund streets and drains. Los Angeles, Oakland, Portland and Kansas City raised 20 per cent of their budget on account of special assessments in 1913. By 1972, US cities with more than 100,000 population met 12 per cent of their budgets through special assessment districts. In the case of New York Avenue metro station in Washington, DC, approximately one-fourth of the financing of construction in 2004 was voluntarily contributed by local business through a self-imposed special assessment on all commercial properties within 2,000 feet of the station's entrances. Business improvement districts, started by Ontario, have been widely used in Canada since the 1960s. They aim at financing capital improvements in designated areas through agreement with owners and/or tenants of a majority of businesses to pay an additional levy. Once an improvement district is established, it resorts to long-term debt for infrastructure based on a dedicated debt-servicing arrangement.

Betterment Levy

Most countries around the world have experimented with betterment levies at some point or other, typically aiming to capture 30–80 per cent of the imputed increase in land value. Such instruments include (a) tax or charge on land value increment in a demarcated benefit area; (b) uniform land tax paid annually without differentiation or discrimination; (c) tax on transaction of land or buildings in the demarcated area; (d) recoupment from purchase of land adjoining projects and resale after development of infrastructure; (e) rent from long-term lease of publicly owned or acquired land; (f) sale of land use and development rights along major infrastructure alignments, with rezoning and enhanced FSI; and (g) set-off or reduction in compensation payable for land acquired for public purpose. The Housing and Town Planning Act of 1909 in the UK established the principle of betterment due to TPS.

In Australia, the NSW Local Government (Town and Country Planning) Amendment Act, 1945, permitted taxing up to 80 per cent of the increase in land values arising from TPS. From 1970 to 1973, a betterment levy was imposed on specified rural lands within the Sydney metropolitan region under the Land Development Contribution Act, 1970, and Land Development Contribution Management Act, 1970. This was a 30 per cent tax on the gain from rezoning of rural land— difference between the capital value of unimproved land on the date of rezoning and that on 1 August 1969. The levy was payable by a landowner when land was sold or planning permission was accorded to undertake development. The tax proceeds were earmarked for city improvement schemes. Johannesburg collects 'development contribution' to recover one-third of the increase in land values due to grant of higher zoning rights. This goes to a dedicated 'town planning fund' to finance capital projects such as road widening, water and sewer networks and purchase of land for parking.

In Colombia, national law permitted betterment levy in 1887. Bogota has successfully used *Contribución de Valorización* to finance public infrastructure since 1921. This is calculated by multiplying certain benefit factors relating to size of property, its use, proximity to investment, etc. Over 50 per cent of Bogota's main road grid was paid for by betterment levy. Reliance on this instrument, however, declined in the 1980s and 1990s due to difficulties in attributing land value increases to public works and court litigations. However, Bogota simplified its betterment levy and adopted a city-wide valorisation fee, differentiated by benefit areas. The new instrument, *Participación en Plusvalías*, introduced in 1997, aims to capture land value increments arising directly from government investments in infrastructure and indirectly from planning and regulatory instruments like zoning and FSI. Municipalities are permitted to capture 30–50 per cent of the land value increments. The proceeds are required to be spent on development works: social housing, infrastructure, open space, mass transit, urban renewal and historic preservation. The new betterment levy has enabled Bogota to revive valorisation as an effective instrument to finance urban infrastructure.

Tax Increment Financing

TIF is a value capture tool that relies on future increments in tax revenues to finance current infrastructure programmes. It is based on 'growth pays' principle. While the concepts and modalities of TIF vary, it essentially allows a local government to ring-fence 'tax increment' within a geographically demarcated area to finance development or renewal that contributes to this increment. Originally started by California in 1951 as an innovative way to raise local matching funds for federal grants, TIF is extensively used in the United States. As many as 49 out of 50 states have a TIF-enabling legislation. Chicago has used TIF to a greater extent than any other large city in the United

States. In the past three decades, TIF has been the primary source of funding to promote local economic development in the city. TIF has been a successful instrument to rejuvenate blight areas, prevent localities from deteriorating into blighted conditions and foster industrial development in the United States. The principle of TIF is adopted by other countries also. In Australia, the instrument is known as value increment financing. TIF is flexible instrument. The tax increments can be used to secure a loan, encourage an upfront investment or undertake development on a pay-as-you-go principle. Sometimes, tax increments are supplemented by special assessment, impact fee or betterment levy. There is a considerable scope for implementing TIF in developing countries like India.

Under a TIF scheme, a public authority or private business proposes a TIF district. It makes a general estimation of land and property values in the district and likely increases due to TIF. The entity examines the suitability of the area for TIF and conducts a study to demonstrate that the proposal conforms to the legal requirements. The local or state government considers the proposal and establishes a TIF authority. This authority delineates the TIF district and prepares DP with cost estimates in consultation with local and state governments, private developers, community and other stakeholders. The plan follows the local and state planning laws. The authority then raises debt through TIF bonds or other instruments to meet the upfront project costs. TIF bonds are often in the nature of 'infrastructure revenue bonds'. Rating of these bonds to meet capital market standards ensures that the TIF project is subjected to rigorous scrutiny. Over a period of time, TIF results in property development, increased land and property values and a rise in tax bases in the district. Tax increments over and above the pre-TIF levels are ring-fenced to service debt. The total taxes from the district revert to the original taxing authority at the end of the TIF term, which may be 5–25 years, depending on development.

A Toolbox of Land-Based Instruments

While theory and international practice provide useful lessons for designing land-based instruments to finance urban public goods, the 'context of political economy' is important for their adoption. Given the structure of India's fiscal federalism enshrined in the Constitution of India, we suggest a toolbox of land-based instruments for assignment to/exploitation by cities, accompanied by broader reforms in municipal finance in India, as follows (see Mohanty 2016, 2019; Vyas, Vyas and Mishra 2020):

1. **VLT**—International experience suggests that a VLT of 0.5–2 per cent can generate significant revenues to debt-finance major urban infrastructure projects. To start with, a VLT at 0.5 per cent of capital value of land in larger cities and 0.2 per cent in smaller towns or even lower, as practised in Andhra Pradesh and Telangana state, may be considered. A time period of 5 years could be allowed to complete construction on a vacant plot following layout approval after which a steeply graduating tax may be levied depending on the period land is held vacant. Further, the tax rate on idle land may be higher than that on built-up property to discourage speculative land hoarding. Properties with more than a certain percentage of land area utilized for building, say 20 per cent, may be exempted from VLT.
2. **Property Tax**—A two-part property tax with higher rate for land than buildings may be considered on the logic that unearned benefits to land significantly exceed those to buildings. Municipal laws in India have traditionally prescribed for components of property tax: general tax, conservancy tax, water tax, drainage tax, light tax, etc. The general tax component, nearly 50 per cent of property tax, is based on capital value of land. This component may be in the form of a progressive LVT linked to the basic value of land determined by the government for the purpose of stamp duty. The civic service–related taxes may be linked to general tax, or total property tax may be based on capital value of land or land and buildings.
3. **RETT**—While local governments are authorized to levy RETT in some countries, payable by seller or buyer or both, stamp duty on property registration tax in India is assigned to states and paid by the buyer. However, the tax is basically a local tax linked to increase in property values due to planned infrastructure investments by local governments. In southern states of India, a

surcharge on stamp duty is levied and shared with local governments; for example, Andhra Pradesh levies a surcharge at 2 per cent of property value and allocates the same to local authorities. All states in India may consider sharing stamp duty with local governments, being a local and land-based tax.

4. **DIF**—Hyderabad is a pioneer in India, which has been implementing impact fee for the last two decades. The city levies such fee for converting land located on designated commercial roads from 'other' uses to 'commercial'. It also levies city-level infrastructure impact fee for built-up area above 15 m height in multi-storied buildings. Fifty per cent of the fee is required to be utilized for infrastructure in the area from which it is collected, and the other 50 per cent for city-wide developments. Gujarat has mandated the levy of impact fee to provide facilities such as parking, sanitation and fire safety under the Gujarat Regularization of Unauthorized Development Act, 2011. A 10 per cent impact fee on the cost of new construction in Mumbai is estimated to finance as much as 40–50 per cent of all regional infrastructure investments needed for two decades. Developments in large city regions must pay for impacts, including those related to infrastructure, environment and affordable housing.

5. **Betterment levy**—Hyderabad collects betterment and external betterment charges while approving layouts and building construction. Betterment charges are linked to on-site or internal infrastructure such as water supply, drainage and roads; external betterment charges are related to off-site or external infrastructure such as major arterial and radial roads, flyovers and regional parks. However, most India cities are yet to utilize betterment as a resource. The case for the levy arises from the fact that land value gains due to spatial planning and infrastructure development tend to be disproportionately large—not amenable for being captured through a generic tax. International experience suggests that a levy rate of 25–30 per cent on betterment in land could be reasonable for cities in India.

6. **Monetization of land**—Since the 1980s, MMRDA has implemented the development of a 553-acre site from marshland and industrial slums to develop a secondary sub-urban commercial

and office node to relieve congestion in central Mumbai—Bandra Kurla Complex (BKC). It has deployed long-term lease of land (for 80 years) to private developers with permission to undertake high-density development. The price per square meter of land sold was ₹30,000 in 1993, ₹42,500 in 1995 (Diamond Bourse), ₹86,000 in 2000 (Citibank), ₹153,000 in January 2006 (Convention Centre) and ₹504,000 in November 2007 (Commercial Complex and Car Park). In just two land auctions of 2006 and 2007 covering 13 hectares, MMRDA generated a sum of about ₹51 billion. The developers in BKC are responsible for all on-site and approach infrastructure at their own cost. MMRDA is using the land monetization proceeds for major regional infrastructure projects, including Mumbai transit. Other cities may implement similar land monetization programmes.

7. **Monetization of development rights**—Karnataka has embarked on innovative mechanisms to monetize development rights for generating resources for Bengaluru MRT system as follows:
Development cess on new layouts/developments—Cess @ 5 per cent of market value of land or/and building in future property developments and new layouts.

Cess on additional FAR—FAR up to 4.0 allowed for all properties lying within an influence area of 500 m on either side of the metro alignment subject to a cess of 10 per cent for residential buildings and 20 per cent for commercial buildings.

TDRs—TDR issued by transit authority in lieu of compensation for acquisition of land for metro rail alignment.

Apart from the above instruments, large Indian cities may consider sale and auctioning of development rights with up-zoning and increase in FSI as in the case of OODC and CEPAC in Brazil. As FSI is very low in Indian cities, monetization of development rights, linked to investment in public transit, holds a considerable promise to usher in urban transformation.

8. **LPS**—TPS in Gujarat presents an elegant scheme for self-financed urban development through value creation and capture based on spatial planning and development—implemented by the government. Magarpatta city presents a self-contained township development scheme with landowners as shareholders and partners in

value-creating development—implemented by the private sector. Both the models deserve to be adopted by states. TPS needs to be simplified with a significant reduction in the time period for completion; private landowners may also be enabled by law to implement TPS. Through a development and construction company formed by farmers as shareholders, the Magarpatta scheme needs to be promoted with proactive facilitation by city and state governments—with covenant for the mandatory inclusion of the SEWS as in TPS in Gujarat.

Municipal Finance Reforms

The 74th Amendment Act, 1992 incorporates the 12th Schedule into the Constitution of India, including 18 legitimate municipal functions. These functions can be divided into four groups: (a) service provision, including operation and maintenance of delivery systems, (b) capital works to address the infrastructure needs of services, (c) social inclusion including slum upgradation and poverty alleviation and (d) conservation of environmental and heritage resources. Public finance principles suggest that finance follows functions. However, ULGs in India are faced with gross mismatch between functions and finances. On the one hand, they are not able to discharge their basic service delivery functions. On the other hand, there is no clarity regarding the modalities to finance other critical urban functions—infrastructure, inclusion and conservation. Such functions, which involve externalities and spillover effects, are important for national economic growth and sustainable development. Ironically, while the level of urbanization and contribution of cities to GDP in India are increasing, the fiscal position of ULGs has been dwindling in real terms, with local taxes being appropriated by state governments over the years. GST has been the latest blow to municipal finances.

Indian municipalities, with revenues at a meagre 1 per cent of GDP are among the weakest globally—compared to 7.4 per cent in Brazil and 6.0 per cent for South Africa. This is closely connected to India's fiscal federalism, which neglects the 'third tier'. After GST subsumed important local taxes such as octroi, entry tax and advertisement tax,

Indian municipalities are left with only one major tax, that is, property tax. Ironically, cities in developed countries have access to a much broader basket of revenue sources, including income tax, sales tax, GST, motor fuel tax, excise tax, payroll tax and a range of land-based taxes and charges apart from sizable transfers. In countries where the assigned tax base is narrow, ULGs receive substantial transfers from central and provincial governments. In the United Kingdom, central transfers often constitute more than 70 per cent of municipal revenues (Mohanty 2014). However, ULGs in India, subject to a narrow tax base, do not have access to large transfers from state and central governments. At the present context of India's fiscal federalism, a local government GST rate or a formula-based local government share in dual GST appears to be the most sensible strategy to strengthen municipal finances. The present central-state GST regime may be replaced by a centre-state-local GST based on the formula: 5 per cent centre: 5 per cent state: 2 per cent local. The local GST may be earmarked for MRT, HSR, grids of arterial and radial roads and other core infrastructure projects, including those connecting rural growth centres and satellite towns with mother cities.

Local public finance literature highlights the following 'golden rules' for designing instruments to finance different types of urban public expenditures (Bahl and Linn 1992):

- Where benefits of public services are measurable and accrue to readily identified individuals in a jurisdiction, user charges are the most appropriate financing instruments.
- Local services such as administration, traffic control and street lighting, which are services to the general public in the sense that identification of beneficiaries and/or measurement of benefits are difficult, need to be financed by taxes on local residents.
- Cost of services for which significant spillovers to neighbouring jurisdictions occur (e.g., health, education and welfare) should be financed substantially by state or national intergovernmental transfers.
- Borrowing is appropriate for financing capital outlays on infrastructure projects, particularly public utilities, roads and transit, where investments required are large and benefits accrue over generations.

'Users pay', 'beneficiaries pay' and 'growth pays' are cornerstones of urban public finance. User charges are 'first-best 'instruments to meet the costs of local public goods. They act as market prices. Where charging is not feasible, 'benefit charges' and 'benefit taxes' on local residents are appropriate. They act as 'surrogate' user charges. As a corollary to the benefit principle, those creating negative externalities must also pay for their mitigation. Thus, 'polluters pay' and 'congesters pay'. General taxes and intergovernmental transfers are necessary when user charges, benefit charges and benefit taxes are not adequate. Borrowing is appropriate for long gestation infrastructure projects. India must design a robust municipal finance system based on the 'golden rules' of local public finance.

City governments and infrastructure authorities must levy water supply, sewerage and drainage user charges on a full cost recovery basis, adopting an increasing block tariff framework with exemption granted up to minimum threshold of service. They must also be enabled to levy 'beneficiaries pay', 'congesters pay' and other benefit charges. Those who benefit from public services must pay towards costs; those who create costs on the society must pay towards their mitigation. Water and sewer benefit taxes are collected by Greater Mumbai Municipal Corporation towards recouping the costs of capital works. However, instruments have not been adopted by most other cities. Most cities collect planning-related fees and charge while approving layouts and buildings; these include permission fee, land use conversion charges, non-agricultural land assessment, internal and EDCs, impact fees, betterment levies, etc. While such revenues are small, the experience of Hyderabad city suggests that with appropriate 'design' of instruments, planning-related revenues can be a major source of municipal finance in growing cities—next to property tax.

Cities in India are not empowered to levy CCs and local motor vehicles taxes or local fuel taxes in lieu to address roadway congestion, reduce peak loads of transport infrastructure, facilitate switchover to cleaner transport modes and raise resources for transport development. They are not pricing transport based on CC principle. As a result, travel behaviour and location decisions have increased motorization while reducing the efficiency of road use. The importance of such charging is eloquently highlighted by Nobel laureate, William S. Vickrey in the following words:

> ...in no other major area are pricing practices so irrational, so out of date, and so conducive to waste as in urban transportation. (Vickrey 1963, 452)

Singapore, London and Stockholm have adopted ERP. Other cities globally have resorted to one-time motor vehicle registration tax, annual motor vehicles tax, licensing fee for automobile ownership, motor fuel levy, pay-at-the-pump charges, highway tolls, truck weight fees, parking charges, carbon taxes and emission charges. Metropolitan cities in developing countries like India may be enabled to adopt similar instruments or have a share in the relevant taxes

While the design of financing instruments is important, structuring of value-creating projects is even more important. As spatial planning and infrastructure capitalize into land values, land-based tools such as LVT, VLT, impact fee, special assessment and betterment levy are ideal to leverage debt for such projects through municipal bonds and other instruments. The benefit principle also makes a strong case for taxing rents accruing to other immobile and quasi-immobile factors. These include scarcity rent, monopoly rent, agglomeration rent, spatial planning and infrastructure-induced rents, etc. When project revenues, benefit charges, benefit taxes, including LVT, and earmarked intergovernmental transfers are suitably combined, there is no reason why urban projects cannot be self-financed. After all, both urban and rural areas cannot be subsidized. Urban areas create rents to many and must generate resources for both urban and rural development and poverty alleviation.

If a worthwhile urban project passes the social benefit-cost test, it must, in principle, lead to adequate value increments due to wider economic impacts through agglomeration and networking externalities. Thus, a strong case exists for designing such projects based on value creation, capture and recycling principles. Project design needs to integrate available resources and instruments: accessibility to transport, zoning, FSI, density, land development and land use based on a flexi-planning framework. Development, regulatory and economic instruments must be combined. Major projects in metropolitan regions lead to large increases in the tax bases of all levels of government due to tax wedge effects. A strong economic case, thus, exists for funding such projects based on intergovernmental partnerships based on escrowing of tax increments. Developed countries like the United States and France have financed major transportation investments, including mass transit, with dedicated motor fuel tax and payroll tax. However, given the present structure of fiscal federalism in India, it will be appropriate that cities have resource to GST. A piggybacked income tax as in the United States could perhaps be considered. Of course, cities will have to reform property tax and user charge systems, while exploiting the land-based instruments assigned. If supported by sustained investments in PT, public health, disaster risk reduction and resilience and environmental and social infrastructure, metropolitan regions can act as powerful engines of sustainable development.

Land Economics and Policy

Addressing the Challenges of Sustainable Development

Cities and Sustainable Development

The central idea in 'sustainable development' is that the future of humanity depends on the ability of current development to cater to the present requirements without compromising the ability of future generations to satisfy their own needs. The concept is at the core of the UN Millennium Development Goals (MDGs) 2015 and UN SDGs (UN-SDGs 2030). Adopted by 193 member states of the United Nations in 2015 including India, the Global Agenda for Sustainable Development 2030 lays out 17 SDGs to be achieved by 2030. It sets out 169 targets and 233 indicators encompassing various dimensions of sustainable development. It identifies the localization of SDGs as a fundamental requirement to attain them. The agenda regards urbanization as among the greatest challenges as well as opportunities for developing countries to accelerate economic growth and reduce poverty. It also recognizes that unplanned and disproportionate urbanization will have adverse spatial, economic, social and environmental consequences. Further, SDGs cannot be attained without transforming the way we finance and govern cities, manage land resources, build urban spaces and integrate rural and urban development. The overwhelming number of people to be added to urban areas in developing countries in the 21st century suggests that the struggle for global sustainability will be won or lost in their cities (United Nations 2018, 2019).

UN-SDG 11 calls for making 'cities and human settlements inclusive, safe, resilient, and sustainable' (Box 8.1). It is a crucial goal, which

Box 8.1: SDG 11: Make Cities and Human Settlements Inclusive, Safe, Resilient and Sustainable

- By 2030, ensure access for all to adequate, safe and affordable housing and basic services and upgrade slums.
- By 2030, provide access to safe, affordable, accessible and sustainable transport systems for all, improve road safety, notably by expanding PT, with special attention to the needs of those in vulnerable situations, women, children, persons with disabilities and older persons.
- By 2030, enhance inclusive and sustainable urbanization and capacity for participatory, integrated and sustainable human settlement planning and management in all countries.
- Strengthen efforts to protect and safeguard the world's cultural and natural heritage.
- By 2030, significantly reduce the number of deaths and the number of people affected and substantially decrease the direct economic losses relative to global GDP caused by disasters, including water-related disasters, with a focus on protecting the poor and people in vulnerable situations.
- By 2030, reduce the adverse per capita environmental impact of cities, including by paying special attention to air quality and municipal and other waste management.
- By 2030, provide universal access to safe, inclusive and accessible, green and public spaces, in particular for women and children, older persons and persons with disabilities.
- Support positive economic, social and environmental links between urban, peri-urban and rural areas by strengthening national and regional development planning.
- By 2020, substantially increase the number of cities and human settlements adopting and implementing integrated policies and plans towards inclusion, resource efficiency, mitigation and adaptation to climate change, resilience to disasters and develop and implement, in line with the Sendai Framework for Disaster Risk Reduction 2015–2030, holistic disaster risk management at all levels.
- Support least developed countries, including through financial and technical assistance, in building sustainable and resilient buildings utilizing local materials.

Source: United Nations. *2030 Agenda for Sustainable Development.*

is closely connected with important SDGs such as no poverty, zero hunger, good health and well-being, quality education, gender equality, clean water and sanitation, reducing inequality, decent work and economic growth, industry and infrastructure, responsible production and consumption, climate action and life on land. It recognizes the crucial role of government in spatial and socio-economic planning, land management, infrastructure development, employment generation, economic growth, poverty alleviation, environmental conservation and disaster resilience and risk reduction in attaining SDGs. The successful implementation of SDGs calls for effective, inclusive and accountable institutions to implement policies and programmes. It is in this context that the role of land and urban policies and governance assumes significance. The policies aim at balancing efficiency, equity, sustainability and financial viability objectives in development. This chapter is focused on land and urban policies in developing countries in the context of SDGs with special focus on India. The remaining parts of the chapter deal with the mechanics of urbanization; anatomy of failure of urban land markets and city governments; key issues of land policy and management; fallacies of modernist planning; and strategies to integrate land, transport and urban economics into land and urban policies. We also suggest broader reforms in urban planning, financing and governance systems to address the challenges of sustainable development.

The Mechanics of Urbanization

The Census of India defines urban areas to include 'statutory towns' and 'census towns'. Statutory towns are places with a municipality, corporation, cantonment board or a notified town area committee, etc. Census towns are places satisfying the following criteria simultaneously:

1. A minimum population of 5,000;
2. At least 75 per cent of the male working population engaged in non-agricultural pursuits; and
3. A population density of at least 400 per square kilometre.

In demographic terms, urban growth is explained by natural increase (births–deaths), net migration (in-migration–out-migration) and reclassification (increase in the population of existing urban area due to extension of boundaries + population of rural areas converted in situ into 'urban'-population of declassified towns, that is, areas converted from 'urban' to 'rural'). Urbanization manifests in (a) 'densification' of existing urban areas with infill development and vertical construction; (b) 'annexation' of villages to existing cities and towns; and (c) 'in situ conversion' of rural areas into 'urban', and 'new towns'.

Urban growth is closely connected with the economics of city regions. These regions act as drivers of growth, attracting entrepreneurs and workers, including migrants. As urbanization occurs, governments also increase the jurisdictions of 'municipalities' and 'UDAs' for the purpose of spatial planning. City regions, thus, evolve due to market forces and government actions. A city region comprises a central city, its suburban peripheries and urbanizing rural hinterlands. Migration to these regions depends on 'poverty-push', 'prosperity-push' and 'prosperity-pull' factors. It is linked to socio-economic conditions in rural areas, employment opportunities offered by cities and towns, urban-rural wage differential, prospects of urban-rural remittance, cost of urban living, access to basic amenities, etc. Reclassification requires that at least 75 per cent of the working age population is engaged in non-agricultural pursuits. However, annexation of suburbs to cities and in situ conversion of rural areas to municipalities are often based on political considerations.

The urbanization process is fuelled by actions of numerous firms, households-workers and developers-builders. These economic actors take decisions regarding location, relocation, land use, reuse, development and redevelopment in pursuit of economic activities. Producers choose location along with investment, technology and input mix for production. They balance benefits of scale and agglomeration with the costs of transporting inputs and outputs. Workers choose employment and residence to balance benefits and costs of living, working and shopping in different locations. Benefits include wages from employer located at a distance from residence and access to transport, learning opportunities, amenities and services. Costs include land, housing, commuting and external diseconomies. Developers decide location, along with building technology and mix of residential, commercial, office and other developments. They balance benefits and costs of land development and construction in alternative sites.

Economic growth, primarily driven by market forces, localizes. Secondary and tertiary activities collocate in city regions to exploit agglomeration and network externalities (Alonso 1964; Brueckner 2011; Glaeser 2008; Mills 1967, 1972; Mohanty 2014, 2019; Muth 1969). Agglomeration externalities, occurring on the supply side, owe to the clustering of firms, households and institutions. Network externalities, arising on the demand side, are connected with the use, integration and merger of networks such as transportation, communication and knowledge. These forces are instrumental in reducing the costs of moving goods, people, information, ideas and knowledge. Cities result in economies of learning, sharing and matching. They nurture skills, act as nurseries of new ideas, attract creative entrepreneurs and skilled workers, support employment in formal and informal sectors and generate tax bases for all governments. Cities lead to human capital externalities (Lucas 1988). Small market towns lead to economies of scale in marketing and distribution of agricultural inputs and outputs. Medium-sized cities result in localization economies of manufacturing, division of labour and specialization. Large cities present urbanization economies associated with large market size, diversity and innovation. Metropolitan regions combine the benefits of specialization, diversity, networking, collaboration, innovation and competition (Mohanty 2014).

Globally, urban areas occupy about 3 per cent of land, contain 55 per cent of population, but generate more than 80 per cent of GDP. As the level of urbanization of a country rises by 10 per cent, its per capita output uplifts by 30 per cent. Per capita incomes are four times larger in countries with the majority residing in cities compared to those in which the majority lives in rural areas (Glaeser 2011). Studies for OECD countries reveal that the doubling of city population is associated with a 2–5 per cent increase in productivity (OECD 2015). Within the United States, workers in metro areas earn 30 per cent more than those in non-metro areas. These relationships do not alter even after correcting for heterogeneity with regard to education, experience, intelligence quotient (IQ) and industry of workers (Glaeser 2011). The contribution of urban regions in India to GDP, estimated at more than 60 per cent, is projected to rise to 75 per cent by 2031. McKinsey Global Institute (2010) projects that Indian cities would generate 70 per cent of all new jobs and 85 per cent of tax revenues of governments through 2030 (see Mohanty 2019).

Metropolitan regions are economic powerhouses in this era of knowledge-based production. They compete nationally and internationally to attract technology, capital, enterprise and skill. The world's top 750 cities accounted for 57 per cent of global GDP and their share would rise to 61 per cent by 2030 (Oxford Economics 2017). In 2016, the 300 largest metropolitan economies in the world, containing 24 per cent of global population, contributed nearly 50 per cent of global GDP. These economies, including nine from India, also concentrated and accelerated economic growth between 2014 and 2016. They explained 67 per cent of real GDP growth and 36 per cent of employment growth in the world, while accounting for 22 per cent of the increase in population (Brookings Institution 2018).

Anatomy of Urban Failure

Economic growth, urbanization and spatial concentration of economic activity move together in the structural transformation process. They are connected with the decisions of multiple actors regarding location and land use. However, land uses interact, leading to external economies and diseconomies. The clustering of economic activities also results in agglomeration economies. However, when spatial concentration is not supported by infrastructure, external diseconomies creep in. These diseconomies manifest as a mismatch between demand for and supply of land and floor space, incompatible land uses, traffic congestion, air and water pollution, slums, poverty, crime, public health hazards, vulnerability to disasters and destruction of natural habitat. They warrant interventions by governments to correct for market failure. However, the inability of governments to internalize externalities subject cities to double jeopardy: market failure and government failure (Mohanty 2019).

Failure of Land Markets

Urban land markets fail in both developed and developing countries due to the peculiar features of land, monopolistic conditions, externalities and public goods. Land is a composite good with spatial, economic, environmental and social characteristics. It is geographically fixed, immobile, permanent, scarce and heterogeneous. The quantity of land is finite, but the availability for particular urban uses can be increased by expanding city boundaries, changing land uses and converting 'rural' land to 'urban' uses. Ironically, it is not land per se but floor space with access to infrastructure that matters for most urban activities. Floor space can be augmented by increasing FSI. However, the right to develop urban land is not entirely a private right. Zoning and DCRs affect the exercise of such rights. Further, the lack of access to connectivity infrastructure discourages development. These factors impact 'location' and 'land use' in complex ways.

Interactions between land uses are traced to backward and forward linkages between secondary and tertiary activities. The use to which a land is put affects its locational attractiveness and, hence, land values in adjoining areas. The commercial use of a plot may increase the value of lands nearby, while lowering that for residential and other uses. Non-commercial use may dampen land values in an area but uplift land values for commercial use in other locations. Installation of infrastructure such as public transit enhances land values along its alignment. However, actions of landowners and users are not priced; so also, public goods. Thus, developed countries impose land use restrictions on grounds such as avoiding uncompensated interferences with neighbouring lands, providing infrastructure, facilitating competition, controlling pollution and congestion, safeguarding heritage and environment, supplying affordable housing and 'recouping' unearned increments in land.

Rampant speculation is a key reason for governments of developing countries to intervene in land markets. As urban activities spill over peri-urban areas, speculators keep their land out of the market so that developers bypass the same and travel farther to purchase land. The extra distance creates additional social costs due to increase in the burden on existing infrastructure and sprawl externalities. Similarly, if landowners somehow know that a high value development is planned near their land, they 'hold out' such land to charge extortionary prices later. More money is made by keeping land idle rather than selling or developing. Speculation in land markets, along with neglect of transport to service land, has led to inconsistent development, uneconomic extension of urban boundaries, longer commuting, environmental decay, energy wastage and increased service costs.

Failure of Governments

Governments typically intervene in land markets with physical instruments such as land use zoning; development control; LA and infrastructure installation; and economic tools such as land taxation, CC, pricing of development rights, VCF and fiscal incentives. However, poorly designed and haphazardly implemented regulations exacerbate market failure in developing countries. This is most conspicuous in their metropolitan regions. These regions are plagued by exorbitant land and housing prices, low consumption of floor space, slums and long neglect of PT and health infrastructure. They are confronted with a mismatch between accessibility, density, affordability, land development and use, leading to sprawl, wasteful commuting and deleterious effects on the environment.

Land market regulations in developing countries include zoning codes allocating land for various uses; layout rules including standards for plot size, road width, public amenities, etc.; building codes including FSI norms and construction standards; planning permission to undertake development; field inspections; fines and penalties for violation of permit conditions; and demolition of unauthorized constructions. Over the years, regulatory controls have proliferated. They are exercised by multiple agencies: ULGs, UDAs, pollution control boards, slum redevelopment authorities, etc. These controls operate at regional, city, zone, local and plot levels. Plot-level controls extend to FSI, plot size, coverage, front, back and side setbacks, width of approach road, building height, etc. FSI is heavily controlled in Indian cities. It is hardly 2 as against 5–15 in central areas of global cities. Such restrictions hinder the operation of urban land markets. Operating through administrative mechanisms, they lead to rent-seeking and corruption.

While regulatory controls over urban land market in India are extensive, cities are subject to chronic under-investment in infrastructure and affordable housing. McKinsey Institute (2010) estimates the requirements at ₹9.74 million crores in 2008 prices for 2010–2030. It suggests that India needs to build 700–900 million m² of residential and commercial space annually and get 2.5 billion m² of roads paved along with 7,400 km of metros and subways constructed by 2030. HPEC (2014) projects the investment requirement of core urban infrastructure sectors for 2012–2031 in 2009–2010 prices at ₹3.1 million crores, including ₹2.3 million crores for roads, transport and traffic-related infrastructure. The projections were made a decade back. However, municipal revenues in India as a percentage of GDP have stagnated at an abysmally low level of 1 per cent for a long time. Thus, cities are unable to meet the demands of growth without reforms in fiscal federalism. Land policy and management issues are closely connected with the broader issues of urban planning, financing and governance.

Land Policy and Management

Land policy and management are concerned with planning, procuring, assembling, financing, developing, renewing, servicing, using, reusing and regulating land and floor space. They aim at optimally using the limited land resources to achieve SDGs. In particular, they target at making land, floor space and infrastructure available for growth-generating activities, while addressing concerns of housing affordability, agricultural productivity, rural livelihoods protection, environmental conservation and climate change. Attempts by the GoI to address land and urban policy issues include Urban Land Policy Committee, 1965, Planning Commission Task Force on Planning of Urban Development, 1983, National Commission on Urbanization, 1988, Draft National Land Utilisation Policy, 2013, NUTP, 2014, URDPFI Guidelines, 2014 and NUPF, 2018. The salient recommendations from these initiatives are presented below.

Urban Land Policy Committee, 1965

The Ministry of Health, GoI, constituted the Urban Land Policy Committee, which gave a report in 1965. This report articulates the following objectives of urban land policy:

- to achieve the optimum social use of urban land;
- to make land available in adequate quantity at the right time and at reasonable prices to both public authorities and individuals for planned urbanization;
- to encourage cooperative community effort and bona fide individual builders in the field of land development, housing and construction;
- to prevent concentration of land ownership in a few private hands and to safeguard the interests of the poor and the underprivileged sections of the urban society; and
- to use land as a resource for financing urban development by recouping the unearned income, which otherwise accrues to private landowners.

The Task Force on Planning of Urban Development set up by India's Planning Commission in 1983 reiterated similar urban land policy objectives as follows:

- to widen the base of land ownership, especially to safeguard the interests of the poor and the underprivileged sections of the urban society;
- to encourage socially and economically efficient allocation of urban land such that urban development occurs in a resource-conserving manner and land is used optimally; and
- to promote flexibility in land use in response to changes resulting from a growing city.

Land policy objectives cut across multiple considerations: efficiency, equity, sustainability and resource mobilization.

The Urban Land Policy Committee, 1965, justified government intervention in land markets to maximize the net benefits of planned urban development to society. It opined that if left to market forces, the social needs for housing and basic services would be overlooked. The Committee argued that compulsory acquisition of land was a must for supply of adequate housing and infrastructure. It proposed large-scale advance acquisition of land to end speculation in land markets and capture unearned increments in land values due to spatial planning and infrastructure investments. The major recommendations of the Committee are presented in Table 8.1.

Following the recommendations of the committee, UDAs were set up by states. They were entrusted with the tasks of preparing master plans for delineated urban areas along with zonal and local land use plans, acquiring land, undertaking land assembly and making serviced land available for planned uses. Not surprisingly, the performance of such authorities has been dismal. Plan achievement has drastically fallen short of target. Excessive regulation has dampened initiative to develop and build. The argument that the space needs of the poor are better addressed in a public sector–led model of urban development turned out to be fallacious. This is amply demonstrated by the experience of DDA.

Draft Land Utilization Policy, 2013

The Department of Land Resources, Ministry of Rural Development, GoI, circulated Draft National Land Utilisation Policy, 2013. The draft policy aimed:

> to ensure optimal utilization of the limited land resources in India for achieving sustainable development, addressing social, economic and environmental considerations and to provide a framework for the States to formulate their respective land utilization policies incorporating state-specific concerns and priorities. (MoRD 2013)

The document recommends classification of lands into six land utilization zones (LUZs): predominantly rural and agricultural areas; areas under transformation; predominantly urban areas; predominantly IAs; predominantly ecological and natural resource areas, landscape conservation and tourism/heritage areas; and major hazard vulnerable areas. LUZs are subjected to land use planning based on DPs for regions and for urban areas, rural areas, IAs, mining areas, etc.

Table 8.1 Committee on Urban Land Policy (1965): Major Recommendations

Subject	Major Recommendations
Measures for developed urban land	• Effective implementation of master plan, zoning and subdivision regulations and urban renewal. • CIP, fiscal plan and land use plan to be integrated into city development plan (CDP).
Measures for undeveloped urban land	• Stringent controls on development outside compact areas to avoid uneconomic stretching of infrastructure. • Extension of public utility to prevent 'spotty development' and encourage compact growth. • Future development in undeveloped areas to be based on 'planned neighbourhoods'. • Conversion tax on change of land use from agriculture to non-agriculture to discourage speculation.
Measures for land in urbanizable limits	• Urbanizable limits to be determined for each city and included in municipal jurisdiction. • Where an extension of municipal limits is not feasible, physical planning be applied to about 8 km beyond such limits. • No change to be permitted in present use of land in an area of 300 feet along all roads and railway lines and in the potential areas in which the town is likely to extend. • A high-powered statutory autonomous authority be set up at state level to gain ownership of land in the city's 'urbanizable limits' through compulsory acquisition of land for orderly urban development.
Measures for land beyond urbanizable limits	• Land use beyond urbanizable limits to be governed by regional land use plan, regulated by an authority, to prevent growth of conurbations, sprawl and spotty development. • Power to control ribbon development by prescribing right of way and disallowing developments within a prescribed distance therefrom be legislated and enforced.
Measures for mopping up unearned increases	• Unearned increases in urban land and property values are 'social surpluses' not to be left to speculators and profiteers. • A modest levy on planning permission; a conversion tax with differentiated structures for conversion to residential, commercial and industrial uses; a broad-based annual tax on unearned increments in land and property values; shifting property tax base from rental value to capital value and a lower tax rate on development along with a graduated higher rate on site value to mobilize unearned increments. • Five years' time to be given for completing construction on vacant plots following the provision of services, and a heavy tax, thereafter, increasing with passage of time.

Source: Report of the Committee on Urban Land Policy (1965), Ministry of Health, Government of India; Mohanty (2014).

For effective land utilization, land uses under DP are categorized into land use management areas (LMAs). LMAs are to ensure protection, regulation, control and guided development or even reserve land in accordance with legal provisions and priority needs of sectors. Key planning considerations for LMAs include optimal utilization of land to promote sustainable development; prevention of conversion of agricultural land to urban uses to ensure food security and protect livelihoods; making land available to support social development; preservation of historic, cultural heritage and natural resource, biodiversity and eco-sensitive areas, covering places of religious, archaeological, scenic and tourist importance; and promotion of guided development to minimize land use conflicts and adverse environmental impacts. The draft policy advocates a regional planning approach to establish a hierarchy of places with infrastructure and services.

URDPFI Guidelines, 2014

The URDPFI guidelines, prepared by the MoUD, GoI, aim at 'promoting balanced and orderly regional and urban planning and development' (MoUD 2015). They acknowledge that urban planning in India is 'rigid' and 'static', with 'little regard to investment planning', and 'taking a very long time'. The guidelines recommend an elaborate planning system comprising (a) core area planning and (b) specific and investment planning. Core area planning includes four interdependent plans: (a) a long-term 'perspective plan' with vision and policy orientation, (b) a sustainability-based long-term 'regional plan' (and 'district plan') aimed at optimization of regional resources for development, (c) a comprehensive long-term settlement plan as 'DP' for urban and peri-urban areas and (d) a short-term rolling 'local area plan' within the framework of DP. Specific and investment planning comprises of three plans: (a) a rolling special purpose plan within the framework of 'DP', (b) annual plans to translate the physical and fiscal resource requirements of DP/local area plan and (c) projects/research focused on execution.

Some welcome features of the URDPFI guidelines are (a) 'DP' to replace 'master plan', (b) 'development promotion' to substitute 'development control', (c) overarching DP for a metropolitan region to be in the form of 'structure plan', (d) 'DP' and 'mobility plan' to be integrated to ensure 'transport oriented spatial planning', (e) planning at local level to be mainly guided by an urban design approach focusing on mobility, accessibility and connectivity, (f) planning process to be simplified and (g) land to generate finance for infrastructure. However, the guidelines have some shortcomings. First, they exacerbate the multiplicity of plans prepared by authorities, leading to overlapping contents, regulations and signals. They ignore the capacity to plan in cities and towns. Second, the guidelines focus on horizontal land and call for projection of requirements for land uses. They underplay the role of density, accessibility, affordability and externalities in spatial organization of economic activity. Third, they neglect the economics of cities and dynamic interactions between market forces, externalities and public policies in producing spatio-economic outcomes.

National Urban Policy Framework, 2018

The MoHUA, GoI, framed NUPF in 2018. This calls for a 'new', 'organic' and 'decentralized' framework for urban planning and a 'new way' of thinking about urban issues and solutions in a 'context-based' manner. The vision of NUPF is as follows:

> The vision underpinning NUPF is to see cities as complex and changing agglomerations of people who are constantly interacting with each other, with socio-economic institutions and with the built environment. The soft and hard infrastructure of the city provides the backdrop for such interaction and are not ends in themselves. The exact optimization of a specific city, therefore, depends crucially on local context and cannot be done through the blind application of some Cartesian ideal. (MoHUA 2018)

NUPF, 2018, presents 10 guiding principles, applied to 10 functional areas of urban space and management: city planning, urban economy, physical infrastructure, social infrastructure, housing and affordability, transportation and mobility, urban finance, urban governance, urbanization and information system and environmental sustainability (see Box 8.2).

> **Box 8.2:** National Urban Policy Framework, 2018: Ten Guiding Principles

Principle 1: Cities as clusters of human capital—invest in clusters of human capital, which vary as per the economic and social context of a particular city.

Principle 2: Cities require a 'sense of place'—pay attention to the unique sense of place, critical for civic identity and pride and adopt planning and urban design that derive from location, socio-economic context, culture and history.

Principle 3: Not static master plans but evolving ecosystems—deal with cities as evolving, organic ecosystems with greater attention to the series of transitions that the city undergoes over time. Mixed and changing land uses are considered a natural part of urban management.

Principle 4: Build for density—anticipate and accommodate density. Proximity to transit or to clusters of human capital naturally attracts higher densities. In new areas, in particular, infrastructure should be pre-built to accommodate high density.

Principle 5: Public spaces that encourage social interactions—we need many shades of safe and accessible public spaces that encourage people to interact with each other. Moreover, we need to think of these spaces specifically for the Indian social context.

Principle 6: Multi-modal PT backbone—promote multi-modal PT and walkability in the city. The diversity of transport solutions and interchangeability is the key and must be tuned to the needs of the specific urban context.

Principle 7: Environmental sustainability—adapt to the local environmental landscape; this requires local knowledge and can benefit from digital mapping and satellite imaging technologies.

Principle 8: Financially self-reliant—encourage cities to leverage their local assets including community savings to generate more financing and revenue sources. The whole range of options needs to be explored from user charges to municipal bond financing to diverse methods of VCF.

Principle 9: Cities require clear unified leadership—implement urban governance structures that empower a unified and clear leadership and reduce the multiplicity of decision-makers. In addition, give a voice to those 'unheard' to promote universally accessible and equitable response.

Principle 10: Cities as engines of regional growth—an interconnected urban network, often driven by a large central node, can generate and sustain high rates of economic growth.

Source: Ministry of Housing and Urban Affairs, Government of India.

NUPF, 2018, envisages that cities propel sustainable development and job creation by clustering economic, social and cultural infrastructure, enhancing social and economic mobility, adopting mixed land use and leveraging local resources. It also expects that cities become inclusive by promoting socio-economic mobility, mixed uses, shared public spaces and PT. NUPF calls for building up rather than out, anticipating density and developing infrastructure accordingly. It advocates making urban planning dynamic, adaptive, iterative and continuous with changing land uses and constant feedback-based adjustment. NUPF further suggests making urban design responsive to historic, geographic and economic contexts and designing public places to facilitate people-to-people interaction.

The basic concepts in NUPF, 2018, are not 'new'. Some are highlighted by Jane Jacobs (1961) in her vehement criticism of modernist urban planning. Others are presented by planning movements in developed countries in the late 20th century: 'new urbanism', 'smart growth' and 'neo-traditionalism'. These movements raised a strong voice against sprawl, sub-urban traffic congestion, longer commuting, segregation and environmental degradation. They called for a planning model that brings home, work, shopping and recreation together; encourages pedestrian traffic; and promotes TOD and mixed land use, while conserving the environment (Knapp and Talen 2005). A key issue with NUPF, 2018, is that it suggests 'principles' and 'thinking', but no concrete actions, to restructure urban planning, financing and governance systems—address the root causes of India's urban problems. In fact, NUPF, 2018, leaves the preparation of urbanization strategy to states based on a view that urban solutions must be 'local' and 'contextual'.

An assessment of the national efforts to address land and urban policies in India suggests that they are disjointed. They do not integrate the principles of land, transport and urban economics and NEG. The view that urbanization is a state subject and should be addressed by state governments is myopic. In fact, in the 'post-GST', 'no octroi-no entry tax' regime, the issues of precarious municipal finances cannot be meaningfully addressed without the centre and states coming together to share GST with local governments. Moreover, metropolitan regions are India's growth engines, and even the Constitution (74th Amendment) Act, 1992, envisages a key role for the central government in metropolitan planning and development. Further, the objective of decentralized planning envisaged in NUPF, 2018, cannot be attained without a pan-India effort to implement the unfinished agenda of the 74th Amendment Act. The Act aims to position elected municipalities as the 'third tier' of government. However, it has deficiencies in regard to matters such as district and metropolitan planning and political and fiscal empowerment of ULGs. Ironically, it is the GoI that pioneered the 74th Amendment based on national consultations. It will be appropriate for the central government to lead another round of national debate to firmly establish local governments as agents of sustainable development. India must adopt the paradigm: 'think globally, act locally'.

Strategy of Urban Development

UN-SDG 11 and many other SDGs underscore the crucial importance of cities in attaining SDGs in developing countries. These countries, whose future is urban, need to balance development and conservation objectives. Cities catalyse economic growth and generate resources for rural and urban development. However, they consume a large quantity of non-renewable rural resources, while causing congestion, pollution and environmental degradation. Thus, cities must be equipped with instruments to address both the economies and diseconomies of density. Economic principles suggest that the society should be concerned with social benefits minus social costs, not costs per se. They emphasize the importance of SLM in addressing land market failure. Three foundational principles of SLM are: conservation of the environment with reference to 'carrying capacity' of the eco-system is non-negotiable; economic growth needs to be people-centric, people-driven and inclusive; and urban development must be value-creating so as to generate adequate resources to address the concerns of both urban and rural areas.

Urban planners and economists differ in the choice of instruments to address market failure. Planners favour regulation and direct intervention through land use and development controls and LA. Economists advocate incentivizing market players through tax-subsidy mechanisms to achieve socially optimal outcomes, while supplying an adequate quantity of public goods. Further, they suggest that regulatory instruments can be more effective when combined with economic tools; for example, residential land use zoning can be effective in promoting affordable housing, if combined with stiff taxation of vacant land to prevent speculative land hoarding. However, form-centric master plans in developing countries have neglected economic instruments. A key direction to reform urban planning in these countries is to incorporate the key principles of land, transport and urban economics and NEG. These disciplines, dealing with allocation of scarce land resources among competing uses, provide valuable lessons to design SLM and land and urban policies. They also present directions for broader reforms in urban planning, financing and governance to attain SDGs.

Land, transport and urban economics and NEG point to five major forces that determine spatial, socio-economic and environmental outcomes in urban areas (Glaeser 2011):

Agglomeration externalities—these arise from the collocation of economic activities in secondary and tertiary sectors, impacting spatial and socio-economic outcomes such as density, diversity, networking, cooperation, collaboration, competition, innovation and growth.

Location choice by firms, households and developers—various actors choose location based on an appraisal of benefits and costs of economic activities such as investing, producing, trading, living, working, earning, consuming, learning, sharing, matching and innovating.

Building technology and FSI—modern construction technology and higher FSI enable developers to substitute capital for costly land by going vertical in central areas, promoting densification, catalysing agglomeration economies and discouraging sprawl.

Transport technology—transport technology and connectivity influence commuting costs and time, facilitate mobility, enhance accessibility and enable cities to function as efficient labour markets. They widen the choice by employers and workers, match jobs and skills, shape city form and functions and make VCF of infrastructure feasible.

Government policies—government interventions affect activities such as land development, redevelopment, use and reuse—through spatial planning, zoning, development regulation, density management, infrastructure investment, public service delivery, land-based taxes and charges, congestion pricing, etc.

Land Economics

The concept of land in economics is much broader than its physical dimensions. It includes all factors with features of immobility and inelasticity in supply. It is a 'spatial', 'economic' and 'environmental' good with multiple features such as 'horizontal', 'vertical', 'accessibility' and linkage to important 'externalities'. The demand for urban land is primarily 'derived' from the needs of floor space by economic actors operating in multiple markets: land, transport, labour, goods and services, etc. The supply of urban land depends on private and public landowners. Three major constraints in the supply of land and floor space are (a) speculative 'holdouts' that lead to withdrawal of strategically located lands from the market, (b) chronic under-investments in transportation infrastructure that keep large extents of land inaccessible and (c) stringent zoning and DCRs that lead to market-wide artificial scarcities. The demand for and supply of land is impacted by externalities linked to collocation, contiguity, density, land use and accessibility to transport. They are influenced by government regulations concerning zoning, development control, infrastructure, conversion of agricultural land to urban use, transfer of property, rent control, land assembly, land taxation, etc. Land economics suggests that government interventions are important, but when poorly designed, they adversely affect the contribution of cities to economic growth and welfare.

Land economics portrays land as an 'input', 'output' and a 'resource' and land rent as 'surplus'. It suggests that high urban land values and housing prices in developing countries reflect the position that land

and housing markets are severely constrained to due to a combination of factors, including low FSI, chronic under-investment in infrastructure and speculative 'hold-outs'. Land economists regard LVT as an ideal instrument to finance urban infrastructure, apart from curbing speculation. The Henry George Theorem (HGT) suggests that under certain conditions, the aggregate spending by government on public goods generates adequate land rents to finance such goods (Arnott 2004; Arnott and Stiglitz 1979; George 1879; Stiglitz 1977). Stiglitz (2012) makes a strong case for stiff taxation of value of land and other natural resources and monopoly rents to reduce not only inequalities but also incentives for rent-seeking.

Urban land is characterized by land in physical dimensions + development right + accessibility to infrastructure, especially transportation + land use + land value and rents + links to externalities. However, urban planning in developing countries through master plans is narrowly focused on horizontal land. It neglects the vertical and accessibility dimensions of land, apart from externalities and unearned land rents. Master planning accords a secondary role to transport, with the primary role assigned to land use. It neglects the significance of PT in enhancing accessibility, promoting density and agglomeration economies, mitigating congestion diseconomies and guiding land development and use. Master plans in India have resorted to very low FSI on the ground that cities lack infrastructure. However, they fail to answer the question: why infrastructure investments cannot be increased to support higher FSI instead of resorting to horizontal expansion of cities and damaging the environment. By neglecting density, accessibility, externalities and land rents, the master plans have not been able to exploit 'benefit taxation', 'CC' and 'VCF' instruments. In spite of strong theoretical merits, the taxation of land rents, scarcity rents, monopoly rents, agglomeration rents and planning and infrastructure–induced rents has not engaged the attention of policymakers in developing countries.

Transport Economics

Transport links markets, including land, housing, transport, labour and goods and services. It connects households to opportunity and firms to prosperity. Along with land use, it shapes city form and functions. A successful urban form is one in which the negative consequences of urbanization and land use changes are outweighed by positive effects due to spatial planning, investment in infrastructure and land management. Dispersed development, characterized by fewer transport options, low densities and separation between residences and workplaces, leads to adverse environmental consequences through congestion; pollution; wastage of energy; segregation between the rich and the poor; overexploitation of land, water and other natural resources; and loss of biodiversity. It also negatively impacts the efficiency of the transport system as the same volume of activities and the same number of commuters demand transport involving increased number and length of trips. Further, the poor who need PT to access employment and housing opportunities are adversely impacted. Non-polluting transport investments in anticipation of economic growth have the potential to make cities efficient, mobile, inclusive and sustainable.

Major UT projects such as MRT, HSR and grids of arterial and radial roads have the potential to catalyse economic growth through direct, indirect and induced effects. They expand labour markets, enhance accessibility to valued locations, increase labour mobility, reduce transaction and time costs, facilitate density and knowledge transfers and increase competition. Paradoxically, the master plans in India have neglected not only transportation planning but also financing. Major UT projects lead to 'accessibility premium' to locations and 'WEBs' to the regional and national economies. Such benefits capitalize into tax bases of all levels of government, making value creation, capture and recycling a versatile strategy to finance transportation investments. The Mohring–Harwitz Theorem (MHT) states that under certain conditions, the revenues from a Pigovian congestion toll suffice to finance the capacity cost of an optimal-sized transport facility (Mohring 1972, 1976; Mohring and Harwitz 1962).

Transport economics argues that the relationship between transportation and land use is two-way. However, the master planning approach takes a one-sided view, that is, land use determines the transportation needs. The opposite view is perhaps more appropriate for a developing country like India as transport can play a key role in 'leading' local economic development by generating externality-induced benefits. Moreover, when investible resources are limited, transport investments must be channelized to guide the location of the most productive economic activities. The role of PT in environmental conservation, mobility of the poor and rise in land values that can finance transport infrastructure constitute other reasons why PT should receive utmost attention in national urbanization policy in developing countries. In fact, public transit presents a huge opportunity to re-engineer cities to make them inclusive. The urban poor, who are weeded out of both formal urban land markets and master plans, need to be provided with adequate space for living, working and vending in transit nodes and corridors to enable them to access remunerative employment and affordable housing.

Urban Economics

Urban economics considers cities as products of trade-offs between agglomeration and dispersal forces. It argues that cities form and grow to reap the external economies of agglomeration. The spatial concentration of economic activity leads to benefits at four levels. Gains internal to individuals arise from wider choices for jobs, higher wages, scope for learning and access to retail facilities, public services and social, cultural and recreational opportunities. Economies internal to firms occur from sharing of fixed assets, intermediate inputs, markets and services, division of labour and specialization. Benefits internal to industry but external to firms, called localization economies, include knowledge spillovers, sharing of inputs and infrastructure and access to markets for industry-specific skills. Economies external to industry but internal to the city arise from larger markets, greater diversity of economic activity, large pool of workers with cross-cutting skills, inter-industry knowledge spillovers and access to regional and national infrastructure networks. The strength of Silicon Valley and Bengaluru can be attributed to exchanges of knowledge between creative people. Large cities lead to benefits from specialization, diversity and competition. However, when the concentration of economic activities exceeds a threshold, external diseconomies arise, manifesting in increased costs of land and housing, congestion, pollution, sprawl, etc.

Urban economics recognizes the role of cities as large labour markets. The larger the urban labour market, the more innovative, efficient and productive a city is likely to be. The development of transport systems and functioning of labour markets are closely connected. Efficient transport ensures mobility, reduces congestion and pollution and leads to smooth movement of labour and goods across the urban region. Transport also affects the functioning of land markets. Transport improvements intensify economic activities in locations with greater accessibility. Further, they open up new areas for residential and non-residential development. Transport ensures that firms and households can choose new location or change existing location to optimize their objective functions. Major UT projects reduce commuting time and costs, expand labour markets, increase labour mobility and promote affordability of locations to firms and households. The basic model of urban economics assumes that people commute to CBD for work in order to get higher wages due to external economies of agglomeration. It offsets the land and housing costs against money and time costs of travel while choosing residential location. The model predicts that land rent, housing price, building height and population density fall with an increase in distance from CBD.

The trade-off between land/housing prices and transport costs—cheaper land/housing versus costlier commuting—has important implications for the role of transport in the design of urban planning. Major UT projects reduce commuting time and costs, increase labour mobility and promote affordability of locations to firms and households. Bertaud (2014) identifies two key objectives of urban planning, namely mobility and affordability:

> Mobility' is the ability to reach any area of a metropolitan area in as short a travel time as possible and "affordability" is the ability of households and firms to locate in whichever area they deem will maximize their welfare. Increasing mobility and affordability are the two main objectives of urban planning. These two objectives are directly related to the overall goal of maximizing the size of a city's labor market, and therefore its economic prosperity. (Bertaud 2014, 21)

New Economic Geography

NEG refers to the combined role of 'first nature geography' and 'second nature geography'. It emphasizes the tension between centripetal and centrifugal forces in the rise of regional agglomerations. Key centripetal forces are (a) market size: producers prefer larger markets due to consumers' preference for a variety of goods and services (demand linkage); a local concentration of intermediate inputs suppliers reduces the costs of other producers (cost linkage); (b) thick labour markets: agglomeration of many economic activities leads to emergence of thick labour markets for specialized skills to match the requirements of competing firms; and (c) pure external economies such as knowledge spillovers that promote learning. Main centrifugal forces include (a) transport costs; (b) immobile factors such as land and natural resources; (c) barriers to trade; (d) rise in land and housing costs; and (e) pure external diseconomies such as congestion. The interactions between agglomeration and dispersal forces shape spatio-economic outcomes—a position very different from that propagated by master planning based on modernist planning theories.

A recent body of research in NEG suggests that economic agglomerations lead to unearned increments to mobile factors in addition to immobile ones like land. It contends that when agglomeration externalities are vibrant, they create 'agglomeration rents' to capital and skilled workers. These can be taxed without the tax base vanishing (Andersson and Forslid 2003; Baldwin and Krugman 2004; Borck and Pfluger 2006; Ludema and Wooton 2000). Stiglitz (2012) refers to other forms of rents, including monopoly rents and natural resource rents. Municipalities can make the beneficiaries of various forms of rents to pay for investments that benefit them disproportionately. Policymakers and planners in developing countries, however, have neglected various forms of rents, including agglomeration rents to raise resources to finance urban development projects. The issues are embroiled in political economy factors.

Restructuring Urban Planning

Master plans of city regions embark on utopian urban forms, ignoring the limitations of financing and implementation instruments. They fail to appreciate a dominant paradigm in economics, namely optimization subject to constraints. This paradigm emphasizes the need to manage urban growth, prioritize objectives and address binding constraints. It advocates SLM to balance development, conservation, inclusion and financing imperatives, focusing on strategic objectives rather than routine land use controls at regional, city, zonal, local and plot levels. These objectives include (a) making serviced land and floor space available for growth and employment-generating activities, including affordable housing; (b) integrating transportation and land use planning to promote density and agglomeration economies, mitigate congestion diseconomies, balance employment and housing, avoid sprawl and unnecessary conversion of fertile agricultural land to urban use and catalyse rural development; (c) undertaking land assembly without relying on compulsory acquisition of land, weighing the options of 'building up' and 'building out' and recognizing landowners as partners in development; (d) incorporating the space needs of the poor for living, working and vending in land use plans; and (e) rooting plan financing strategy in the design of value creation, capture and recycling schemes. Land, transport and urban economics refer to spatial, economic, social, environmental, financial and other constraints in achieving SDGs. Abysmal urban finance and deficient urban governance are overarching constraints for suboptimal urban planning and development outcomes in developing countries.

Globally, cities containing 50 per cent of the population produce 80 per cent of global GDP. However, they account for 75 per cent of natural resource consumption, 80 per cent of energy and 75 per cent of carbon emissions (UNEP 2015; UN-Habitat 2016). Further, density leads to public health hazards via contagion effects of communicable diseases like Covid-19. The dense metropolitan cities of India are subject to serious issues of environment and public health due to land use–led spatial planning and neglect of infrastructure. Pollution in Delhi and devastating floods in Hyderabad in August 2000 and October 2020, Chennai in November 2015, Bengaluru in July 2016 and October 2020, and Mumbai in July 2005 and August 2017 reveal that not only urban planning but also infrastructure financing and governance systems have not kept pace with urbanization. The incidents highlight the importance of SLM in city regions, led by proactive investment in infrastructure and focused on inclusive growth and conservation. Cities have to be equipped with public health, PT, disaster management and other infrastructure to make them deliver desired outcomes. They need to be disaster resilient and, in a position, to cope with unforeseen calamities, including epidemics and pandemics like Covid-19. However, Indian cities are subject to chronic underinvestment in public goods and merit goods due to abysmal finances and weak governance structures (Mohanty 2014, 2016, 2019).

SLM suggests that the starting task in planning for sustainable development is to assess the ground realities, constraints and opportunities they present. Planners need to study the size, composition and growth in population of city regions and their income distribution structure; patterns of land use, density, transport and development; challenges of land, water, energy, environment and climate change; and state of urban finances. These considerations make it imperative for city regions to adopt a compact, PT–led and TOD strategy, while avoiding sprawl and personalized automobile-dependent urbanization. However, urban planners in developing countries have favoured horizontal expansion of cities, driven by anti-density perspectives of modernist planning. They exercise extreme controls over FSI in central city areas, while neglecting PT. This is at odds with SLM principles, which make a strong case for public transit and transport–land use integration. SLM advocates densification of strategic nodes in cities to gain from agglomeration, while avoiding unwarranted annexation of fertile agricultural lands to urban limits. In this regard, planners need to study the signals transmitted by market prices at regular intervals to design regulatory, developmental and economic interventions. They must monitor spatial trends and patterns in land values, housing prices, office rents, transport costs, etc. and their impacts on emerging land development and land use patterns. All the solutions to urban land market failure problems cannot be attained through regulatory controls.

Case for Strategic Urban Planning

Location and land use decisions of numerous actors in a city region are determined by complex and dynamic interactions between market forces, externalities and public policies. Thus, a deterministic and static master plan with rigid land use prescriptions at multiple levels is not suitable to promote SLM and sustainable development. Ill-conceived and poorly crafted controls on FSI and land use stifle the operations of market forces and dampen people-driven and developer-led initiatives. Accordingly, a two-tier planning approach is considered adequate: strategic or structural planning at regional level and TPS at local area level. The strategic plan may focus on conservation of natural and heritage resources and phased development of core infrastructure, including public transit, commuter rail, HSR, water supply, sewerage, drainage, gas, broadband connectivity, etc. TPS may focus on TOD and SLM, integrating PT, labour mobility, accessibility and affordability of locations, land use, density, development, inclusion and VCF as part of urban design. A strong case exists for the government to facilitate LPS led by private developers incentivized by government policies and actions such as infrastructure connectivity, density bonus, zoning changes and fiscal dispensations.

The SLM approach warrants that planners in a developing country must first assess the 'carrying capacity' of the ecosystem. The conservation of heritage and non-renewable resources is non-negotiable. It must be the starting point in the plan-making process for sustainable development. The regional conservation plan may be followed by regional transportation plan. Transport receives priority over other land management tools due to its critical role in environmental sustainability, social equity, economic efficiency and resource generation objectives. The regional transportation plan may include existing and proposed national, state and district highways, railways, air and other transport networks, integrating BRT, LRT, MRT, HSR and a regional grid of arterial and radial roads to be developed in phases. Traffic-generating land uses such as commercial, institutional and high-density housing may be located around public transit nodes and corridors to facilitate transit ridership, make transit system viable and promote TOD. Allocation of land for high-income housing may be the last step in the planning process. A structural planning approach will provide the flexibility needed by decentralized actors to respond to the GEM, including major PT investments.

Re-engineering Cities with Transit

A transport-led and TOD strategy has the potential to re-engineer cities in developing countries like India through SLM. It calls for delineating land for regional transit, HSR, arterial and radial road networks well in advance so as to add infrastructure inexpensively on a 'just-in-time' basis as urbanization occurs. This approach does not rely on a top-down master planning approach that prescribes rigid controls up to the plot level. It relies on land development between arterial roads and around transit corridors by households and developers, facilitated by LPS. Land delineated for transportation networks could be procured in the planning process based on a value creation and capture approach. The Sardar Patel Ring Road in Ahmedabad with land secured through the TPS presents a good example. The revised DP for Ahmedabad metropolitan area has demarcated a 1-km stretch around the 76-km-long ring road as R-AH zone, permitting FSI of 4 for the construction of residential units of 36–80 m² of built-up area. This is a pioneering effort to integrate PT, density and land use to promote IZ and affordable housing—worth emulation by all cities in the country.

Major UT projects lead to accessibility benefits to locations and WEBs to the economy. They lead to a massive transfer of resources to property owners from future buyers and renters apart from benefiting them through transit construction subsidy. Making such projects financially viable calls for transportation-land use integration to facilitate value increment financing. However, the transit agency may not possess the instruments to utilize the windfall gains in property values due to their investments. Thus, the design of TOD with appropriate intergovernmental partnerships is important. It calls for flexible, incentive-linked zoning instruments that permit beneficial changes in land use and FSI in transit nodes and corridors; for example, TOD can be facilitated by permitting access of large developments to service roads linking highways and rail corridors. Similarly, increasing FSI in transit-impact zones, say, 500 m of MRT alignment and converting land use in such zones from single-family residential to commercial, institutional or multi-family residential can incentivize TOD. Access to PT within 15 min of walk and a commuting time to work up to 1 h may be regarded as a guide to implement TOD.

Metropolitan cities in India are executing MRT projects to address their mobility concerns. The full benefits of such projects, with capacity to handle 50,000–80,000 PHPDT can be reaped only by densifying transit nodes and corridors. This calls for changes in zoning in transit-impact areas and development of feeder infrastructure to ensure last-mile connectivity. However, metro projects in India are executed in isolation without partnerships between transit authorities, other infrastructure entities, planning and development authorities and municipalities. The success of these projects depends on complementary policies—discouraging automobile ridership, encouraging PT, developing town centres and subcentres, enhancing regional connectivity and imposing a graduated VLT to curb speculation in land. In order for a transit project to generate the largest beneficial impacts, the transit and local authorities must work closely. The local government must be in a position to exploit land management tools to promote dense developments around transit nodes and corridors to support transit ridership. It must also be equipped with fiscal instruments to capture land value increments to repay the debt incurred for financing. The need for flexible land use planning and complementary policies is amply demonstrated by successful public transit projects around the world such as Hong Kong, Singapore, Seoul, Toronto, Copenhagen, Curitiba and Bogota.

Land Assembly with Land Pooling

Compulsory acquisition of land for planned urban development is not going to be smooth under the LA Law, 2013, in India. Moreover, one cannot justify why landowners-farmers, who contribute the limited land they possess for value creation through cities, should not be made partners in development. Thus, city regions should explore other land assembly options along with overall liberalization of density, FSI and land use to balance vertical development and horizontal expansion. Such options include strategic densification of CBD and select other centres; renewal of derelict areas and infill development; planned expansion with LPS; ring towns and satellite towns connected to large cities by limited access expressways, regional transit, commuter rail or HSR to be developed in phases; and new towns on emerging industrial growth corridors. SLM suggests that land assembly be guided by overriding priority to conservation, 'leading' role of PT, TOD, mixed land use, IZ and VCF of infrastructure. Some best practices include TPS in Gujarat; land pooling with farmers as shareholders in Magarpatta city, Pune; city-wide liberalization of FSI linking it to objective parameters such as road width, plot size and impact fee and zoning incentive-linked road widening scheme in Hyderabad; RA-H zone in Ahmedabad, integrated transportation-land use planning in Copenhagen (finger plan); transit-based urban design in Curitiba and auctioning of development rights under the scheme of CEPAC in Brazil.

Case for Inclusionary Zoning

Not only markets but also master plans have failed the poor, depriving them of the 'right to the city'. These plans have not allocated adequate space to the LIGs for living, working and vending. They ignore the informal economy that engages the bulk of the urban poor. Unrealistic space norms such as minimum size of development, maximum FSI, minimum size of plot and dwelling unit, maximum plot coverage, minimum setback, minimum number of parking spaces per unit of housing, minimum permissible width of approach road and other standards have led to an inequitable planning regime in India in which some have gained while many have lost. In contrast, the assignment of higher FSI and higher value land uses such as commercial, office or high-density residential to some locations has resulted in huge windfalls to a lucky group of landowners. The gainers are not required to compensate the losers such as those whose lands are reserved for conservation. The master planning model has perpetrated inequality, leading to artificial scarcity of land and floor space not only for the poor and LIGs but also the middle class.

Cities in India must explore the instruments of IZ and IH adopted by developed countries. Growth must mitigate its impacts, including the need for affordable housing. There is a strong case for allocating land to LIGs in the planning process as in TPS in Gujarat. TOD, combined with TPS, presents a huge opportunity to re-engineer cities and reconnect the poor to economic opportunities. Zoning incentives may be designed to promote strategic densification of transit nodes and corridors to provide affordable housing and workplaces for the disadvantaged groups. In this context, the R-AH zone in Ahmedabad provides an innovative example to promote inclusionary affordable housing. The RA-H zone permits high density affordable housing around the 76-km-long Sardar Patel Ring Road. Access to highways, IZ, density bonus and fiscal incentives to developers under income tax and GST rules have succeeded in creating affordable housing stock for the LIGs. India must explore denser and taller housing near transit while planning for TOD.

Revamping Urban Finance

A fundamental policy issue in India is that both rural and urban development cannot be subsidized. If the plight of the underprivileged in rural areas has to be substantially improved in national interest, cities must generate adequate resources not only for urban services but also for rural development and poverty alleviation. This realization must guide policymakers in endowing cities with a basket of 'own' taxes, revenue-shared taxes, charges, transfers and other instruments to finance infrastructure and services. However, with revenues at a meagre 1 per cent of GDP, Indian municipalities are among the weakest globally in terms of resource raising power and fiscal autonomy (Mohanty 2016). With the central-state GST subsuming key local taxes such as octroi, entry tax and advertisement tax, ULGs in India are left with only one major tax, namely property tax. No doubt, property tax is under-exploited and reforms in the tax are overdue. However, unlike developed countries, ULGs in India do not have access to a broad basket of revenue sources: income tax, sales tax, GST, excise duty, turnover tax, motor fuel tax, payroll tax, etc. Transfers from central and state governments are not satisfactory. International practice suggests that a combination of land-based taxes, other benefit taxes, general taxes, user charges for utility services, formula-based transfers, borrowing, development financing, VCF and CC instruments is appropriate for municipalities in developing countries.

The design of a robust financing system for the 'third tier' in India calls for drastic reforms in fiscal federalism, including a 'municipal finance list' in the Constitution of India. A strong case exists for enabling ULGs to have access to GST based on the principle of benefit taxation. At present, the dual GST scheme may be replaced by a three-part formula: 5 per cent (centre)-5 per cent (state)-2 per cent (local government). Land-based taxes and shared GST may be dedicated to a long-term, say, 30-year regional and urban infrastructure plan, including MRT, commuter rail, HSR and regional grids of arterial and radial highways linking cities, suburbs and rural growth centres. Subject to GST sharing, municipal finance reforms in India may be guided by two key principles: benefit taxation and TIF.

Principle of Benefit Taxation

In public finance theory, benefit taxes are regarded as ideal instruments to finance public goods (Bahl and Linn 1992; Lindahl 1919; Mohanty 2016, 2019; Wicksell 1896). The generalized benefit principle makes a strong case for financing city development and services with 'users pay', 'beneficiaries pay', polluters pay', 'exacerbaters pay', 'congesters pay' and 'growth pays' instruments. As cities create benefits to economic agents due to spatial planning, infrastructure investment, agglomeration externalities, economic growth, etc., they ought to have access to appropriate benefit taxes. Property tax is a benefit tax to meet the costs of collective civic services. Vehicles and fuel taxes for highways and water and sewer benefit taxes for water supply and sewerage projects are special benefit taxes. Income, payroll, excise and GSTs are general benefit taxes in connection with living, working and transacting in the city (Bahl and Linn 2014). As central and state governments gain by way of huge increments in their tax bases due to investments in major infrastructure projects in metropolitan regions, they need to share the costs of such projects based on the benefit principle.

Land-based revenues are well suited to raise seed money to leverage debt financing for lumpy urban infrastructure projects, especially PT. Benefits from these projects capitalize into land values due to enhanced 'accessibility', 'serviceability' and increased 'intensity' of development, often facilitated by favourable changes in land use and FSI or 'upzoning'. Paradoxically, cities in India have not exploited land-based instruments such as LVT, LVIT, capital value–based property tax, VLT, impact fee, betterment levy, special assessment district, planning obligations, development contributions, purchasable development rights, TIF, etc. They have not attempted to tax 'land rents', 'monopoly rents' and 'agglomeration rents' generated by urban planning and development processes. While a tax on vacant land can be a powerful tool to promote land uses for growth-generating activities and affordable housing, hardly any city has resorted to such instruments. Similarly, TPS based on land pooling and self-financing of urban expansion and renewal with inclusion have not been adopted by states other than Gujarat.

Tax Increment Financing Model

The theory of public finance suggests that borrowing is the most appropriate instrument to finance lumpy infrastructure projects such as MRT and HSR whose benefits spread over generations and jurisdictions. However, the debt incurred for such projects, whether executed by a public authority or PPP, will have to be repaid. This calls for escrowing revenues: project and general. In this regard, a TIF approach, often considered 'the only game in the town' in the United States, is worth adopting by Indian cities. TIF aims at earmarking the future revenue increments due to infrastructure investments and supporting policies to repay the debt incurred for financing. It focuses on value-creating development or renewal in a designated area with the public authorities 'ring-fencing' a part or whole of the incremental taxes, charges and special levies made possible by such projects. The success of TIF depends on its design, especially financing and cost recovery. In the case of major urban projects, TIF revenues could be supplemented by other sources such as viability gap funding, dedicated taxes, charges and fees and transfers.

Reforming Urban Governance

Local government institutions in India are weak. The country has 278,974 local bodies comprising 253,098 Panchayati Raj Institutions

(PRIs), 13,964 traditional bodies and 4,545 ULGs (www.lgdirectory. gov.in accessed August 30, 2019). PRIs include 654 panchayats at the district level, 6,713 panchayats at the block or intermediate level and 253,098 panchayats at the village level. The ULGs include about 220 municipal corporations established for larger cities, about 1700 municipalities for smaller cities and towns and the rest being nagar panchayats for areas in rural-urban transition. Empowerment of these local governments and good urban governance will unleash a huge amount of energy and leadership to own, localize and implement the global agenda for sustainable development.

Municipalities as the Third Tier

Indian cities are faced with institutional, human resource and technical capacity constraints to deliver good governance. With precarious finance, outdated planning and weak public service delivery systems, they are subjected to elaborate controls by state governments. Unlike developed countries, municipalities in India are not empowered with functions, finances and functionaries to act as self-governed institutions. A popular textbook in urban economics makes the following observations regarding local government in the United States (Brueckner 2011):

> In the United States, most of the public goods and services that people consume are provided by local jurisdictions, not by the federal or state government. The federal government provides national defense, interstate highways, national parks, and some other less visible public goods and services. State governments provide highways, parks, and higher education through systems of public universities. But it is local governments that provide elementary and secondary education, police and fire protection, mass transit, city streets, recreational facilities, public health facilities, sewers and sanitation, and other goods and services. These goods play a bigger role in people's daily lives than the goods provided by higher levels of government. (Chapter 8: Local Public Goods and Services, 159)

The above description applies to local bodies in most developed countries. Several developing countries have also taken initiatives to decentralize and empower local governments. However, municipalities in India do not have the autonomy to deliver performance with accountability. They are unable to discharge mandate due to overlapping responsibilities, mismatch between functions and finances and weak governance structure. The country needs to complete the unfinished agenda of democratic decentralization envisaged in the Constitution (74th Amendment) Acts, 1992. A national consensus is needed to firmly establish municipalities as the 'third tier', led by a directly elected mayor for 5 years and supported by a team of professional urban managers.

Metropolitan Governance Framework

Metropolitan regions are subject to important externalities and spill-over effects. They are multi-governmental and coordination is critical for internalizing externalities and correct for failure of metropolitan markets. However, the structure of metropolitan governance in India is highly fragmented. This has led to serious problems in planning, financing and implementation—most conspicuous in the case of regional functions like PT and conservation. The authorities involved in planning and development of the NCR include DDA, DMRC, Delhi Urban Art Commission, New Delhi Municipal Committee, three municipal corporations, Delhi Jal Board, Delhi Urban Shelter Improvement Board, GNCTD, NCR Planning Board, and Ministries of GoI, especially Housing and Urban Affairs, Home and Railways. Coordination between these authorities is a major issue due to the political, legal, administrative and bureaucratic complexities involved. Metropolitan fragmentation adversely affects the provision of infrastructure to growth-generating firms and environmental conservation service delivery to people, especially the poor. The governance structures of metropolitan regions in London, New York, Tokyo and Barcelona highlight the importance of a strong political autonomy and public accountability framework at the metropolitan level. Such frameworks are missing in India. The country may explore a strong metropolitan mayor system as in Greater London.

Addressing Capacity Constraints

Unlike central, state and district administration, well-defined cadres do not exist in municipalities in India to discharge various functions.

ULGs depend on state governments for posting of chief executive officer and other key personnel. These personnel are transferred at the mercy of state government. They often lack professionalism to discharge functions such as transport–land use integration, PPP structuring, resource mobilization through municipal bonds, and application of new technology such as big data analytics, artificial intelligence and machine learning to improve civic services. Performance measurement and management, independent regulatory oversight and social accountability mechanisms to facilitate the effective functioning of municipal officials are absent in municipalities.

The expertise to plan for urban regions, metropolitan areas, districts, cities, census towns and large villages likely to become urban centres in India is severely limited by the lack of physical, transportation, environmental, social and economic planners. With 7,935 cities and towns, including 53 metropolitan cities requiring MDPs and more than 650 districts requiring DDPs as mandated by the Constitution (74th Amendment) Act, 1992, India needs a multi-fold increase in the number of town and country planners from the current level of about 6,000. The report of the committee of experts for the preparation of policy guidelines to energize architecture and town planning education in India set up by the Ministry of Human Resource Development, GoI, July 2011 estimated that India would need about 300,000 qualified town and country planners by 2031. A total of 15,000 planners need to be trained every year as against less than 1,000 at present. This calls for strengthening planning education in the country to create a pool of town and country planners.

Summary and Conclusion

Land economics has not received the importance it deserves from policymakers and planners. There is perhaps no branch of economics that is so relevant, yet so neglected in developing countries. Land economics is not even taught in universities. This is disturbing as land is instrumental for planned urban development in these countries whose future is 'urban'. Land acts as a platform for cities to deliver spatial, economic, social and environmental functions. Further, as

Stiglitz–Piketty debate highlights, urban land is a prominent source of inequality in wealth. Lack of access to land is also a major cause of poverty in rural areas in developing countries, including India. However, land policy issues are grossly neglected in these countries. An integrated approach to land management combining developmental, regulatory and economic instruments has not emerged. Infrastructure development to service land has been plagued by chronic under-investment for decades. While land taxation to finance infrastructure curbs speculation in land markets, it has not engaged the attention of politicians and bureaucrats. Urban planning through master plans has adopted a narrow view of land, undermining the role of transport, density and externalities in land development and use. Because master planning is focused on regulatory controls over land markets, it lacks economics.

Urbanization presents a unique opportunity for developing countries to promote sustainable development. City regions act as locomotives of growth. They enable rural-urban migrants and commuters to overcome abject poverty. They generate public finance for rural and urban development, but density and land use in cities lead to congestion, pollution, public health hazards and adverse impacts on food, water, energy and climate change. Public policy needs to address both positive and negative effects of urbanization and spatial concentration. However, master planning has been unduly obsessed with urban costs and controls to correct negative externalities. It fails to recognize a fundamental principle of economics that the society ought to be concerned with 'net social benefits', that is, social benefits – social costs, not costs per se. The principle suggests that urban growth needs to be managed, rather than being controlled and confined to a rigid spatial frame. It is in this context that the present book advocates SLM tools to manage density and land use. It calls for incorporating the principles of land economics and closely related disciplines of transport economics and urban economics into urban planning and development strategies. Recognizing the pivotal role of cities in national transformation, the book also suggests broader reforms in urban planning, financing and governance in developing countries.

Pivotal Importance of Cities

The role of cities as catalysts of external economies of agglomeration and economic growth is well recognized. What is not understood is their role in rural transformation—through creation of employment for rural-urban migrants and commuters and generation of public finance for rural development and poverty reduction. The great urbanist Jane Jacobs observes:

> The hard truth is there is no decent way of overcoming rural poverty where people have no access to productive city jobs. That was true in the day of Scottish clearances and is true still. It has been true in the case of the rich United States and is equally true in the case of the World Bank's poor clients. (Jacobs 1984, 92)

Referring to cities as tax bases, Jacobs (1984) calls them 'the greatest yielders of revenues in a nation or empire'. She informs that when the United States income tax was first adopted in 1913, a third of the nation's total tax yield came from New York State alone, most of it from NYC. She argues that until a nation has well-developed and productive cities, it cannot afford programmes for basic necessities or transfer payments to the rural poor. The crucial role of cities in catalysing externalities, generating public finance and addressing rural poverty makes a compelling case for strengthening urban planning, financing and governance systems in developing countries.

Fallacies of Master Planning

Cities are inherently dynamic. Urban outcomes reflect interactions between market forces, externalities and public policies. As Jacobs (1961) observes, cities are integrated systems in which many variables interact. The elements of a city function synergistically. They enable decentralized actors to organize into something greater than the sum of their individual parts. Thus, a static master planning model that destines the city to a mechanically predetermined form ignoring its evolution, is ill-suited to deal with land market failure. Moreover, as land economics portrays, the concept of land is much broader than that adopted by master planning. Land is a highly heterogenous good with spatial, economic, environmental and social characteristics. It has multiple dimensions: horizontal, vertical, access to infrastructure and links to externalities. Land performs multiple roles in planned urban development process—as an input, an output and a resource. The demand for land is largely 'derived' from the needs of economic activities for floor space. The supply of land and floor space depends on several factors, including speculation in land market, access to infrastructure, especially transport, FSI and land use controls and land prices.

Urban planning, which is narrowly focused on land use in developing countries, neglects the other even more important dimensions of land such as density, accessibility, affordability and externalities. The heterogeneous nature of land and complexities of land markets suggest that the survey-analysis-project-plan technique, propagated by eminent planner Patrick Geddes, is fraught with methodological problems. This technique limits land to its horizontal dimensions, while projecting economic activities and their land use requirements, 20–25 years ahead. Land economics, on the contrary, regards land as a composite good represented by:

> Land in physical dimensions + use permissible under zoning + FSI or density permissible under development regulations + accessibility to transportation and other infrastructure that depends on public investment + linkages to externalities that arise due to the collocation of numerous economic agents + land value and rents that depend on demand and supply, access to infrastructure, present and future use potential.

The broader view of land suggests that long-term projections of economic activities, which form the basis of land use proposals by master planners, are likely to be erroneous. Further, rigid land use controls at regional, city, zone, local and plot levels are unwarranted. They seriously distort the signals transmitted by the market and curtail the degrees of freedom with market players.

A Two-Tier Planning Strategy

Master planning in India has led to a scarcity of serviced land and floor space for economic growth and affordable housing. It has resulted in sprawl, environmental degradation, social exclusion, corruption and deadweight welfare losses. Land and urban economics advocate shifting from a top-down, technocratic, prescriptive, rigid, land use–based and comprehensive planning to decentralized, people-driven, responsive, flexible, transport-led and strategic planning paradigm aimed at promoting development rather than controlling it. India needs to liberalize master planning that remains untouched by economic liberalization reforms from the 1990s. The country must also proactively invest in regional and UT infrastructure projects, including MRT, commuter rail/HSR to redensify and re-engineer cities. These projects lead to economy-wide benefits not captured by standard benefit-cost analysis.

Indian cities are under-planned and over-regulated. They are under-planned due to the neglect of infrastructure, especially transport to support and attract growth. By neglecting investment in transport, they have not exploited the synergy between transport, land use, density, development, inclusion and VCF. Cities are over-regulated due to their restrictive zoning and FSI regimes. The master plans have undermined the role of market forces in growth while disregarding the limitations of regulatory instruments. They constrain decision-making regarding 'location' and 'land use' by firms and households. The adverse effects of over-regulation of land markets are exacerbated by under-investment in transport due to neglect of urban finances. This book suggests a two-tier planning approach instead of land use controls at regional, city, zonal, local and plot levels. The first tier aims at a regional strategic or structural plan, focused on conservation of national, state and regional heritage and environmental resources and core regional infrastructure networks, especially public transit, HSR and a grid of arterial and radial roads to be developed in phases. The second tier envisages a series of LPS at the local level led by TOD, guided by SLM, incentivized by government and driven by developers, including people. It aims to integrate transportation, land use, density, development, inclusion and VCF. This book calls for implementing urbanization as a 'project'.

Urbanization as a Project

Urbanization project is complete in the developed world but ongoing in developing countries. Every project has its economics that calls for aligning objectives, constraints and instruments. Overriding considerations of sustainable development make a compelling case for transport-led and transit-oriented urban development strategy. This strategy is aimed at establishing connectivity, expanding labour market, enhancing labour mobility, catalysing economic growth, facilitating employment and housing for the poor, conserving the environment and promoting VCF. Subject to the leading role of transport, urban renewal, infill development, expansion and new township schemes may combine developmental, regulatory and economic instruments. While master planning is narrowly focused on land use, planning for urbanization as a project calls for integrating transportation, land use, density, local economic development, social inclusion, environmental conservation and financing strategy. Flexibility is required in attracting investment and growth while designing self-financing schemes. The logic put forth by urban planners that flexible planning will lead to discretionary changes in land use is flawed. Administrative issues must be tackled by reforming governance rather than by perpetuating inefficiencies that hurt growth. Countries like the United States, the United Kingdom and Australia allow zoning incentives for projects with potential to generate large social benefits relative to social costs.

Major projects like MRT, HSR and a grid of arterial and radial roads lead to important externalities. They influence economic activity, location, land use, investment, input mix and production. Such projects need to be appraised taking into account direct, indirect and induced effects. Regulations and permissions under the planning system also generate trade-offs between benefits and costs. Conventional benefit-cost analysis is inadequate to evaluate major urban investments and regulatory instruments. The wider economic impacts of urban planning, design and development need to be taken into account. Further, benefit taxation and VCF ought to be integral parts of project design. A well-structured project that passes the social benefit-cost test must be able to generate adequate resources for its financing.

Urban Planning as a Resource

Cities in developing countries have not utilized urban planning as a resource. This is due to the narrow interpretation of land and neglect of land, transport and urban economics. Master planning predetermines land use and density; it is not suited to exploit the links between transport, density, land use and plan financing. Urban economics suggests that collocation and density catalyse agglomeration economies in central locations and facilitate knowledge-led growth. Transport economics refers to WEBs of major transport investments by enhancing access to economic mass. Such investments lead to accessibility premiums to locations that capitalize into land values and rents. Land economics refers to unearned increments to land, including monopoly rent, scarcity rent, location rent and agglomeration rent that can be utilized to leverage debt financing of infrastructure. Economics principles suggest strategic densification of cities linked to transportation investment with focus on a few centres rather than spreading development too thinly. However, poorly managed density leads to negative externalities and welfare losses. The strategy to increase density needs to be combined with investment in transit and complementary policies such as taxation of vacant land and CC to promote TOD. Density, land use and TOD must be planned together along with connectivity infrastructure and pricing of development rights rather than being 'pre-determined'. Gainers must pay; losers must be compensated.

Value Increment Financing Partnerships

The current finances of ULGs in India are precarious, locking cities in a low-level equilibrium trap. Thus, a strategy of urban development that relies on future revenue streams from well-designed projects makes good sense. This strategy warrants structuring of value-creating projects with intergovernmental partnerships, involving the private sector where beneficial. Ironically, central and state governments reap huge gains from major projects in metropolitan regions such as MRT and HSR. Generating WEBs, these projects lead to sizable increases in tax bases: income tax, corporation tax, GST, sales tax, excise duty, property transfer tax, motor vehicles tax, etc. Thus, a value increment financing partnership between local, state and central governments to implement projects is desirable. The repayment of debt for such projects may be linked to land-based taxes, impact fees, betterment levies, special assessments, CC and dedicated funds from central and state governments. Examples of dedicated funds include fuel tax in the United States, transport tax in France and earmarked transfers from governments in other countries. In the present context of India, a city share in GST, which has subsumed local taxes such as octroi and entry tax is appropriate for sustained funding of major urban infrastructure projects, including MRT and HSR. India may also explore a 'piggy-backed' income tax as in the United States to strengthen municipal finance.

Landowners as Development Partners

The view that landowners gain without risking or economizing is myopic. In developing countries like India, pervasive imperfections in land markets, poor land records, prolonged court litigations and periodic booms and busts in property markets suggest that landowners and developers do shoulder major risks. It is desirable that they are taken into confidence as partners in the design of LPS and other land development schemes. Compulsory acquisition of land in the past was in the spirit of command and control–based master planning. It was vehemently opposed by landowners and farmers as it led to compensation to landowners at below-market rate. There is also no justification why landowners, contributing land for value creation in cities, should not benefit from planned urban development. Schemes like Magarpatta city, led by farmers as shareholders-developers need to be incentivized, with the additional incorporation of IZ. The government may take proactive action to promote 'ease of doing development'.

Innovations and Best Practices

While innovation is the hallmark of great cities, there are many good practices that can be adopted and replicated across India. They include, but are not limited to TPS (Gujarat); landowners-farmers as shareholders in urban development (Magarpatta city); drastic liberalization of FSI linked to objective parameters such as road width, plot size and impact fee (Hyderabad); integrated transportation-land use planning linking accessibility, affordability, mobility, density and development (Copenhagen, Curitiba, Seoul and Toronto); auctioning of development rights through CEPAC (Brazil); urban strategy, zoning and FSI as resources to finance metropolitan transit (Hong Kong, Singapore and Bengaluru); public-private partnership for construction of metro linked to land as a resource (Hyderabad); IZ with allocation of land to weaker sections through TPS (Gujarat) and R-AH zone along Sardar Patel Ring Road that combines density, TOD, IZ and affordable housing (Ahmedabad).

Think Globally, Act Locally

International experience suggests that well-governed, compact, dense, diverse, dynamic and networked city regions act as drivers of sustainable development. They compete with other regions and countries to attract entrepreneurs, skilled workers and investments for economic growth. Distinguished by multi-modal PT infrastructure networks, hub and spoke-patterned spatial development, transport–land use integration, labour market mobility and knowledge-led drivers of growth, these regions are endowed with robust planning, financing and governance systems. They combine autonomy and accountability in the implementation of regional functions. If city regions, especially metropolitan areas are to drive SDGs, democratically elected and empowered ULGs and metropolitan governments must be put in place. They must also be able to make sustained investments in public health, PT and disaster resilience infrastructure in anticipation of economic growth, exigencies and calamities. Further, they must be in a position to structure and implement land and development schemes, integrating local resources and instruments.

Public authorities in India have resorted to land use–led urban planning for seven decades, disregarding the principles of land, transport and urban economics. The results are far from being satisfactory. They must implement transport-led and transit-oriented planning and development to re-engineer city regions for at least the next three decades. Urbanization needs to be implemented as a project to exploit the synergy between accessibility, affordability, density and land use in locations, mobility in the labour market, land and infrastructure development, social inclusion, value creation, capture and recycling strategy and economic growth drivers. Urban renewal, densification, infill development, expansion and new township development schemes may be designed as self-financed projects. Key directions for urban sector reforms include incorporation of land economics into urban planning and development; investment in PT in anticipation of growth; transport-led and transit-oriented urban development, exploitation of potential of property tax, VLT and other land-based taxes, benefit taxation, a city GST rate, a municipal finance list in the Constitution of India and TIF; empowered ULGs and metropolitan governments led by directly elected mayors; and professionalization of urban management. India must firmly establish the 'third tier' to localize the UN-SDGs, guided by the global approach to sustainable development: 'think globally and act locally'.

Bibliography

Ahluwalia, Isher, R. Kanbur, and P. K. Mohanty. 2014. *Challenges of Urbanization in India*. New Delhi: SAGE Publications.
Allmendinger, P. 2009. *Planning Theory* 2nd Edition. Basingstoke: Palgrave Macmillan.
Alonso, William. 1964. *Location and Land Use*. Cambridge, MA: Harvard University Press.
Andelson, Robert V., ed. 2000. *Land-value Taxation around the World*. Malden, MA: Blackwell.
Anderson, John E. 2009. 'A Review of the Evidence on Land Value Taxation'. In *Land Value Taxation: Theory, Evidence, and Practice*, edited by Richard F. Dye and Richard W. England. Cambridge, MA: Lincoln Institute of Land Policy.
Andersson, Fredrik, and Rikard Forslid. 2003. 'Tax Competition and Economic Geography'. *Journal of Public Economic Theory* 5: 279–303.
Angel, Shlomo. 2008. 'An Arterial Grid of Dirt Roads'. *Cities* 25: 146–162.
———. 2012. *Planet of Cities*. Cambridge, MA: Lincoln Institute of Land Policy.
Arnott, R. 2004. 'Does the Henry George Theorem Provide a Practical Guide to Optimal City Size?' *The American Journal of Economics and Sociology* 63: 1057–1090.
———. 2012. 'What Planners Need to Know about the "New Urban Economics"'. In *Oxford Handbook of Urban Economics and Planning*, edited by Nancy Brooks, Kieran Donaghy and Gerrit Jan-Knapp. Oxford: Oxford University Press.
Arnott, R., and Joseph E. Stiglitz. 1979. 'Aggregate Land Rents, Expenditure on Public Goods, and Optimal City Size'. *Quarterly Journal of Economics* 93: 471–500.
Arthur, W. Brian. 1990. 'Positive Feedbacks in the Economy'. *Scientific American* 262 (February): 92–99.
Atkinson, A. B., and Joseph E. Stiglitz. 1980. *Lectures on Public Economics*. New York, NY: McGraw Hill.
Augustyn, Robert T., and Paul E. Cohen. 1997. *Manhattan in Maps*. New York, NY: Rizzoli International Publications.

Bahl, Roy, and Johannes Linn. 1992. *Urban Public Finance in Developing Countries*. New York, NY: Oxford University Press.

———. 2014. *Governing and Financing Cities in the Developing World*. Cambridge, MA: Lincoln Institute of Land Policy.

Bahl, Roy, Jorge Martinez-Vazqez, and Joan Youngman, eds. 2008. *Making the Property Tax Work: Experiences in Developing and Transitional Countries*. Cambridge, MA: Lincoln Institute of Land Policy.

Bahl, Roy W., Johannes F. Linn, and Deborah L. Wetzel, eds. 2013. *Financing Metropolitan Governments in Developing Countries*. Cambridge, MA: Lincoln Institute of Land Policy.

Baldwin, Richard, and Paul Krugman. 2004. 'Agglomeration, Integration and Tax Harmonization'. *European Economic Review* 48: 1–23.

Ballaney, Shirley. 2008. *The Town Planning Mechanism in Gujarat, India*. Washington, DC: World Bank.

Barlowe, R. 1986. *Land Resource Economics: The Economics of Real Property*. Englewoods Cliffs, NJ: Prentice Hall.

Bauer, Catherine. 1934. *Modern Housing*. Boston, MA: Houghton Mifflin.

Bentley, E. G. and S. Pointon Taylor. 1911. *A Practical Guide in the Preparation of Town Planning Schemes*. London: George Philip & Son.

Bertaud, Alain. 2003. 'The Use and Value of Urban Planning'. Available at http://alain-bertaud.com (accessed on 1 November 2017).

———. 2014, 19 February. *Cities as Labor Markets* (Working Paper No. 2). New York, NY: Marron Institute of Urban Management.

———. 2018. *Order without Design: How Markets Shape Cities*. Cambridge, MA: MIT Press.

Bertaud, Alain, and Jan K. Brueckner. 2005. 'Analyzing Building Height Restrictions—Predicted Impacts, Welfare Costs'. *Regional Science and Urban Economics* 35 (2): 109–125.

Bird, R. M., and E. Slack. 2015. 'Local Taxes and Local Expenditures: Strengthening the Wicksellian Connection'. In *Interaction between Local Expenditure Responsibilities and Local Tax Policy: The Copenhagen Workshop*, edited by Junghun Kim, Jorgen Lotz and Niels Jogen Mau, 43–66. Sejong: The Korea Institute of Public Finance.

Boadway, Robin W., and David Wildasin. 1984. *Public Sector Economics*, 2nd edition. Boston, MA; Toronto: Little, Brown & Company.

Borck, Rainald, and Michael Pfluger. 2006. 'Agglomeration and Tax Competition'. *European Economic Review* 50: 647–668.

Boulding, K. E. 1992. *Towards a New Economics, Critical Essays on Ecology, Distribution and Other Themes*. Brookfield, VT: Edward Elgar.

Brookings Institution. 2015. *Global Metro Monitor 2014*. Metropolitan Policy Program. Washington, DC: Brookings.

———. 2018. *Global Metro Monitor 2018*. Metropolitan Policy Program. Washington, DC: Brookings. Available at https://www.brookings.edu/research/global-metro-monitor-2018/ (accessed on 25 June 2020).

Brueckner, Jan. 2011. *Lectures in Urban Economics.* Cambridge, MA: MIT Press.
Brueckner, Jan K., and Kala Seetharam Sridhar. 2012. 'Measuring Welfare Gains from Relaxation of Land Use Restrictions: The Case of India's Building-height Limits'. *Regional Science and Urban Economics* 42: 1061–1067.
Brulhart, Marius, and Federca Sbergami. 2009. 'Agglomeration and Growth: Cross-Country Evidence'. *Journal of Urban Economics* 65 (1): 48–63.
Buchanan, J. M. 1963. 'The Economics of Earmarked Taxation'. *Journal of Political Economy* 71: 457–469.
Buckley, Robert. 2005. 'Macro Linkages with Municipal Finance: An Overview'. Available at http://www.worldbank.org/uicconference (accessed on 24 August 2021).
Burrows, E. G., and M. Wallace. 1999. *Gotham: A History of New York City to 1898.* Oxford: Oxford University Press.
Button, Kenneth. 2010. *Transport Economics*, 3rd ed. Cheltenham: Edward Elgar.
Castle, E. N., M. M. Kelso, J. B. Stevens, and H. H. Stoevener. 1980. 'Natural Resource Economics'. In *Survey of Agricultural Economics Literature*, edited by L. R. Martin, Vol. 3. Minneapolis, MN: University of Minnesota Press.
Census of India 2011, Office of the Registrar General, Government of India, New Delhi.
Centre for Civil Society. 2009. *State of Governance: Delhi Citizen Handbook 2009.* New Delhi: Centre for Civil Society.
Chamberlin, Edward H. 1933. *The Theory of Monopolistic Competition*, 1st ed. Cambridge, MA: Harvard University Press.
Chauvin, Juan Pablo, Edward Glaeser, Yeran Ma and Kristina Tobio. 2016. What Is Different About Urbanization in Rich and Poor Countries? Cities in Brazil, China, India and the United States. Harvard University and NBER. Available at https://scholar.harvard.edu (accessed on 30 July 2017).
Cheshire, P. C., and C. A. L. Hilber. 2008. 'Office Space Supply Restrictions in Britain: The Political Economy of Market Revenge'. *The Economic Journal* 118 (529): F185–F221.
Cheshire, P. C., Max Nathan, and Harry G. Overman. 2014. *Urban Economics and Urban Policy: Challenging Conventional Policy Wisdom.* Northampton, MA: Edward Elgar.
Cheshire, P. C., and S. Sheppard. 1998. Estimating Demand for Housing, Land, and Neighbourhood Characteristics, Oxford Bulletin of Economics and Statistics, 60, 357–382.
Christaller, Walter. 1933. *Central Places in Southern Germany.* Englewood Cliffs, NJ: Prentice Hall.
Coase, R. H. 1960. 'The Problem of Social Cost'. *Journal of Law and Economics* 33: 1–44.
Combes, Pierre-Philippe, Gilles Duranton, Laurent Gobillon, Diego Puga, and Sebastien Roux. 2012. 'The Productivity Advantages of Large Cities: Distinguishing Agglomeration from Firm Selection'. *Econometrica* 80 (6): 2543–2594.

Corbusier, Le. 1929. *The City of Tomorrow and Its Planning*. London: John Rodker.
———. 1933. *The Radiant City*. London: Faber and Faber Limited.
D'Aspremont, C., J. Jaskold Gabszewicz, and Jacques-Francois Thisse. 1979. 'On Hotelling's "Stability in Competition"'. *Econometrica* 47 (5): 1145–1150.
Danish Ministry of the Environment. 2015. *The Finger Plan: A Strategy for the Development of the Greater Copenhagen Area*. Copenhagen: The Nature Agency.
Delhi Development Authority. 2015. *Master Plan for Delhi—2021*. Available at http://52.172.182.107/BPAMSClient/seConfigFiles/Downloads/MPD2021.pdf (accessed on 24 August 2021).
De Soto, H. 2000. *The Mystery of Capital: Why Capitalism Triumphs in the West and Fails Everywhere Else*. New York, NY: Basic Books.
Duranton, Gilles, and Diego Puga. 2004. 'Micro-Foundations of Urban Agglomeration Economies'. In *Handbook of Urban and Regional Economies*, Vol. 4, edited by J. Vernon Henderson and Jacque Thisse. Amsterdam: North-Holland.
Duranton G., J. V. Henderson and W. Strange. 2015. Eds. *Handbook of Urban and Regional Economics 5*. North Holland.
Dye, Richard F., and Richard W. England. 2010. *Assessing the Theory and Practice of Land Value Taxation*. Cambridge, MA: Lincoln Institute of Land Policy.
Faludi, Andreas. 1973. (ed). *A Reader in Planning Theory*. Oxford: Pergamon Press.
Finance Commission of India. 2009. *Report of the Thirteenth Finance Commission*. New Delhi: Government of India.
———. 2015. *Report of the Fourteenth Finance Commission*. New Delhi: Government of India.
———. 2020. *Report of the Fifteenth Finance Commission*. New Delhi: Government of India.
Florida, Richard. 2002. *The Rise of the Creative Class*. New York, NY: Basic Books.
———. 2005. 'The World Is Spiky'. *The Atlantic Monthly* 296: 48–51.
———. 2008. *Who's Your City? How the Creative Economy Is Making Where to Live the Most Important Decision of Your Life*. New York, NY: Basic Books.
———. 2011. 'Globalisation: Part I'. In *Wiley-Blackwell Companion to Human Geography*, edited by John A. Agnew and James S. Duncan. New York, NY: Wiley.
Florida, R., T. Gulden, and C. Mellander. 2008. 'The Rise of the Mega Region'. *Cambridge Journal of Regions, Economy and Society* 1 (3): 459–476.
———. 2012. 'Global Metropolis: Assessing Economic Activity in Urban Centers Based on Night-time Satellite Images'. *The Professional Geographer* 64 (2): 178–187.
Food and Agriculture Organization of the United Nations (FAO). 1995. *Planning for Sustainable Use of Land Resources—Towards a New Approach*. FAO Land and Water Bulletin 2. Rome: FAO.
Friedman, Thomas K. 2006. *The World Is Flat: A Brief History of the Twentieth Century*. New York, NY: Farrar, Strauss and Giroux.

Fujita, Masahisa. 1989. *Urban Economic Theory: Land Use and City Size*. Cambridge: Cambridge University Press.

Fujita, M., and T. Mori. 1997. 'Structural Stability and Evolution of Urban Systems'. *Regional Science and Urban Economics* 42: 399–442.

Fujita, M., and Jacques-Francois Thisse. 2002. *Economics of Agglomeration: Cities, Industrial Location, and Regional Growth*. Cambridge: Cambridge University Press.

Fujita, M., Paul Krugman, and Anthony J. Venables. 1999. *The Spatial Economy: Cities, Regions, and International Economy*. Cambridge, MA: MIT Press.

Fuller, Brandon, and Paul Romer. 2014. *Urbanization as Opportunity* (Marron Institute of Urban Management Working Paper No. 1). New York, NY: New York University. Available at https://marroninstitute.nyu.edu (accessed on 15 September 2017).

Geddes, Patrick Sir. 1915. *Cities in Evolution: An Introduction to the Town Planning Movement and to the Study of Civics*. London: Williams & Norgate.

George, Henry. 1879. *Progress and Poverty*. Centenary Edition. 1979. New York, NY: Robert Schalkenbach Foundation.

———. 1897. *The Science of Political Economy*. New York, NY: Doubleday.

Gibbon, Sir G. 1937. *Problems of Town and Country Planning*. London: Allen & Unwin.

Glaeser, Edward L. 2008. *Cities, Agglomeration and Spatial Equilibrium*. Oxford: Oxford University Press.

———. 2011. *Triumph of the City: How Our Greatest Invention Makes Us Richer, Smarter, Greener, Healthier, and Happier*. New York, NY: Penguin Books.

Glaeser, Edward L., and Abha Joshi-Ghani. 2015. *The Urban Imperative: Towards Competitive Cities*. New Delhi: Oxford University Press.

Graham, D. J. 2007. 'Agglomeration, Productivity and Transport Investment'. *Journal of Transport Economics and Policy* 41 (3): 317–343.

Hagman, Donald G., and Dean J. Misczynski, eds. 1978. *Windfalls for Wipeouts: Land Value Capture and Compensation*. Chicago, IL: American Society of Planning Officials.

Hall, Peter. 1988. *Cities of Tomorrow: An Intellectual History of Urban Planning and Design in the 20th Century*. Oxford: Blackwell Publishing.

———. 2019. 'Looking Backward, Looking Forward: The City Region in the Mid-21st Century'. *Regional Studies* 6: 803–817.

Harris, C. D. 1954. The market as a factor in the localization of industry in the United States, Annals of the Association of American Geographers 44(4), 315–348.

Heady, E. O. 1952. *Economics of Agricultural Production and Resource Use*. Englewood Cliffs, NJ: Prentice-Hall.

Heilburn, J., and P. A. McGuire. 1987. *Urban Economics and Public Policy*. New York, NY: St. Martin's Press.

Helpman, E. 1998. 'The Size of Regions'. In *Topics in Public Economics: Theoretical and Applied Analysis*, edited by D. Pines, E. Sadka, and I. Zilcha, 33–54. Cambridge: Cambridge University Press.

Henderson, J. Vernon. 1974. "The Sizes and Types of Cities." *American Economic Review* 64(4): 640–56.

———. 1988. *Urban Development: Theory, Fact, and Illusion*. New York, NY: Oxford University Press.

———. 2005. 'Urbanization and Growth'. In *Handbook of Economic Growth*, edited by Philippe Aghion and Steven N. Durlauf. Amsterdam: Elsevier.

High Powered Expert Committee (HPEC). 2014. *Report on Indian Urban Infrastructure and Services*. The High Powered Expert Committee (HPEC) for Estimating the Investment Requirements for Urban Infrastructure Services. New Delhi: HPEC.

Hirschman, Albert O. 1958. *The Strategy of Economic Development*. New Haven, CT: Yale University Press.

Hoover, Edgar M. 1948. *The Location of Economic Activity*. New York, NY: McGraw-Hill.

Hotelling, H. 1929. 'Stability in Competition'. *The Economic Journal* 39 (153): 41–57.

Howard, Ebenezer. (1898) 1902. *Garden Cities of Tomorrow*. London: S. Sonnenschein.

Hubacek, Klaus, C. J. Jeroen, and M. van den Bergh. 2006. 'Changing Concepts of "Land in Economic Theory": From Single to Multi-disciplinary Approaches'. *Ecological Economics* 56: 5–27. Available at https://www.cooperative-individualism.org and www.sciencedirect.com (accessed on 15 March 2020).

Isard, W. 1956. *Location and Space Economy*. Cambridge, MA: MIT Press.

Jacobs, Jane. (1961) 1992. *The Death and Life of Great American Cities*. New York, NY: Vintage Books.

———. 1970. *The Economy of Cities*. New York, NY: Vintage Books.

———. 1984. *Cities and the Wealth of Nations*. New York, NY: Vintage Books.

Jevons, W. S. 1865. *The Coal Question: An Enquiry Concerning the Progress of the Nation and the Probable Exhaustion of Our Coal-Mines*. London: Macmillan.

Kennedy, C. A. 2011. *The Evolution of Great World Cities: Urban Wealth and Economic Growth*. Toronto: University of Toronto Press.

Knapp, Gerrit, and Emily Talen. 2005. 'New Urbanism and Smart Growth: A Few Words from the Academy'. *International Regional Science Review* 28 (2): 107–118.

Koopmans, T. C. 1957. *Three Essays on the State of Economic Science*. New York, NY: McGraw-Hill.

Koster, H. R. A, P. Rietveld, and J.N. van Emmerren. 2011. 'Is the Sky the Limit? An Analysis of High-Rise Office Buildings'. SERC Discussion Paper No. 86. London, SERC.

Krugman, Paul R. 1991a. *Geography and Trade*. Cambridge, MA: MIT Press.

———. 1991b. 'Increasing Returns and Economic Geography.' *Journal of Political Economy* 99 (3): 483–99.

———. 1993. 'First Nature, Second Nature, and Metropolitan Location'. *Journal of Regional Science* 33 (2): 129–144.

Krugman, Paul R., and A. J. Venables. 1995. 'Globalization and the Inequality of Income'. *Quarterly Journal of Economics* 110: 857–880.

Kuznets, Simon. 1955. 'Economic Growth and Income Inequality'. *American Economic Review* 45: 1–28.

Lall, Somik V., M. Freire, B. Yuen, R. Rajack, and L. J. Helluin. 2009. *Urban Land Markets: Improving Land Market for Successful Urbanization*. London: Springer.

Lincoln Institute of Land Policy. 2011. 'Land-Based Financing for Brazil's Municipalities'. Land Lines. Available at https://www.lincolninst.edu/publications/articles/land-based-financing-brazils-municipalities (accessed on 24 August 2021).

Lindahl, Erik R. 1919. *The Justness of Taxation*. Lund: University of Lund.

Lösch, Auguste. 1940. *The Economics of Location*. New Haven, CT: Yale University Press.

Lucas, Robert E. Jr. 1988. 'On the Mechanics of Economic Development'. *Journal of Monetary Economics* 22 (1): 3–42.

Ludema, Rodney, and Ian Wooton. 2000. 'Economic Geography and the Fiscal Effects of Integration'. *Journal of International Economics* 52: 331–357.

Mackie, Peter, Daniel Graham, and James Laird. 2011. 'The Direct and Wider Impacts of Transport Projects: A Review'. In *A Handbook of Transport Economics*, edited by Andre de Palma, Robin Lindsay, Emile Quinet and Roger Vickerman. Cheltenham: Edward Elgar.

Mahadevia, Darshini, Rutul Joshi, and Rutul Sharma. 2009. *Approaches to the Lands for the Urban Poor, India*. Ahmedabad: Centre for Urban Equity, CEPT University.

Mallach, Alan. 1984. *Inclusionary Housing Programs: Policies and Practices*. New Brunswick, NJ: Centre for Urban Policy Research, Rutgers University.

Malthus, T. R. (1798) 1926. *Essay on the Principle of Population*. London: Macmillan.

Marriot, Oliver. 1967. *The Property Boom*. London: H. Hamilton.

Marshall, Alfred. 1890. *Principles of Economics*. London: Macmillan.

———. 1920. *Principles of Economics*, 8th ed. London: Macmillan.

Marx, K. (1867) 1909. *Capital, A Critique of Political Economy*, Vol. III. Chicago, IL: Kerr.

McCluskey, J. William, and Riel C. D. Franzsen. 2013. 'Property Taxes in Metropolitan Cities'. In *Financing Metropolitan Governments in Developing Countries*, edited by Roy W. Bahl, Johannes Linn, and Deborah L. Wetzel. Cambridge, MA: Lincoln Institute of Land Policy.

McKinsey Institute. 2010. *India's Urban Awakening: Building Inclusive Cities, Sustaining Economic Growth*. Chennai: McKinsey and Company.

———. 2014. *Understanding India's Economic Geography*.
Meek, R. L. 1962. *The Economics of Physiocracy*. Cambridge, MA: Harvard University Press.
Melo, P. C., D. J. Graham, and R. Noland. 2009. 'A Meta-analysis of Estimates of Urban Agglomeration Economies'. *Regional Science and Urban Economics* 39: 332–342.
Menger, K. (1871) 1923. *Grundsatze Der Volkswirtschaftslehre*. Wien/Leipzig: Holder-Pichler-Tempsky/G. Freitag.
Mill, John Stuart. (1848) 1909. *Principles of Political Economy* (Ashley edition). London: J. M. Dent.
Mills, E. S. 1967. 'An Aggregate Model of Resource Allocation in a Metropolitan Area'. *American Economic Review* 57: 197–210.
———. 1972. *Urban Economics*. Glenview, IL: Scot Foresman.
Ministry of Agriculture and Farmers' Welfare. 2019a. *Agricultural Statistics at a Glance 2018*. New Delhi: Government of India.
———. 2019b. *Agricultural Census 2015–16 Phase I. All India Report on Number and Area of Holdings*. New Delhi: Ministry of Agriculture and Farmers Welfare, Government of India.
Ministry of Finance (MoF), Government of India. 2017. Economic Survey 2014–15. In *From Competitive Federalism to Competitive Sub-Federalism: Cities and Dynamos*, 300–314. Available at https://www.indiabudget.gov.in/budget2017-2018/es2016-17/echap14.pdf (accessed on 24 August 2021).
Ministry of Health (MoH), Government of India. 1965. *Report of the Committee on Urban Land Policy*. New Delhi: Manager of Publications.
Ministry of Human Resource Development (MHRD), Government of India. 2011. *Report of the Committee of Experts in Town Planning and Architecture for Policy Guidelines to Energize Architecture and Town Planning Education in the Country*. New Delhi: Government of India.
Ministry of Rural Development (MoRD), Government of India. 2013. *Draft Land Reforms Policy 2013*. New Delhi: Government of India.
Ministry of Statistics and Program Implementation. *Nine-fold Classification of Land Use*. New Delhi: Government of India. Available at http://mospi.nic.in/45-nine-fold-classification-land-use (accessed on 6 July 2020).
Ministry of Housing and Urban Affairs (MoHUA). 2018. National Urban Policy Framework 2018. https://smartnet.niua.org (accessed January, 2020).
Ministry of Urban Development (MoUD), Government of India. 2014. *National Urban Transport Policy, 2014*. Available at https://www.changing-transport.org/wp-content/uploads/E_K_NUMP_India_2014_EN.pdf (accessed on 24 August 2021).
———. 2015. *Urban and Regional Development Plan Formulation and Implementation (URDPFI) Guidelines*. Available at http://mohua.gov.in/upload/uploadfiles/files/URDPFI%20Guidelines%20Vol%20I.pdf (accessed on 24 August 2021).
———. 2018. *National Urban Policy Framework*. Available at https://smartnet.niua.org/nupf (accessed on 24 August 2021).

Ministry of Urban Development (MoUD), Government of India and the World Bank. 2013. 'Land Based Fiscal Tools and Practices for Generating Additional Financial Resources'. Capacity Building for Urban Development Project (CBUD). Available at https://smartnet.niua.org/sites/default/files/resources/Final-Report-LBFT_28Aug2014%20%281%29.pdf (accessed on 24 August 2021).

Mishra, A. K. 2019a. 'Cities, Transport and Agglomeration: Addressing the Urban Mobility Challenges in India'. *Growth and Change* 50 (3): 1–19.

———. 2019b. 'Henry George and Mohring–Harwitz Theorems: Lessons for Financing Smart Cities in Developing Countries'. *Environment and Urbanization ASIA* 10 (1): 13–30.

Mishra, A. K., and P. K. Mohanty. 2018. 'Urban Infrastructure Financing in India: Applying the Benefit and Earmarking Principles of Taxation'. *Journal of Social and Economic Development* 20: 10–19.

Mohring, H., and M. Harwitz. 1962. *Highway Benefits: An Analytical Framework*. Evanston, IL: Northwestern University Press.

Mohanty, P. K. 2014. *Cities and Public Policy: An Urban Agenda for India*. New Delhi: SAGE Publications.

———. 2016. *Financing Cities in India: Municipal Reforms, Fiscal Accountability and Urban Infrastructure*. New Delhi: SAGE Publications.

———. 2019. *Planning and Economics of Cities: Shaping India's Form and Future*. New Delhi: SAGE Publications.

Mohanty, P. K., and A. K. Mishra. 2014. 'Cities and Agglomeration Externalities'. *Environment and Urbanization ASIA* 5 (2): 235–251.

Mohanty, P. K., B. M. Mishra, R. Goyal, and P. D. Jeromi. 2007. *Municipal Finance in India—An Assessment* (Study No. 26). Mumbai: Department of Economic Analysis and Policy, Reserve Bank of India.

Mohring, H. 1972. 'Optimisation and Scale Economies in Urban Bus Transportation'. *American Economic Review* 62: 591–604.

———. 1976. *Transport Economics*. Cambridge, MA: Ballinger.

Mohring, H., and M. Harwitz. 1962. *Highway Benefits: An Analytical Framework*. Evanston, IL: Northwestern University Press.

Moses, L. 1958. 'Location and the Theory of Production'. *Quarterly Journal of Economics* LXXII: 259–272.

Mumford, Lewis. 1938. *The Culture of Cities*. New York, NY: Harcourt Brace and Company.

———. 1961. *The City in History*. San Diego, CA: Harcourt.

Musgrave, Richard A. 1959. *The Theory of Public Finance*. New York, NY: McGraw Hill.

Muth, Richard. 1969. *Cities and Housing*. Chicago, IL: University of Chicago Press.

Myrdal, G. 1957. *Economic Theory and Under-developed Regions*. London: Duckworth.

———. 1974. 'What Is Development?' *Journal of Economic Issues* 8 (4): 729–736.

Nathan, Max, and Harry G. Overman. 2011. *What We Know (and Don't Know) about the Links between Planning and Economic Performance* (Spatial and Economic Research Centre [SERC] Policy Paper No. 11). London: London School of Economics. Available at www.spatialeconomics.ac.uk (accessed on 30 September 2017).

National Sample Survey Office, Ministry of Statistics and Program Implementation, Government of India. 2006. *NSS 59th Round (January–December 2003): Household Ownership Holding in India, 2003.* Available at http://mospi.nic.in/sites/default/files/publication_reports/491_final.pdf (accessed on 24 August 2021).

———. 2010a. NSS 65th Round (July 2008–June 2009) *Report No. 534: Some Characteristics of Urban Slums.* Available at http://www.indiaenvironmentportal.org.in/files/Some%20characteristics%20of%20urban%20slums%20 2008-09.pdf (accessed on 24 August 2021).

———. 2010b. NSS 65th Round (July 2008–June 2009) *Report No. 535. 2010. Housing Conditions and Amenities in India 2008–09.* http://www.indiaenvironmentportal.org.in/files/Housing%20Condition%20and%20Amenities.pdf

———. 2011. *NSS Report No. 538: Level and Pattern of Consumer Expenditure 2009–10.* December 2011. Available at http://mospi.nic.in/sites/default/files/publication_reports/NSS_Report_538.pdf (accessed on 24 August 2021).

———. 2012. *NSS Report No. 539: Informal Sector and Conditions of Employment in India, NSS 66th Round*, January 2012. Available at http://mospi.nic.in/sites/default/files/publication_reports/nss_rep_539.pdf (accessed on 24 August 2021).

———. 2014. *NSS 68th Round (July 2011–June 2012): Employment and Unemployment Situation in India*, January 2014. Available at http://mospi.nic.in/sites/default/files/publication_reports/nss_rep_563_13mar15.pdf (accessed on 24 August 2021).

———. 2015. *NSS 70th Round (January–December 2013): Household Ownership and Operational Holdings in India 59th Round (January–December 2003). Report on Household Ownership Holdings in India.* Available at http://mospi.nic.in/sites/default/files/publication_reports/Report_571_15dec15_2.pdf (accessed on 24 August 2021).

———. 2016. *NSS 70th Round (January–December 2013): Household Assets and Liabilities in India.* Available at http://mospi.nic.in/sites/default/files/publication_reports/nss_Report_570_1.pdf (accessed on 24 August 2021).

Nico, Calavita, and Alan Mallach, eds. 2010. *Inclusionary Housing in International Perspective: Affordable Housing, Social Inclusion and Land Value Recapture.* Cambridge, MA: Lincoln Institute of Land Policy.

Nourse, Hugh O. 1968. *Regional Economics.* New York, NY: McGraw Hill.

OECD (Organisation for Economic Co-operation and Development). 2015. *The Metropolitan Century: Understanding Urbanisation and Its Consequences,* OECD, Paris.

Oxfam India. 2020. *Time to Care: Wealth Inequality and Unpaid Care Work for Women in India.* New Delhi: Oxfam India.

Oxford Economics. 2017. 'Global Cities 2030—Future Trends and Market Opportunities in the World's Largest 750 Cities'. Available at https://www.oxfordeconomics.com (accessed on 31 August 2017).

Pallander, Tord. 1935. *Beitrage zur Standortstheoire*. Uppsala: Almqvist & Wiksells.

Parker, Geoffrey G., Marshall W. Van Alstyne, and Sangeet Paul Choudary. 2016. *Platform Revolution—How Networked Markets are Transforming the Economy and How to Make them Work for You*. New York, NY: W. W. Norton & Company.

Patel, Shirish B. 2005. 'Housing Policies for Mumbai'. *Economic & Political Weekly* 40 (33): 3669, 3671–3676.

———. 2016. 'Housing for All by 2022'. *Economic & Political Weekly* 51 (10). Available at https://nhb.org.in/en/housing-for-all-by-2022/ (accessed on 24 August 2021).

Pennance, F. G. 1967. *Housing, Town Planning and the Land Commission* (Hobart Paper No. 40). London: Institute of Economic Affairs.

Peterson, George E. 2009. *Unlocking Land Values to Finance Urban Infrastructure*. Washington, DC: World Bank.

Peterson, Sarah Joe. 2014. *Tax Increment Financing: Tweaking TIF for the 21st Century*. Washington DC: Urban Land, The Urban Land Institute.

Pigou, A. C. 1927. *A Study in Public Finance*. London: Macmillan.

Piketty, Thomas. 2014. *Capital in the Twenty-First Century*. Cambridge: The Belknap Press of the Harvard University Press.

Planning Commission, Government of India. 2008. *Eleventh Five Year Plan 2007–2012*. New Delhi: Government of India.

———. 2013. *Twelfth Five Year Plan 2012–2017*. New Delhi: Government of India.

———. 2014. *Report of Expert Group to Review the Methodology for Measurement of Poverty*. New Delhi: Government of India.

Polanyi, K. 1957. *The Great Transformation*. New York, NY: Farrar & Rinehart.

Porter, Michael E. 1990. *The Competitive Advantage of Nations*. New York, NY: Free Press.

Pred, Allan R. 1966. *The Spatial Dynamics of U.S. Urban-Industrial Growth, 1800–1914: Interpretive and Theoretical Essays*. Cambridge, MA: MIT Press.

Prest, A. R. 1981. *The Taxation of Urban Land*. Manchester: Manchester University Press.

Puga, Diego. 2010. 'The Magnitude and Causes of Agglomeration Economies'. *Journal of Regional Science* 50: 203–219.

Ramachandran, H. 2017. Intensity of Use of Land in Urban Residential Areas. Working Paper 199, Institute for Studies in Industrial Development (ISID), New Delhi.

Renner, George T. 1951. *World Economic Geography: An Introduction to Geonomics*. New York, NY: Crowell.

Ricardo, D. (1817) 1951. 'The Works and Correspondence of David Ricardo'. In *On the Principles of Political Economy and Taxation*, Vol. I, edited by P. Sraffa. Cambridge: Cambridge University Press.

Robinson, Joan. 1934. *Imperfect Competition*. London: Macmillan.
Romer, Paul M. 1986. 'Increasing Returns in Long-Run Growth'. *Journal of Political Economy* 94 (5): 1002–1037.
———. 1994. 'The Origins of Endogenous Growth'. *Journal of Economic Perspectives* 8 (1): 3–22.
Rosenthal, Stuart S., and William C. Strange. 2004. 'Evidence on the Nature and Sources of Agglomeration Economies'. In *Handbook of Regional and Urban Economics*, Vol. IV, edited by J. Vernon Henderson and Jacque Thisse, 2119–2171. Amsterdam: Elsevier.
Rostow, W. W. 1960. *The Stages of Economic Growth*. Cambridge: Cambridge University Press.
Ryan-Collins, Jose, Toby Llyod, and Laurie Macfarlane. 2017. *Rethinking the Economics of Land and Housing*. London: Zed Books Ltd.
Salon, Deborah, and Sharon Shewmake. 2011. 'Opportunities for Value Capture to Fund Public Transport: A Comprehensive Review of the Literature with a Focus on East Asia'. ADB and ITDP. Available at https:/www.itdp.org (accessed on 5 March 2016).
Salzberg, Andrew, Richard Bullock, Ying Jin, and Wanli Fang. 2013. *High-Speed Rail, Regional Economics and Urban Development* (China Transport Topics No. 08). Beijing: World Bank.
Sandroni, P. 2010. 'A New Financial Instrument of Value Capture in Sao Paulo: Certificates of Additional Construction Potential'. In *Municipal Revenues and Land Policies*, edited by Gregory Ingram and Yu-Hung Hong. Cambridge, MA: Lincoln Institute of Land Policy.
SECC (Socio-economic and Caste Census) 2011, Ministry of Rural Development, Government of India https://secc.gov.in.
Schultz, T. W. 1953. *The Economics Organization of Agriculture*. New York, NY: McGraw Hill.
Smith, Adam. 1976. *An Inquiry into the Nature and Causes of the Wealth of Nations*. Chicago, IL: University of Chicago Press (Cannan's edition of the Wealth of Nations was originally published in 1904 by Methuen & Co. Ltd. First Edition in 1776).
Smolka, Martim O. 2007. *La regulacion de los mercados de suelo en America Latina: Cuestiones claves*. Reported in Peterson (2009): *Unlocking Land Values to Finance Urban Infrastructure*. Washington, DC: World Bank.
———. 2013. *Implementing Land Value Capture in Latin America (Policy Focus Report): Policies and Tools for Urban Development*. Cambridge, MA: Lincoln Institute of Land Policy.
Solow, R. M. 1956. 'A Contribution to the Theory of Economic Growth'. *Quarterly Journal of Economics* 70: 65–94.
Starrett, D. 1978. Market allocations of location choice in a model with free mobility. *Journal of Economic Theory* 17: 21–37.
Stein, Clarence S. 1939. *Toward New Towns for America*. Cambridge, MA: MIT Press.

Stiglitz, Joseph E. 1977. The Theory of Local Public Goods. In: Feldstein, M.S and R.P. Inman eds. The Economics of Public Services. McMillan, London, 274–333.

———. 2012. *The Price of Inequality: How Today's Divided Society Endangers Our Future*. New York, NY: W. W. Norton

———. 2015. 'The Origins of Inequality, and Policies to Contain It'. *National Tax Journal* 68 (2): 425–448.

Suzuki, Hiroaki, Jin Murakami, Yu-Hung Hong, and Beth Tamayose. 2015. *Financing Transit Oriented Development with Land Value Capture*. Washington, DC: World Bank.

Suzuki, Hiroaki, Robert Cervero, and Kanako Iuchi. 2013. *Transforming Cities with Transit: Transit and Land-Use Integration for Sustainable Urban Development*. Washington, DC: World Bank.

Taylor, N. 1998. *Urban Planning Theory since 1945*, London, Sage.

Town and Country Planning Organization (TCPO), Government of India. 2007. 'Model Guidelines for Urban Land Policy'. Available at http://www.cmamp.com/CP/FDocument/GuidelinesULP.pdf (accessed on 24 August 2021).

United Nations. n.d. *2030 Agenda for Sustainable Development*. Available at https://sustainabledevelopment.un.org (accessed on 16 July 2018).

———. 1976. *The Vancouver Action Plan*. Vancouver: United Nations Conference on Human Settlements.

———. 2018. *The Sustainable Development Goals Report 2018*. New York, NY: United Nations, Department of Economic and Social Affairs.

———. 2019. *World Urbanization Prospects: The 2018 Revision*. New York, NY: United Nations, Department of Economic and Social Affairs.

United Nations Convention to Combat Desertification (UNCCD). 1994. *United Nations Convention to Combat Desertification in Countries Experiencing Serious Drought and/or Desertification, Particularly in Africa*.

United Nations Environment Program (UNEP). 2015. *Cities and Buildings*. Nairobi: UNEP-DTIE—Sustainable Production and Consumption Branch.

United States Department of Commerce. 1926. *A Standard State Zoning Enabling Act*. Advisory Committee on Zoning. Washington, DC: United States Government Printing Office.

———. 1928. *A Standard City Planning Enabling Act*. Washington, DC: United States Government Printing Office.

United States Department of Housing and Urban Development (USDHUD). 1993. *Impact Fees and the Role of the State: Guidance for Drafting Legislation*. Collingdale, PA: Diane Publishing.

United States Environmental Protection Agency (US EPA). 2004. *What Is Smart Growth?* Smart Growth. Available at https://www.epa.gov/sites/production/files/2014-02/documents/smartgrowth (accessed on 4 March 2016).

United States National Commission on Urban Problems. 1969. *Building the American City: Report of the National Commission on Urban Problem to the*

Congress and to the President of the United States. Washington, DC: U.S. Government Printing Office.

UN-Habitat. 2016. *World Cities Report 2016—Urbanization and Development: Emerging Futures.* Nairobi: United Nations Human Settlement Program.

University of Hyderabad-Human Settlements Management Institute (UoH-HSMI). 2017. *Land-based Instruments for Financing Smart Cities in India.* Hyderabad: HUDCO Chair Program.

Venables, Anthony J. 1996. 'Equilibrium Locations of Vertically Linked Industries'. *International Economic Review* 37: 341–359.

———. 2007. 'Evaluating Urban Transport Improvements: Cost–benefit Analysis in the Presence of Agglomeration and Income Taxation'. *Journal of Transport Economics and Policy* 41: 173–188.

Vickerman, R. 2008. 'Transit Investment and Economic Development'. *Research in Transportation Economics* 23: 101–115.

Vickrey, William S. 1963. 'Pricing of Urban and Suburban Transport'. *American Economic Review* 53 (2): 452–465.

Vidal de la Blache P.1921. *Principice de geographie humaine.* Paris: Armand Colin.

von Thünen, J. H. 1826. *The Isolated State.* Hamburg: F. Perthes.

Vyas, I., H. N. Vyas, and A. K. Mishra. 2020. 'Land-based Financing of Cities in India: A Study of Bengaluru and Hyderabad and Directions for Reforms'. *Journal of Public Affairs* 1–13. Available at https://dx.doi.org/10.1002/pa.2378 (accessed on 24 August 2021).

Wallis, John J. 2000. 'American Government Finance in the Long Run: 1790 to 1990.' *Journal of Economic Perspectives,* Volume 14, Number 1, Winter 2000: 61–82.

Walras, Leon. 1899. *Elements d'economie politique pure.* Lausanne: Corbaz, Paris: Guillaurain, and Basle, H. Georg: 1874–1877, translated as *Elements of Pure Economics or the Theory of Social Wealth* by W. Jaffe, Homewood, 111: Irwin, 1954.

Walters, L. C. 2011. *Land and Property Tax: A Policy Guide.* Nairobi: UN-Habitat and the Global Land Tool Network.

Weber, Alfred. (1909) 1971. *The Theory of the Location of Industries,* 2nd ed. Chicago, IL: University of Chicago Press.

Wicksell, Knut. (1896) 1964. 'A New Principle of Just Taxation'. In *Classics in the Theory of Public Finance,* edited by R. Musgrave and A. Peacock, 72–118. London: Macmillan.

Williamson, Jeffrey. 1965. 'Regional Inequality and the Process of National Development: A Description of the Patterns'. *Economic Development and Cultural Change* 13 (4): 1–84.

World Bank. 2004. *Doing Business: Removing Obstacles to Growth.* Washington DC: The World Bank.

———. 2009. *World Development Report 2009: Reshaping Economic Geography.* Washington, DC: World Bank.

———. 2013. *India: Urbanization Beyond Municipalities*. Washington, DC: World Bank.

———. 2015. *Leveraging Urbanization in South Asia: Managing Spatial Transformation for Prosperity and Livability*, Conference Edition. Washington, DC: World Bank.

———. 2020. *Doing Business 2020: Comparing Business Regulation in 190 Countries*. Washington, DC: World Bank.

World Economic Forum (WEF). 2019. Schwab K. (ed) *The Global Competitiveness Reports 2019*. WEF, Switzerland.

Wright, Frank Lloyd. 1958. *The Living City*. New York, NY: Horizon Press.

Wright, Henry. 1935. *Rehousing Urban America*. New York, NY: Columbia University Press.

About the Author

Prasanna K. Mohanty is honorary professor of economics in University of Hyderabad. He teaches land economics, urban economics and transport economics. He is also honorary executive chair of National Institute of Urban Management and adviser to Centre for Good Governance, Hyderabad. He has been a director in the central board of Reserve Bank of India (RBI).

An officer from the Indian Administrative Services, Dr Mohanty was chief secretary to the Government of Andhra Pradesh. He worked as mission director for Jawaharlal Nehru National Urban Renewal Mission (JNNURM), Government of India, director general for Centre for Good Governance, Hyderabad, commissioner of metropolitan cities of Hyderabad and Visakhapatnam and vice-chairman of Hyderabad Urban Development Authority.

Dr Mohanty did MA in economics from Delhi School of Economics and MA and PhD in economics from Boston University. He was also Rockefeller Foundation Postdoctoral Fellow at Harvard University. He has authored *Planning and Economics of Cities: Shaping India's Form and Future* (2018–2019), *Financing Cities in India: Municipal Reforms, Fiscal Accountability and Urban Infrastructure* (2016) and *Cities and Public Policy: An Urban Agenda for India* (2014) and co-edited *Urbanisation in India: Challenges, Opportunities and the Way Forward* (2014)—all published by SAGE. Dr Mohanty led the seminal RBI Development Research Group study *Municipal Finance in India: An Assessment* (2007).

Index

agglomeration diseconomies, 21
agglomeration economies, 20
agglomeration index, 188
agricultural economics, 13
agricultural land(s), 13, 16, 33, 37,
   43, 61, 115, 122, 125, 134,
   167, 175, 189, 190, 197, 225,
   231, 276, 289
agricultural landholdings, 192
Arnott, Richard, 57

backward linkages between economic
   activities, 5
beneficiaries pay principle, 41
benefit taxation (principle of),
   295–296
betterment levy, 257
Boulding, Kenneth, 7
Broadacre City concept of Frank
   Lloyd Wright, 148
bus rapid transit (BRT), 200, 203,
   207, 212, 222, 290

capital in industry, importance of, 10
central business districts (CBDs), 30,
   43, 73, 121
characteristics of land
   accessibility dimension, 38
   derived demand, 39
   development rights, 40

durability of structure, 39
economic value of land, 42
externalities, impact of, 41
horizontal dimension, 38
immobility, 37
inelastic in supply, 38–39
land as collateral for credit, 42
land rent as surplus, 41
locational fixity, 37
planning and regulations, 41
property rights, 40
uniqueness, 37
vertical dimension, 38
Christaller, Walter
   central place theory (CPT), 16,
   86–89
cities, 6, 10, 16, 17, 23, 29, 54, 60,
   87, 88, 141
   clustering in, 18
   organized complexity of, 180
   attract poor people for
      employment, 57
   changes in land cover and use, 56
   consume rural resources, 189
   diverse, 20
   dual, 158
   emergence in west, 103
   failure in developing countries,
      182
   importance of, 301

innovations and best practices, need to adopted, 306–307
land acts as a platform for, xxi
land-based financing of, xxi
metropolitan, 4, 137, 173, 201
over-regulation in, xxii
products of processes, 180
reasons for change in, 33
slums and squatter settlements prone to natural calamities, 21
source of land rents in, 26
value of land, 37
vertical development in, 200
City Beautiful movement by Daniel Hudson Burnham, 147–148
city(ies), functions of
economic, 56
environmental, 56
social, 57
classical economics, 7–9
Coase theorem, 14
Committee on Urban Land Policy (Report of) 1965, 232, 273–274
communication economies, 20
Covid-19 pandemic, 33

Delhi Development Authority (DDA), 159, 214
Delhi Development Authority Act 1957, 159, 171, 215
demand (needs versus effective), 49–51
density bonus, 223
development contribution, 113
development control, regulations on, 171–172
development gains tax (DGT), 178, 228
development impact fee, 257
differential fertility (or diversity of land), 8
Draft National Land Reforms Policy 2013, 4, 276

economic geography, 21, 73
economic theory, land in, 7
economies of agglomeration in spatial economy, types of
economies of scale, 76
localization economies, 77
urbanization economies, 77–79
environmental economics, 13–15
defined, 6
extensive margins, of cultivation in rural land, 28
external economies of agglomeration, 21
externalities (negative and positive) and market failure, 55
on demand side, 47–49

face-to-face communication, 18
firms cluster, 20
floor area ratio (FAR), 26
floor space index (FSI), 26, 29, 36, 40, 44, 139, 142, 190
food chain theory, 7
forward linkages between economic activities, 5

garden cities concept of Ebenezer Howard, 146
Geddes, Patrick, 71
George, Henry, 8–9, 57
on land values, 231
greenhouse gas (GHG) emission, 13, 43

Hall, Peter, 145
high-speed rail (HSR), 26, 66, 184, 190, 200, 203, 204, 207, 212, 222, 223, 224, 186, 260, 284, 290, 295, 296, 303, 305, 306
Hirschman, Albert, 109
home market effect (HME), 103
Hotelling, H., 78
model of spatial competition, 93–100

housing, 4
  inclusionary, 156
  stock of wealth as ratio of GDP, 3
human geography, 73
Hyderabad Metropolitan Development Plan 2031, 168

Industrial Revolution, 7
industrializing cities, problems of, 145
information and communication technology (ICT), 109
Institute of Town Planners, India (ITPI), 160
intensive margins, of cultivation in rural land, 28
isodapane, concept of, 83

Jacobs, Jane, 150
Jevons, William, 9

labour market economies, 20
land assembly and development, 214–216
  farmers as shareholders, 218–219
  land pooling scheme, 216–218, 292–293
  public land management, 220–221
  road widening scheme in Hyderabad, 220
land development, charges levied in
  developer exactions, 244
  development contributions, 248
  impact fees, 245–246
  internal and external charges, 244–245
  planning obligations, 247
  town planning schemes (TPS), 248
land economics, 282–283, 299
land market(s), economic framework, 64–65
  benefit taxes and charges, 67
  land value taxation (LVT), 65–66
  location and land use incentives, 69
  pricing of development rights, 68
land market(s), regulatory frameworks
  direct intervention by government, 64
  land use zoning, 62
  master planning, 58–61
  planning permission, 62–63
land market(s)
  and role of government, 54–58
  challenges in policies and management in developing countries, 69–45
  failure of, reasons for, 44–54
  issues in developing countries, 45–48
land pooling scheme, 259
land use patterns, 16, 118
  in India, changing trend of, 191–197
  in spatial economy, 115
  rural, 119
  urban, 121
land use planning, assessment of
  anti-density perspective, 175
  community participation, 180
  exclusion of urban poor, 177
  financing strategies, 178
  human resource constraints, 180
  institutional fragmentation, 179
  lengthy process of planning, 176
  narrow definition of development, 175
  neglect of conservation and transportation, 177
  objectives-instruments mismatch, 172–175
  poor plan implementation, 179
  segregation of land uses, 177–178
  technocratic plan formulation, 176
land use planning

defined, 145
in India, evolution of, 157–168
practice, origin of, 152–157
land use
  Alonso–Muth–Mills (AMM) urban model of, 122–134
  and land cover, difference between, 197
  causes of, 134–138
  conversion tax, 228
  decisions by economic agents, 141
  impact on socio-economic and environmental outcomes, 197–199
  policy lessons for, 138–144
  theoretical perspectives, 115
  von Thünen rural model of, 115–122
land use–transport feedback cycle, 208
land value capture (LVC), 228
land value capture (LVT) tools
  aim of, 249
  betterment levies, 253–254
  development rights, lease or sale of, 250–251
  joint development mechanism (JDM), 252
  lease/sale of project-related land, 250
  monetization of land assets, 251
  sale of developer land, 249–250
  special assessment districts, 252–253
  tax increment financing (TIF), 255
land value increment tax (LVIT), 228, 241
land value tax (LVT), 41, 65–66, 178, 228, 233–239
land-based financing
  practice in countries, 233
  theories of, 229–233
land-based taxes, 228

aim of, 233
land value increment tax (see Land value increment tax (LVIT)), 241
land value tax (see land value tax (LVT)), 233
planning/development gains tax (PGT/DGT) (see Planning/development gains tax (PGT/DGT)), 243
property tax, 239
real estate transfer tax (see Real estate transfer tax (RETT)), 240
vacant land tax (see Vacant land tax (VLT)), 240
land
  and inequality, 25–27
  as gift of nature, 7
  defined, 1–3
  economics, 27
  fundamental form of wealth, 3
  public and private sector role in, 5
  source of disparity, 4
  use, 18
landlessness, 4, 194
landowners, 61, 62, 64, 66, 68, 153, 183, 199, 200, 209, 210, 217, 218, 231, 252, 258, 270, 293
  as development partners, 306
  as shareholders in township development, 219
  entitled to TDR, 220
  private, 54, 63, 273, 282
  public, 282
light rail transit (LRT), 207
linkages in industrial growth, role of, 110
local public goods, 47
localization economies, 20, 93, 105, 111
location theory(ies), 73–76
location theory(ies) See also Weber, Alfred, 78

Index

location theory(ies)
  designing development strategy, 109–78
  features of, 105–109
  Weber–Moses location–production triangle, 83–86
Losch, August, 78
  on economic landscape, 22
  demand cone, 93
  on transport costs, importance of, 24
  profit maximization theory, 16, 89–93

mainstream economics, 17, 23
management of land, issues in developing countries, 32
marginal social benefit (MSB), 47
marginal social cost (MSC), 47
market structure, characteristics of, 28
Marshall, Alfred, 9, 11
  externalities in industrial agglomeration, importance, 75–76
Marshallian externalities, 22
Marx, Karl, 8
  on land rents, 232
mass rapid transit (MRT), 69, 200, 203, 205, 207, 210, 212, 222, 223, 224, 260, 284, 290, 291, 295, 296, 303, 304, 305, 306
Master Plan of Delhi 2021 (MPD 2021), 168
master planning, 136, 138, 142, 152, 160, 177, 178, 182, 285, 287, 291, 300
  aims of, 224
  fallacies of, 301–302
  in India, 160–168, 174, 183, 211
  model in developing countries, 34
  of cities in developing countries, 175

perpetrated inequality, 293
secondary role to transport, 71
two-tier planning strategy, 303
material index (MI), concept of, 81
Menger, Carl, 9
merit goods, 49–51
metropolitan agglomerations, 32
Mill, John Stuart, 8, 230
Mohring-Harwitz Theorem (MHT), 284
monetization
  of land, 258
  of development rights, 258
monopoly power, 51–52
multidimensional nature of land, 5
municipal finance, reforms in, 259–234
municipal land transfer tax (MLTT), 240
Myrdal, Gunnar, 109

National Urban Policy Framework (NUPF) 2018, 32, 35, 272, 277–280
neoclassical economics, 9–12
new economic geography (NEG) of Paul Krugman, 5–6, 12, 30, 73, 100–105, 110–111, 287
  core building blocks of, 22
  defined, 23
  emphasizes second nature geography, 22
non-motorized transport (NMT), 200
not-in-my-backyard (NIMBY) syndrome, 61

Pigovian congestion, 284
Pigovian subsidy, 49
planning/development gains tax (PGT/DGT), 178, 228, 241–243
Porter, Michael, 76
price of land, 5
private marginal benefit (PMB), 48

private marginal cost (PMC), 48
property tax, 228, 239, 256
public finance, 27
public goods, 47

quasi-rent, 11

Radiant City of Le Corbusier, 149
real estate economics, 16
real estate transfer tax (RETT), 228, 240, 257
regional economics, 16–21, 73
rent(s), 11
  economic, 28
  land, 8, 9
  location, 24
  monopoly, 8, 25
  scarcity, 8
  seeking, 25
rezoning, 208, 250, 251, 253
Ricardian theory of rent, 28
Ricardo, David, 230
Robinson, Joan, 11
rural land, 36
  conversion for urban use, 44
  focus areas of, 13
  use for non-agricultural activities, 198
  use in growing urban regions, 13
rural-urban transition, 33

scale economies, 20
self-organizing process, 23
site value tax (SVT), 228
Smith, Adam
  land as principal source of revenue and wealth, 7
  taxation of land rents, 229–230
  theory of land rent, 8
  Wealth of Nations, The, 229
social evolution concept of Patrick Geddes, 147

social marginal benefit (SMB), 48, 49
social marginal cost (SMC), 48
Socio-Economic and Caste Census (SECC) 2011, 4
spatial transformation in developed countries, challenges of, 186–191
specialization economies, 20
speculation in land, 54
Standard State Zoning Enabling Act of 1926, United States, 136
supply of floor space, 43
survey-analysis-plan technique, 71
sustainable land management (SLM), 34, 189, 289
  and urbanization strategy, 221–186
  components of, 200
  defined, 15
  focus areas of, 15, 199
  for rural areas, 199–200
  FSI liberalization in Hyderabad, 212
  grid of arterial road networks, 204–205
  investment in core infrastructure, 201
  land allotment for affordable housing projects, 213–214
  new towns on growth corridors, 212–213
  origin of, 199
  public health, importance of, 201
  re-engineering of cities with transit, 204
  role of transport, 201–203
  strategic densification of cities, 209–211
  transit oriented development (TOD), 205–207
  transport–land use integration, 207–209

Index

tax increment financing (TIF) model, 228, 249, 296
taxation of land, 54, 230, 283
technological and pecuniary externalities, Scitovsky's distinction between, 23
Town and Country Planning Act of 1947, United Kingdom, 34, 59, 62, 63, 136, 137, 152
traditional economic geography, 22
transferable development rights (TDR), 40
transport economics, 24, 283–285
transport in land, economic importance of, 142–143
transport, time, transaction and tariff (4 Ts), 140

UK Planning and Compulsory Purchase Act 2004, 60
UN Millennium Development Goals (MDGs) 2015, 264
UN Sustainable Development Goals (SDGs) 11, 264–266
UN Sustainable Development Goals (SDGs) 2030, 264
United States National Commission on Urban Problems, 232
up-zoning, 219, 223, 258, 296
Urban and Regional Development Plan Formulation and Implementation (URDPFI) Guidelines 2014, 168–171, 272, 276–277
Urban and Regional Development Plans Formulation and Implementation (URDPFI) Guidelines 2014, 160
urban and rural population, in India, 188
urban areas, 4, 16, 20, 27, 77, 122, 142, 145, 174, 194, 203, 248 and limitations on quantity of land, 39

creation of rents, 262
defined, 266
demand for land in, 43
land uses in, 134
occupy 3 per cent of land, 268
peri, 53
urban development, 13, 31, 32, 34, 35, 36, 53, 56, 58, 67, 69, 70, 133, 136, 160, 167, 171, 174, 187, 190, 215, 216, 222, 264
urban development authorities (UDAs), 174, 271, 274
Urban Development Plans Formulation and Implementation (UDPFI) Guidelines 1996, 160
urban development
in coastal areas, 198
strategy of, 280–282
transit-oriented, 206
urban economics, 5, 16–21, 73, 139, 285–287
urban failure, anatomy of
failure of governments, 271–272
land market, 269–271
urban finance, 294–296
urban governance, need to reform
metropolitan governance framework, 298
muncipalities as third tier, 296–298
to address capacity constraints, 298–299
urban growth, 43, 58, 189, 198, 206, 243, 267
urban land, 25, 27, 28, 42, 43, 53
as a resource, 227–229
demand, 30
dimensions of, 40
failure in developing countries, 5
global energy consumption, 56
markets in developing countries, 70
monopolistic market, 29

peri, 2, 15
rent as source of inequality, 26
rise in prices, 57
rising values of, 3
urban local bodies (ULBs), 196
urban local governments (ULGs), 228, 260, 265
urban planning, 10, 34, 35
    and development through master plans, 32
    as a resource, 305
    as technical activity, 59
    in developing countries, 2
    in India, 137
    legal tools for, 135
    modern/modernist, 59, 149–152
    new paradigm for, 180–161
    origin of, 145
    re-engineering cities with transit, 291–292
    restructuring of, 287–289
    role in land use, 134
    strategic, 290
urban revolution, 7, 27
urbanization, 5, 6, 15, 20, 28, 32, 39, 43, 70, 157, 300–301
urbanization economies, 20, 83, 93, 105, 111
urbanization
    as a project, 304–305
    deforestation due to, 198
    exclusionary, 43, 142, 177
    in India, 188
    management of scarce land resources, 189
    mechanics of, 266–269
    opportunity for developing countries, 190
    strategy, 34
    supply of land for, 28

vacant land tax (VLT), 65, 178, 228, 240, 256

value capture financing (VCF), 209
value increment financing partnerships, 306
Vancouver Action Plan of the United Nations Conference on Human Settlements 1976, 233
Vickrey, William S., 262

Walras, Leon, 9
Weber, Alfred, 24
    agglomeration, introduction of, 19
    least cost theory of location, 16, 78, 79–83
    pure theory of industry location, 78
wider economic benefits (WEBs), 190
World Bank
    role of governance in ease of doing business, 112
World Economic Forum (WEF)
    competitiveness, pillars of, 112–113

zoning, 5, 28, 30, 32, 33, 36, 41, 53, 56, 58, 60, 70, 134, 135, 167, 178, 205, 254, 262, 270, 282
Zoning for Quality and Affordability (ZQA), New York, 157
zoning
    codes, 59
    flexible, 207
    for land use, 21, 26, 29, 36, 39, 62, 113, 117, 181, 271, 281
    incentive, 68, 113, 210, 219
    inclusionary, 68, 156, 157, 161, 190, 200, 214, 291, 293, 294, 306, 307
    mixed-use, 222
    re-, 251
    restrictive, 140
    spot, 170